World History CHALLENGE!

A CLASSROOM QUIZ GAME

THIRD EDITION

WALCH PUBLISHING

Kathy Sammis

1 2 3 4 5 6 7 8 9 10

ISBN 0-8251-4357-8

J. Weston Walch, Publisher
P.O. Box 658 • Portland, Maine 04104-0658
walch.com

Printed in the United States of America

Contents

To the Teacher

World History Challenge! generates real enthusiasm as it addresses the fundamentals of world history. It is designed to be used for several purposes: as a fun and easy way to reinforce what is being studied, as a study guide, and as a review of the unit or a culminating activity. It challenges your students to remember important facts and encourages them to enjoy themselves in the process.

The format of *World History Challenge!* is similar to that of a popular television game show. A student is given the answer and is asked to provide the question. Questions are divided into categories, and the fact given as a question is actually stated ("Legendary ruler of Bronze Age Crete"), not asked. Then the student response is given as a question ("Who was Minos?"). Many students will already be familiar with the format.

How to Use This Book

Each topic, or game, consists of four general categories. Each question in each category has a point value. The easiest questions are worth 5 points, more difficult questions are worth 10 points, and the most difficult questions are worth 15 and 20 points. Categories do not always include the same number of questions in each game, nor are the values of the questions always exactly divided among 5, 10, 15, and 20 points.

Before you play the game with your students, it may prove effective to allow them to find the answers to, or study, the questions first. You may wish to reproduce the questions for a series of assignments, and then use a game as an evaluation, a further review, or a culmination of the unit. You may find that using the questions without a game is adequate. For these reasons, the answers are presented separately at the back of the book rather than with the questions.

Here are the directions for a typical game:

- Put the categories for the game to be played on the board with the point-value range.
- Divide the class into teams. Play begins when one student asks for a question from a given category with a given point value. For instance, the student might say, "I want a 10-point question from the 'Phoenicians' category."
- The game leader then reads a 10-point question from the requested category.
- Any student on the team may answer. The first person on the team to raise his or her hand is called on. (It may be the student who asked for the category to begin with.)
- If the answer is correct, record points for the team. The student who answered chooses the category and point value for the next question.
- If the answer is wrong, subtract the point value of the question from the team score. A student from the other team now has the chance to answer the question. Whoever answers the question correctly chooses the category and point value for the next question.
- If no one can answer the question, give the correct answer to the group. The student who last successfully answered a question chooses the next category and point value.
- When all the questions of a given point value have been used within a category, erase that point value. Continue with the other questions until the category is completely used.
- When all the questions in a category have been used, erase that category from the board. Continue until all the categories are erased and the game is over.

Feel free to modify *World History Challenge!* If you have stressed something in your class that is not included in this game, it is easy to add questions. Your students will quickly learn how to make questions for you in order to extend the game. Your class can play the same game more than once, which will help them remember material more easily.

No matter how you use *World History Challenge!* it is an entertaining and stimulating way to review, and it's an excellent change-of-pace activity. You'll find your students eager to play over and over again.

WORLD HISTORY CHALLENGE!

Questions

1 Prehistoric Times and the Concepts of History

	Historical Vocabulary	The Ages of Prehistory	Our Human Ancestors	Prehistoric Life
5	1. Period of the human past before writing was invented 2. The story of the human past 3. Development that separates prehistory from recorded history 4. Folktales that explain the past 5. The way of life of a people 6. The number of people who live in a given area	1. Period when the northern continents were buried under ice and snow 2. Before the birth of Christ 3. Anno Domini, the years after the birth of Christ 4. First period of human history 5. What C.E. stands for	1. Continent where the earliest humanlike remains have been found 2. Muscular prehistoric people who were *not* ancestors of modern humans 3. Prehistoric people who closely resembled modern humans 4. Characteristic that allowed humans to use their hands freely 5. Skill that allowed humans to pass along knowledge	1. Earliest (Paleolithic) ways of getting food 2. A shaped stone 3. Earliest clothing material 4. Resource used both for cooking and as a weapon 5. Neanderthal shelters 6. Huge woolly creature, often hunted
10	7. Person who studies the human past 8. The study of people, their environments, and their resources 9. Scientist who studies the earth 10. Scientist who studies the remains of ancient peoples and civilizations 11. Society centered around cities 12. Any surviving object made by early people	6. What B.C.E. stands for 7. Huge, slowly moving masses of ice and snow 8. Years in between glacial times 9. Exceptionally long period of time 10. Period of time figured from some particular date	6. Characteristic that allowed humans to store and use more information than animals 7. One of the facial characteristics that made a Neanderthal different from a Cro-Magnon 8. "Skillful human" 9. "Upright human" 10. "Wise human"	7. How Neanderthals disposed of their dead 8. Prehistoric wall art 9. Neolithic ways of securing food 10. New, Neolithic living arrangement 11. Neolithic invention used for cooking and food storage 12. Neolithic clothing material

15

13. Large, extended kinship unit
14. Digging into the earth to find ancient remains
15. To decode an ancient language
16. Careful hunting for facts or evidence
17. Idea about how something happened
18. To determine how old a historical find is

11. The Old Stone Age
12. The New Stone Age
13. Period of 1,000 years
14. These were formerly used to date archaeological sites.
15. Radioactive element used to date ancient objects

11. Prehistoric dweller on a Southeast Asian island
12. Prehistoric dweller of China
13. When *Homo sapiens* emerged
14. When Cro-Magnon people emerged
15. The color of this depended on the climate where people lived.

13. Neolithic material that began to replace stone
14. Neolithic invention that was the basis of transportation
15. Neolithic invention that was a machine to weave cloth
16. Material mixed with clay to produce pottery
17. People who wandered from place to place, as Old Stone Age people did
18. Hardened lava from volcanoes, used as mirrors

20

19. Scientist who studies languages and written records
20. Scientist who studies the origin and development of human beings
21. Term for father-related society
22. Term for mother-related society
23. Scientist who studies fossilized remains of early life

16. The shift from food hunting and gathering to food producing
17. When the Stone Age ended
18. When the Neolithic Age began
19. Years of the Paleolithic Age
20. When the last Ice Age ended

16. People who have lived in Australia since prehistoric times
17. A 3.5-million-year-old female humanlike skeleton found in Ethiopia
18. River in western Germany where Neanderthal remains were first found
19. Term for creatures that walk upright

19. Methods of shaping stone in the Old Stone Age
20. Method of shaping stone in the New Stone Age
21. Neanderthal religious belief about death
22. First domesticated animal
23. Mobile way of life that depended on large herds of livestock

NOTES

2 Mesopotamia: The Fertile Crescent

	River Valley Life	Cultural Developments	Mesopotamian Places	Mesopotamian People
5	1. Wide, fertile river mouth 2. Highly developed form of culture 3. Recurring river valley events that enriched the soil 4. Population centers 5. Groups of people identified by their status 6. Geographical areas where the earliest civilizations developed	1. Principal building material in Sumer 2. Sumerian writing material 3. System that linked the different parts of both the Assyrian empire and the Persian empire 4. Form of money used for Persian trade 5. Basic political division in Sumer—made up of a city and its surrounding lands and villages 6. Sumerian wedge-shaped writing	1. The "land between the rivers" 2. Easternmost of Mesopotamia's twin rivers 3. Westernmost of Mesopotamia's twin rivers 4. Principal city of the Babylonian empire 5. Arc of rich-soil land where Mesopotamia was located	1. People who created the earliest known civilization 2. Warlike people from Asia Minor who were the first conquerors of Babylon 3. Warfare specialists who destroyed Babylon and created a huge empire 4. First ruler of the Persian Empire 5. Mesopotamian writers
10	7. Soft metal used by early cultures 8. Mixture of copper and tin that gave its name to an age 9. Strong metal first used widely by the Hittites that gave its name to an age 10. Method of watering crops during dry seasons 11. Devices used for flood control 12. Cooperative system that developed as people worked together	7. Architectural element invented by Sumerians 8. Governors of Sumerian cities 9. The Babylonian collection of laws 10. Group of states or nations under one ruler, first created by Sargon 11. Artisan's device for shaping jugs and bowls, first used by Sumerians 12. Vast Assyrian collection of clay tablets (one of the world's first)	6. The two Far Eastern lands that traded with Mesopotamia 7. Mesopotamia's twin rivers emptied into this body of water. 8. Present-day country that includes most of Mesopotamia 9. Southern Mesopotamia, home of the earliest known civilization 10. Capital city of the Assyrian empire	6. People who created the mightiest Mesopotamian empire 7. Sumerian priest-king who was the hero of the world's oldest written story 8. Ruler who joined Sumer and Akkad, creating the world's first empire 9. Ruler of the first Babylonian empire 10. People who captured Ninevah and rebuilt Babylon

15	13. Economic system created by surplus products 14. Principal occupation of the earliest river valley dwellers 15. Devices developed to reckon and mark time 16. Invention spurred by the need for records 17. Two projects that required group cooperation in river valleys	13. Divisions of the Assyrian empire 14. Chaldean studies of the stars and planets 15. Kingship passed down from father to son 16. Owner of each Sumerian city's land 17. Pyramid-temple at the center of each Sumerian city	11. Western boundary of the Babylonian empire 12. One of the Seven Wonders of the Ancient World, located in Babylon 13. Capital city of Persia 14. Present-day country that includes Persia 15. African country that traded with Mesopotamia	11. Ruler of the second Babylonian empire 12. Former allies defeated by the Persians around 550 B.C.E. 13. Ruler of the Persian empire at its peak 14. Son of Darius who invaded Greece 15. Great Persian religious leader
20	18. Vital transportation method developed by the Sumerians 19. New system in which certain people specialized in specific types of work 20. Simplified picture of a thing 21. Picture that stands for an idea 22. Picture that stands for a sound	18. Sumerian development in mathematics 19. Basic principle of justice under Babylonian law 20. Basic principle of Hittite justice 21. Belief in a number of gods, common among ancient people 22. Persian provinces	16. Area where Mesopotamia's twin rivers began 17. Great city-state of Sumer 18. Easternmost boundary of the Persian empire at its peak 19. Famous Persian transportation route 20. Desert land to the south of Mesopotamia	16. Class of people who had more rights in Babylonia than in other Mesopotamian countries 17. Major occupation of the Assyrians 18. Assyrian king who created a notable early library 19. Son of the first Persian ruler; he conquered Egypt 20. Supreme god of the Assyrians
NOTES				

3 Egyptian Civilization

	Geography and Sites	Religion	Government and Rulers	Culture
5	1. Continent Egypt is part of 2. Egypt's major river 3. Body of water into which Egypt's major river empties 4. Region formed by the mouth of Egypt's major river 5. Type of land that bordered Egypt's river valley 6. Colossal statue of a crouching lion with a human head	1. Religious status of the Egyptian ruler 2. Tombs built to house the deathless rulers 3. This process preserved bodies for the afterlife. 4. Buildings constructed to honor gods, especially Amon-Re 5. God of the sun 6. God of the underworld; personification of the Nile	1. Boy-king whose unopened tomb was discovered in C.E. 1922 2. Hereditary groups who took some power away from Egyptian rulers 3. Egyptian ruler 4. Type of marriage practiced by Egyptian rulers 5. A series of rulers from a single family; ancient Egypt had 31 of these over 2600 years 6. Ruler who united northern and southern Egypt (c. 3000 B.C.E.)	1. Ancient Egyptian system of writing 2. Paperlike Egyptian writing material 3. Artifact that showed how to decipher Egyptian writing 4. Economic basis of Egyptian power and wealth 5. Source of wealth for Egypt in addition to agriculture
10	7. Largest of the Egyptian kings' tombs 8. Ancient kingdom of southern Egypt 9. Ancient kingdom of northern Egypt 10. New Kingdom capital city in central Egypt 11. Series of great waterfalls in Egypt's major river 12. Site of the Great Pyramid, plus other pyramids	7. Fertility goddess; wife of Osiris 8. New single god decreed by Ikhnaton 9. Collection of magic spells to help achieve life after death 10. Pharaohs' burial places during the Middle Kingdom 11. Each god's symbol, revered and mummified 12. Major preoccupation of Egyptian religion	7. New name of the ruler who established belief in a single god 8. Wife and sister of Ikhnaton (Akhenaton) 9. Last strong ruler of ancient Egypt 10. First era of ancient Egyptian history; the Pyramid Age 11. Second era of ancient Egyptian history 12. Third era of ancient Egyptian history; a period of conquest	6. Healing science in which Egyptians became proficient 7. Centers of government and religion 8. Material Egyptians used to write with 9. Building material of Egyptian villagers 10. Animal introduced to Egypt by the invading Hyksos

15	13. Land to the south that became part of Egypt during the empire 14. Type of resource scarce in Egypt, usually traded for 15. This kept many Egyptian manuscripts and artifacts preserved for centuries. 16. Body of water on Egypt's eastern boundary 17. Total length of Egypt's major river	13. Sacred insect 14. God of Thebes 15. Chief Egyptian god 16. Son of Re, also of Osiris and Isis 17. Where all the pyramids were built	13. Leader who conquered Egypt in 332 B.C.E. 14. Original owner of all Egyptian land 15. King entombed in the Great Pyramid 16. Man who discovered King Tut's tomb 17. Prince who drove out the Hyksos and began the New Kingdom	11. Hereditary writing and recordkeeping professional 12. Time of year when the river flood began 13. Mathematical skill developed by Egyptians to measure land 14. Type of calendar developed by Egyptians; an improvement over the lunar calendar 15. Important crop in both ancient and modern Egypt
20	18. Two Middle Eastern areas that became part of Egypt's empire during the New Kingdom 19. Land that joined Egypt with western Asia 20. Capital city of the Old Kingdom 21. Great center for advanced study (especially astronomy and religion) 22. New capital city established by Ikhnaton (Akhenaton or Amenhotep IV)	18. Monster that devoured sinful souls 19. Device used by god Osiris to judge a soul 20. Belief in a single god 21. Belief in a number of gods 22. A sacred bull worshipped by the ancient Egyptians	18. Female ruler who expanded trade and public building 19. Ruler who expanded Egyptian rule into Syria and Palestine 20. Southern kingdom that ruled Egypt from c. 750 to 670 B.C.E. 21. Asian people who ruled Egypt from c. 1700 B.C.E. to 1600 B.C.E. 22. People who conquered Egypt in c. 670 B.C.E.	16. Devices used to build the pyramids 17. Homes of wealthy Egyptians outside the city 18. Storage buildings for grain from good harvests 19. The two building materials for the pyramids 20. Approximate number of pyramids built
NOTES				

4 Civilization in Ancient India and China

	Peoples	Places	Early Indian Culture	Early Chinese Culture
5	1. Family members whom Shang people revered 2. Persons for whom ancient Chinese developed contempt 3. What the Chinese considered all foreigners to be 4. Ruling families in China 5. Bandit leaders who controlled large areas of China 6. Living family members who were most respected in China	1. River whose valley was the site of India's first civilization 2. Northernmost of China's two greatest rivers 3. Southernmost of China's two greatest rivers 4. Major body of water on China's eastern boundary 5. Major Indian river that flows southeasterly	1. What the Aryans did to the Harappan cities 2. Indian social structure that began under the Aryans 3. Structures used to control the rivers 4. India's seasonal wind 5. Most Harappan gods were of this gender. 6. Harappan improvement in brick making	1. Source of our knowledge about earliest Chinese history 2. Structures used to contain a river's high water levels 3. The northern river sometimes did this when flooding. 4. Material produced for wealthy people's clothing 5. Creatures that produced silk 6. Legendary creatures that were driven out of China's river valleys
10	7. Class of people who lived in Chinese cities 8. Class of people who lived outside of Chinese cities 9. People whose civilization flourished in India between 2500 and 1500 B.C.E. 10. Indo-Europeans who invaded northern India around 1500 B.C.E. 11. Type of people the Aryans were—definitely not city dwellers	6. "China's sorrow" or "the great sorrow" 7. Large sea on China's eastern boundary 8. Desert in the north of China 9. Major pass through India's northwestern mountains 10. Body of water into which the Indus River empties	7. Unique feature of Harappan cities' design 8. Crop used to make cloth, first grown by Harappans 9. "Modern" system that kept Harappan cities sanitary 10. Center of each Harappan city 11. Grain-storage buildings in Harappan cities 12. Main crop of the Aryans on the central Indian plain	7. Two grains grown by the ancient Chinese 8. Material used for war chariots, weapons, and works of art 9. Forces in nature that the Shang worshipped 10. Improved metal used by the Zhou for weapons and tools 11. Strongest connection among Chinese people

15	12. First historical dynasty of China 13. Class of people just below the Shang rulers 14. Stone Age inhabitant of China 15. Most admired members of early Aryan society 16. Aryan priests	11. Mountains northeast of India and southwest of China 12. One of ancient India's large cities, in ruins today 13. Geographic term for India, rather than "country" 14. One of the three geographical factors that kept Eastern peoples isolated 15. Chinese term for the land of the two major river valleys	13. Harappan cities were built on this feature as another form of flood protection. 14. How streets were laid out in Harappan cities 15. Artifacts that contain most of the known examples of Harappan writing 16. The Aryan period in Indian history, from 1500 to 1000 B.C.E. 17. Written language of the Aryans	12. Main economic base of the Shang dynasty 13. Type of calendar used by the Shang, adjusted as necessary 14. Building material that was abundant along the Chinese rivers 15. Ancient Chinese term for divine right to rule 16. Centers of early Chinese cities
20	17. Physical characteristic of Aryans that separated them from the people they conquered 18. Legendary first dynasty of China 19. People who overthrew China's first historical dynasty 20. Officials in charge of the Shang calendar 21. Legendary founder of the Xia kingdom	16. India's northwestern mountain range 17. Broad area populated by the spreading Aryans 18. Capital city of an early Chinese dynasty 19. Large river south of China's two greatest rivers 20. Mountains to the northwest of China	18. The Aryans' collections of sacred knowledge 19. Huge watertight tank in a Harappan city 20. Indus Valley religion 21. Basic unit of earliest Aryan society 22. Greatest, longest Indian epic	17. Items that were inscribed with questions for ancestors 18. Writing as an art, practiced by the ancient Chinese 19. Number of written characters a well-educated Chinese had to know 20. Material that gave the Huang He (Yellow River) its color and name 21. Social and economic division that weakened the Shang dynasty

NOTES

5 Ancient Greece

	Origins and Geography	Politics and Society	The Era of City-States	The Hellenistic Age
5	1. Ancient seafaring people of Crete 2. Primary occupation of the Minoans 3. Ocean south of Greece that surrounds Crete 4. Geographic features that separated Greek city-states 5. Geographic feature of Italy's northern border	1. Geographic and political center of Greek life 2. Earliest form of city-state government 3. Form of government developed in Athens 4. Lowest Athenian class 5. People of Athens who spent their lives secluded at home 6. Sole occupation of male Spartan citizens	1. South-central, militaristic city-state 2. Attican city-state that developed as a democracy 3. Wars with a powerful empire of Asia Minor (490–479 B.C.E.) 4. Leader who sailed an army across the Aegean to Greece in 490 B.C.E. 5. Persian leader who sent his army back to Greece in 480 B.C.E.	1. Ruler of Macedon who united the Greek city-states 2. Philip's son and successor 3. Empire conquered by Alexander 4. Northern African country conquered by Alexander 5. Culture spread by Alexander
10	6. Legendary ruler of Bronze Age Crete 7. People who replaced the Minoans as the chief power of the Aegean world 8. Ten-year conflict between the Myceneans and the people of Troy 9. Epic poem about the Trojan War 10. People who conquered the Myceneans around 1000 B.C.E. 11. Sea that separated Greece and Asia Minor	7. Greek word for the city-state 8. Fortified hilltop at a city's center 9. A city's open meeting area, usually the marketplace 10. Form of government in Sparta 11. Set of principles and rules for governing; Athens had one 12. Spartan slaves	6. Statesman who led Athens to its greatest heights 7. Athenian leader who drew up a code of laws 8. Athenian leader whose name today means a wise lawmaker 9. Athenian leader who established nearly complete democracy 10. Battle in which the Greeks defeated the Persians in 490 B.C.E.	6. Athenian orator who vigorously opposed Philip 7. Cause of Philip's death 8. Alexander's Greek tutor 9. Easternmost extent of Alexander's empire 10. Cause of Alexander's death 11. Structure in Egypt's Alexandria; one of the Seven Wonders of the Ancient World

15	12. Sea that formed Greece's western border 13. Most famous of Alexander's new cities, in Egypt 14. Economic activity made necessary by Greek geography 15. Major city of ancient Crete 16. Mountainous land north of Greece	13. Where male Spartan citizens lived from age 7 to age 30 14. Fate of unhealthy or imperfect Spartan babies 15. Fate of Athenian debtors, abolished by Solon 16. What Athenian girls were taught 17. The five governing officials of Sparta 18. One of the two ruling bodies in Sparta	11. Defensive alliance led by Athens 12. Thirty-year war between Athens and Sparta 13. Event in addition to war that destroyed Athens 14. City-state that overthrew Spartan rule in 371 B.C.E. 15. Greek rulers who seized power by force, often backed by the poor	12. Philip's ambition in life 13. City-state where Philip was held hostage as a youth 14. Alexander's major influence on the world 15. Special infantry formation of the Greek and Macedonian armies 16. Battle in which Philip gained control of Greece
20	17. Peninsula on which Greece is located 18. Southern portion of ancient Greece 19. Region of Greek city-states in Asia Minor and on Aegean islands 20. Italy's central mountain range 21. Large island at the toe of Italy	19. Body of Athenian citizens that passed laws 20. Athenian body that proposed laws and handled daily affairs 21. Spartan form of money 22. Athenian ideal of education 23. Greek term for non-Greeks	16. Mountain pass defended by Spartans in 480 B.C.E. 17. Sea battle in which Athenians defeated Persians in 480 B.C.E. 18. Final, decisive battle that ended the wars in 479 B.C.E. 19. Athenian ruler who introduced land reform and was supported by the lower classes 20. Athenian warships	17. Alexander's age when he came to power 18. Northern portion of Alexander's empire after its division 19. Southern portion of Alexander's empire after its division 20. Eastern portion of Alexander's empire after its division 21. Alexandria's renowned center of learning

NOTES

6 Ancient Rome

	Origins and Geography	Government and Society	Leaders	Expansion, Decline, and Fall
5	1. Number of hills on which Rome was built 2. Rome's river 3. The Italian peninsula extended into this sea. 4. Creature who cared for Rome's legendary twins as infants 5. Sea on Italy's east coast	1. Roman form of government in which the citizens who voted held power 2. Roman upper class 3. Roman lower class 4. Extended period of peace that Augustus brought to Rome 5. Popular public meeting places, for both men and women 6. Popular public entertainment staged by the government	1. Famed soldier and politician who became sole ruler and was later assassinated 2. The day Caesar was assassinated 3. Caesar's top general, who fell in love with Cleopatra 4. Caesar's grandnephew and political heir 5. "Exalted One," Octavian's new title	1. General of Carthage who invaded Italy in 218 B.C.E. 2. Mountain range crossed by Hannibal and his troops 3. Large animals that crossed the mountains with Hannibal 4. New, eastern capital established by Constantine 5. Peoples whose tribes invaded the Roman Empire 6. Fierce Asiatic tribe that drove other tribes toward the empire
10	6. Legendary twins who fought to become Rome's first king 7. Invading people who founded Rome 8. Northern people who took over Rome from its founders 9. People who established city-states on islands south of Italy 10. Etruscan method of making marshes useful 11. Bridge-building element Latins borrowed from Etruscans	7. Professional public fighters 8. Rulers who held absolute power for no more than six months 9. Joint officials who were chief executives and military leaders 10. Rome's main public square 11. Basic unit of the Roman army	6. Octavian's status as absolute ruler of the Roman Empire 7. Emperor blamed for the Roman fire of C.E. 64 8. Brothers who were "reformer" tribunes 9. Senator and general who opposed Marius and seized Rome 10. Co-ruler defeated by Caesar in Greece	7. Leader of the Huns; "the Scourge of God" 8. Great commercial power that fought with Rome 9. The wars between Rome and Carthage 10. Geographic area where Carthage was located 11. Roman general who defeated Hannibal 12. Reforming ruler who divided the empire's administration into East and West

15	12. Etruscan system of government 13. River Caesar was ordered not to cross on his way back to Rome 14. Western boundary of the Roman Empire at its height 15. Southern boundary of the Roman Empire at its height 16. Northern land invaded by Caesar, secured under Claudius	12. Elected officials who protected plebeians' rights 13. Class that expanded as the large estates grew 14. Class that was driven from the countryside to the cities 15. Basic principles of Roman law 16. Water-transporting systems	11. One of Caesar's two close friends who became his killers 12. Famous general who extended the empire to its greatest size; the second Good Emperor 13. The third Good Emperor, who had a defensive wall built in Britain 14. Last of the Good Emperors; a Stoic philosopher 15. Adopted son and successor of Augustus	13. Strong ruler who moved the capital to the East 14. Tribe permitted to cross the Danube into imperial territory that later sacked Rome 15. Germanic chief whose army sacked Rome 16. Major political reason for Rome's fall 17. Major economic reason for Rome's fall
20	17. Region north of Rome, today's France 18. Body of water on the eastern and northern boundaries of the Roman Empire at its height 19. The two rivers that were the northern boundary of the Roman Empire at its height 20. One of Rome's two main hills 21. Source of Etruscans' written language	17. Roman road improvement 18. Basic occupation of people in the Roman Empire during the peaceful years 19. Method of succession developed during the empire 20. Type of housing for Rome's lower classes 21. Social and economic division that weakened both the republic and the empire	16. Insane successor of Tiberius 17. Succession of five wise and able rulers 18. Old lawyer/ruler who adopted his successor in C.E. 96 19. Orator and politician who supported Pompey 20. Conflict that broke out while Marius and Sulla were contending for power	18. Major social reason for Rome's fall 19. Area north of Greece acquired by Rome in 148 B.C.E. 20. The two islands to the west of Italy lost by Carthage in the First Punic War 21. What Romans did to destroy Carthaginian land 22. Series of emperors enthroned and assassinated by the army

NOTES

7 Greek, Hellenistic, and Roman Culture

	Science and Religion	Architecture, Sculpture, and Painting	Literature and Theater	Philosophy and History
5	1. Ruler of the gods, Greek or Roman 2. Wife of the gods' ruler, Greek or Roman 3. Greek goddess of wisdom and protector of Athens 4. Greek sporting festival held every four years to honor Zeus 5. Greek "Father of Scientific Medicine"	1. Rome's great ampitheater; site of gladiator fights 2. Central hill of Athens; site of exceptional temples 3. Artifacts on which the best-preserved Greek paintings were found 4. Athens' renowned temple, dedicated to Athena	1. Where Greek plays were performed 2. Form of literature and entertainment invented by the Greeks 3. Drama about people's suffering 4. Plays that focus on humor 5. Epic poet credited with composing the *Iliad* and the *Odyssey*	1. Greek study of the meaning of life and the nature of the world 2. Questioning philosopher condemned to death by poison 3. Student of Socrates, founder of a renowned school 4. Student of Plato, brilliant philosopher, scientist, and logician 5. Plato's book about the ideal state or government
10	6. Doctors' pledge developed by a Greek physician 7. Mathematician who developed fundamental rules of geometry 8. Mathematician and philosopher who developed an enduring theorem about right triangles 9. Doctor who compiled a widely used medical encyclopedia 10. Alexandrian authority on astronomy	5. Greatest Greek fine art 6. Familiar Greek statue of an athlete by Myron 7. Domed building in Rome built in honor of gods 8. Baths built for thousands of bathers 9. Roman oval arena; site of chariot races	6. Semilegendary slave and fable writer 7. Female lyric poet from the island of Lesbos 8. Earliest and greatest writer of Greek stage comedies 9. The language of ancient Romans 10. Roman epic poem about Aeneas, modeled after the *Iliad*	6. Step-by-step questioning to arrive at a final conclusion, the truth 7. Roman historian who wrote an account about early Germans 8. Renowned Roman lawyer, politician, and orator 9. Roman emperor, military leader, and author of the Stoic *Meditations* 10. The "Father of History," the first great Western historian

15

11. Ptolemy's theory of the universe, accepted until the 1600s
12. Scientist who developed the first two steps of the scientific method
13. Scientist who mastered the use of the lever and compound pulley
14. Geographer who accurately calculated the earth's size
15. Astronomer who concluded that the earth revolved around the sun

10. Roman city, destroyed by a volcano, that has yielded many preserved art treasures
11. Roman architectural elements not used by the Greeks
12. First of Greece's greatest sculptors
13. Artist who specialized in large, formal sculpture of deities
14. Famed sculptor of graceful human forms

11. Roman epic poet, author of the *Aeneid*
12. Roman poet who wrote odes, satires, and epistles
13. Author of love lyrics and legends in verse
14. Roman development in writing

11. Famous historian of the Peloponnesian War
12. Greek ideal of aesthetics and thought
13. Plato's school
14. Aristotle's school
15. Roman who wrote a multivolume history of Rome

20

16. Scientist who believed that all matter is made up of atoms
17. What Greek scientists lacked
18. Aristotle's method of grouping similar plants and animals
19. Belief in a number of gods, a feature of Greek and Roman religion

15. Style of architecture based on Greek and Roman buildings; style of the U.S. Capitol
16. Roman sculpture form in which images project from a flat background
17. Colorful Minoan and Roman wall paintings
18. Minoan and Roman artworks created with small pieces of glass, stone, and/or tile

15. Father of Greek tragedy
16. Writer of tragedies, including *Oedipus Rex*
17. Most realistic of the three great writers of tragedy
18. Family of languages that developed from Latin

16. Author of the *Commentaries* on the Gallic war, later emperor
17. Greek author of *Parallel Lives*
18. Roman schools for advanced studies
19. Philosophy that focused on living a vice-free life
20. Philosophy that focused on virtuous conduct and the absence of pain

NOTES

8 Near Eastern Worlds and the Rise of Christianity

	The Phoenicians	The Hebrews	Christianity	Near Eastern Places
5	1. Main occupation of Phoenicians 2. Timber used to build Phoenician ships and for trade 3. Basic politicial division in Phoenicia 4. Landforms that physically separated the different groups of Phoenicians 5. Phoenicians used these to protect their cities. 6. Center of activity in a Phoenician city	1. Religion of the Hebrews 2. The Hebrews' different idea about God 3. Leader who brought the Hebrews out of Egypt 4. God's laws as given to Moses 5. Land Moses led the Hebrews to 6. The Hebrews' God	1. Christ, the Messiah 2. People among whom Christianity began 3. How Jesus was put to death 4. People who controlled Palestine when Jesus lived 5. The savior the Jews waited for 6. The archbishop of Rome, head of the Latin church	1. Village birthplace of Jesus 2. Town where Jesus grew up 3. Western boundary of Phoenicia and Palestine 4. Loose union of city-states; nation of seafarers 5. Land the Hebrews left under the leadership of Moses 6. Body of water the Hebrews crossed during their exodus
10	7. A skill the Phoenicians were renowned for 8. Early Phoenician herding peoples who came from the desert 9. Early rulers of Phoenician city-states 10. Expensive Phoenician item much sought after in trade 11. Phoenicia's permanent settlements in faraway places	7. Leader who brought the Hebrews to Canaan in about 1900 B.C.E. 8. The Hebrews' journey out of Egypt 9. Binding agreement between God and Abraham 10. The two main occupations of the Hebrews in Canaan 11. King who established Jerusalem as the capital of Israel and wrote many psalms 12. Wise king who built a huge temple at Jerusalem	7. Main message of Jesus 8. "Do unto others as you would have them do unto you." 9. Rising from the dead, as Jesus is said to have done 10. What Jesus said his relationship to God was 11. Religious practice early Christians refused to follow 12. Title that some Jews gave Jesus, which alarmed the Romans	7. Hebrew capital city; site of Solomon's temple 8. Land where Christianity developed and Hebrews lived 9. Two of Phoenicia's city-states 10. Phoenicia's greatest colony 11. Area where Carthage was located 12. Land the Hebrews first settled in and later returned to

15	12. Phoenicia's most important contribution to Western culture 13. Phoenicians spread this throughout the Mediterranean world. 14. Egyptian method of preserving dead bodies, adopted by the Phoenicians 15. Continent that Phoenicians may have sailed around 16. Phoenician kings had to share power with these bodies.	13. Spiritual leaders who delivered messages from God to the people 14. Jewish teachers 15. Most sacred Hebrew text; its five books record the early history and laws of the Hebrews 16. Portion of the Bible that tells the story of the Hebrews 17. Peoples the Hebrews fought for Canaan	13. The Latin churches as a group, after the split of C.E. 1054 14. The Greek churches as a group, after the split of C.E. 1054 15. Portion of the Bible that tells about the life and teachings of Jesus 16. The four books of the Bible about the life of Jesus 17. Roman emporer in power during Jesus's life	13. Mountain where Moses received the Ten Commandments from God 14. Northern Hebrew kingdom 15. Southern Hebrew kingdom 16. Palestine's major river 17. Land to which the people of Judah were forced to move in 586 B.C.E.
20	17. Shellfish that was the source of Phoenicia's purple dye 18. A Phoenician princess, who was the legendary founder of Carthage 19. Natural resource Phoenicia lacked and had to trade for 20. Phoenician gods 21. Large Mediterranean island with a Phoenician colony, a center of trade	18. The Hebrew people's 12 divisions 19. Leaders of the 12 tribes 20. First king of the Hebrews 21. Ethical basis of Jewish society 22. Three Hebrew prophets who have books of the Bible named after them	18. First Christian missionary to the gentiles; a former persecutor of Christians 19. Disaster that was blamed on the Christians 20. Roman emperor who encouraged the growth of Christianity 21. Decree that made Christianity legal in C.E. 313 22. Emperor who made Christianity the official religion of the Roman Empire	18. Modern country that includes part of Phoenicia 19. Modern country that includes part of Palestine 20. Mountains that bordered Phoenicia on the east 21. Modern country where Carthage once was located 22. Land the Hebrews first migrated from 23. Desert land the Hebrews first came to after leaving Egypt
NOTES				

9 Early Cultures in Europe

	The Germans	The Franks	Britain and Ireland	The Vikings
5	1. Primary occupation of German men 2. Members of German society who did most of the work 3. Basic unit of German society 4. German tribe that used its kingdom in North Africa as a base for pirate raids 5. Form of government set up by invading Germans 6. Fierce nomadic people from Asia who invaded Europe	1. Religion the Frankish king and his warriors converted to 2. Institution that supported the Franks after they converted 3. Modern-day country that takes its name from the Franks 4. Religion the invading Arabs hoped to spread throughout Europe 5. English translation of both Charlemagne and Karl der Grosse	1. Early inhabitants of Britain, who were conquered by Romans 2. Three Germanic tribes that invaded Britain around 450 3. Tribe that gave its name to England 4. A land the Celts fled to from Britain 5. Famed missionary who brought Christianity to Ireland 6. Status of most English people	1. Europeans' term for Vikings 2. Far northern Europe 3. A characteristic of Vikings that terrified Europeans 4. What the Vikings used much of their abundant timber for 5. Occupation of seafaring Vikings in addition to raiding 6. Primary occupation of Viking men
10	7. Term formerly used for the Early Middle Ages 8. River valley along the Roman Empire's border where many Germans settled 9. Chief German god 10. God of war and thunder 11. East Goths, driven westward by the Huns	6. River along which the Franks lived 7. King who first brought all Franks under one rule 8. Two characteristics shared by most Franks that helped them to feel united 9. Modern country that developed from the Western Frankish kingdom 10. Modern country that developed from the Eastern Frankish kingdom 11. Leader who defeated the invading Arabs	7. The two peoples of northern Britain (modern Scotland) 8. Body of water crossed by the tribes that invaded Britain 9. Centers of culture in Ireland 10. Head missionary to the Anglo-Saxons 11. Center of the Christian church in England, as established by Augustine 12. King of Wessex who fought the invading Vikings	7. An advantage of Viking raids for Europeans 8. The three kingdoms of the Vikings 9. Vikings had none of these for their children. 10. King of the gods 11. God of thunder and lightning

15

12. West Goths; they captured and plundered Rome
13. A German tribe gave its name to this word; it means the willful and senseless destruction of property.
14. European country occupied by Romans, then Vandals, then Visigoths
15. State of European society after the German invasions destroyed the Roman Empire
16. Why the Germans didn't write their own history

12. Battle of 732 in which the invading Arabs were defeated
13. First Frankish king personally crowned by the pope
14. Frankish king who became "Emperor of the Romans"
15. Two of the invading peoples defeated by Charlemagne
16. Charlemagne made this available even to some lower-class children

13. English term for invading Vikings
14. Epic Anglo-Saxon poem
15. Local districts of England
16. Officials who governed local districts in England
17. Body of water between Britain and Ireland
18. Important kingdom in northern England

12. Body of water crossed by Viking raiders heading toward Russia
13. Norwegian adventurer who founded a colony on Greenland
14. The two North Atlantic islands colonized by Norwegian Vikings
15. Eric the Red's son, who sailed to North America
16. Vikings' name for the spot on the coast of North America where they landed
17. Body of water the Vikings crossed to get to Greenland and North America

20

17. Where German warriors expected to spend their afterlife
18. Visigoth king who led the sack of Rome in 410
19. Source of German law
20. German tribe that moved across the Alps into northern Italy
21. German tribe that moved into central Gaul

17. Charlemagne's only surviving son
18. Agreement that divided the empire among Charlemagne's three grandsons
19. Capital of the Frankish kingdom under Clovis
20. Charlemagne's capital city
21. Asian invaders who reminded Europeans of the Huns

19. Important kingdom in central England
20. Important kingdom in southern England
21. Pope who decided to convert the Anglo-Saxons to Christianity
22. Anglo-Saxon king who allowed the missionaries to teach about Christianity
23. Northeastern region of England ruled by the Vikings

18. Viking letters of the alphabet
19. Heroic or mythic poems of the Vikings
20. Heroic stories of the Vikings
21. Danish ruler who became king of England
22. Area of France where Danes settled in large numbers

NOTES

10 The Rise and Spread of Islam

Points	Peoples and Places of the Arab Empire	Governing the Arab Empire	Islamic Culture	Religious Beliefs
5	1. Peninsula on which the early Arabs lived 2. Climate of the early Arabs' homeland 3. Birthplace of Muhammad 4. Christians' term for the Muslim people who conquered Spain 5. Major occupation of Arabian nomads	1. Founder of the Arab Empire 2. How the Arabs treated people they conquered 3. Official language of the Arab Empire 4. Term for a successor of Muhammad 5. The first 100 years in power of the Abbasids, 750–850	1. Type of mathematics invented by Muslim scholars 2. Type of numbers introduced to Europeans by Arab mathematicians 3. Health-care field in which Arabs excelled 4. Things that could not be pictured by Islamic artists	1. The one God of Islam 2. Muslim book of scriptures, the sacred word of God as revealed to Muhammad 3. Muslim house of worship 4. Muhammad's status 5. Food forbidden to Muslims 6. Beverage forbidden to Muslims
10	6. Nomads of Arabia 7. City to which Muhammad fled and established his leadership 8. City captured by Muhammad that became the center of Islam 9. Body of water on the west coast of Arabia 10. Continent whose northern border was conquered by the Arabs 11. Western European country that became part of the Arab Empire	6. Muhammad's early profession 7. Method of choosing the first caliphs 8. How the title of caliph was passed on after the early caliphs 9. Source of income for the Arab Empire 10. Battle in which the Arabs were turned back from their invasion of Europe	5. Artistic use of flowing Arabic script 6. Muslim scientists who tried to turn tin and lead into silver and gold 7. Muslim scientists who gave many stars their names 8. Muslim scientists who determined the earth might be round 9. Popular collection of Persian tales	7. Number of times per day Muslims must pray 8. Position in which Muslims must pray 9. Muslims must do this for the needy. 10. What Muslims must do during the daylight hours of the holy month 11. Men learned in Islamic faith and law

15	12. Empire to the east of Arabia taken over by the Arabs 13. Empire to the north of the Arab Empire extending from Asia Minor into Europe 14. Near Eastern countries to the north of Arabia taken over by the Arab Empire 15. African country to the west of Arabia that became part of the Arab Empire 16. River on which Baghdad was built	11. Muhammad's daughter, who established her own dynasty in North Africa and western Arabia 12. Muhammad's loyal friend, follower, and first successor 13. Muhammad's son-in-law, the last of the Rightly Guided Caliphs 14. Muhammad's flight from Mecca to Medina in 622 15. Dynasty that ruled as hereditary caliphs for 90 years	10. European country that became a point of contact for Europeans and Muslim culture 11. Events that brought Europeans into contact with Muslim culture 12. Slender towers built next to Mosques 13. Navigation instrument perfected by Muslim scientists 14. Arab encyclopedia of medicine used in European medical schools for 500 years	12. Muhammad believed Allah was the same god that these two religious groups worshipped. 13. Pilgrimage to Mecca 14. Heavenly creature whose voice spoke to Muhammad 15. Holy shrine of Mecca that contains a sacred cubelike black structure 16. What the word *Islam* means
20	17. Wealthy businesswoman who married Muhammad 18. Original name of the city of Medina 19. New capital of the Umayyad caliphs, in Syria 20. New capital built by the Abbasid caliphs 21. Spanish city that was a center of learning under the Arabs	16. Group of Muslims who favored caliphs chosen only from Muhammad's own family 17. Group of Muslims who favored electing any eligible, pious Muslim as caliph 18. Group that defeated the Umayyads to rule the empire 19. Term for one of the three parts of the later empire 20. Muslim body of law, incorporating religious, criminal, and civil matters	15. Famed Persian scholar, astronomer, and poet, author of the Rubáiyat 16. Great physician and author of collection of medical knowledge 17. Weapons from Damascus that became world famous 18. Revered Muslim shrine in Jerusalem built in the 600s using Byzantine domes and arches 19. Library, academy, and translation center in Baghdad, a center for scholars	17. Islamic creed that Muslims must recite 18. Muslim prayer leader 19. Muslim holy month 20. Meaning of the word Muslim 21. Event that marks the first year of the Muslim calendar

NOTES

11 The Byzantine and Eastern Empires

Points	Byzantine Territory and People	Byzantine Culture	Important People of the Eastern Empires	Landmarks of the Eastern Empires
5	1. Emperor who moved the capital of the Roman Empire from Rome 2. Capital city of the Byzantine Empire 3. Ancient city, site of Constantinople, that gave the empire its name 4. City Constantinople was patterned after 5. Empire that the Byzantine Empire was originally part of 6. Greatest of the Byzantine emperors	1. Major unifying force of the empire 2. Important arteries that passed through Constantinople 3. Pictures made of many bits of colored stone or glass 4. Small religious pictures kept in homes and churches 5. Central feature of Constantinople's magnificent church	1. People who settled much of eastern Europe 2. Northern warriors and traders who settled in Russia, also called Varangians 3. Central Asian people who took control of Russia 4. Greatest leader of the Mongols, grandfather of the destroyer of Kiev 5. Term for the Russian ruler, adopted by Ivan III 6. People who were formerly free peasants	1. Northern body of water crossed by the Vikings to reach Russia 2. Body of water that was Russia's gateway to the Mediterranean 3. Vast grassy plains of eastern Europe 4. The European and Asian landmass 5. Original home of the Mongols
10	7. Sea south of Russia whose entrance Constantinople controlled 8. Western sea whose entrance Constantinople commanded 9. Justinian's wife, a steely adviser 10. Magnificent Byzantine church whose name means "Holy Wisdom" 11. European country won back by Justinian's army 12. Coastline recaptured by Justinian's army	6. Approximate number of years the Byzantine Empire existed 7. The Church in the East, after the split of 1054 8. Source of the emperor's power, according to the emperor 9. Class of people whose rights were expanded at Theodora's urging 10. Constantinople's public arena that often filled with rowdy fans	7. Viking who became the Prince of Novgorod 8. Prince of Kiev who chose Eastern Orthodox Christianity as Russia's official religion 9. Missionary who gave the Russians their alphabet 10. Scholarly ruler who organized the first Russian code of law 11. Term for a Mongol leader	6. Main physical characteristic of the northern region of early Russia 7. River at the eastern edge of early Russia 8. River that flowed past Kiev and into the Black Sea 9. Landbound sea of Russia 10. Northern Russia town; home of Rurik

15	13. People from the West who attacked the empire 14. People from the East who attacked the empire 15. Major non-European portion of the empire 16. Strategic strait on which Constantinople was located 17. People who captured Constantinople in 1453	11. Common spoken language 12. Head of the Church in Constantinople 13. The Church in the West, after the split of 1054 14. Head of the Eastern Orthodox Church 15. People who spread Christianity to neighboring lands	12. Class of Russian people who became socially isolated during Mongol rule 13. Prince of Moscow who ended Mongol control of Russia in 1478 14. Successor of Ivan III who added much territory to Russia but became mentally unstable 15. Nomadic, freedom-loving settlers who expanded Russia to the west 16. Band of Vikings who gave their name to Russia	11. Southernmost town on the trading route through Russia 12. Mountains that separated Europe and Asia 13. Trading post that grew during the Mongol occupation 14. Mountains that separated eastern Europe and Russia 15. Mountains that bordered Russia on the south
20	18. Present-day name of Constantinople 19. Commander of the Byzantine army under Justinian 20. Leading missionary of the Byzantine Empire 21. Emperor who banned the use of icons 22. People defeated by Justinian's army to secure the empire's eastern borders	16. Religious official with whom the head of the Eastern Orthodox Church clashed 17. Uniform body of civil law, based on Roman law and legal opinions 18. The two major defenses of Constantinople 19. Learning and culture preserved and passed on by the Byzantine Empire 20. An inflammable liquid that was the secret weapon of the Byzantine navy	17. Early ruler of the Kievan state 18. Local princes and nobles who helped to rule Russia 19. First Russian ruler to convert to Christianity 20. Term for the group of Mongols who overran Russia 21. Prince of Moscow who defeated the Mongols in 1378	16. Source of much early Russian culture 17. Eastern European country to the west of Russia; bordered the Baltic Sea 18. Eastern European country to the west of Russia, south of Poland 19. Center of the Russian branch of the Eastern Orthodox Church 20. Central Russian river that flowed into the Sea of Azov
NOTES				

12 Empires of India and China

Points	Indian People, Politics, and Places	Indian Religion and Culture	Chinese Government and Politics	Chinese Thought and Culture
5	1. Rulers of northern Indian states 2. Hero and/or heroine of the *Ramayana* 3. Major river of northeastern India 4. Major river of northwestern India 5. "Great" Persian ruler who briefly controlled northeastern India around 500 B.C.E.	1. Major religion of India that developed slowly over a long period of time 2. The rebirth of the soul in another being 3. Social class system closely woven into Hinduism 4. Cause of human suffering, renounced by Buddha 5. Members of the lowest class in the Indian social system	1. Massive structure built to guard against invasion 2. System of choosing governmental officials 3. "Useless" items burned by the thousands by the first emperor 4. Northern Chinese river 5. Central Chinese river	1. Invention in C.E. 105 that made books more widely available 2. China's most valuable trade item 3. Basis of the Chinese economy 4. The Chinese philosopher K'ung Fu-tse 5. One-wheeled cart invented during the Han period, still used worldwide
10	6. Dynasty that ruled the first great Indian empire 7. Rulers who controlled India during a "golden age" from C.E. 320 to about 550 8. Feature of both Maurya and Gupta rule that ensured peace and prosperity 9. Plateau region of southern India conquered by Maurya forces 10. Most honored Maurya ruler, who converted to Buddhism and promoted peace 11. People whose kingdoms were located in the southernmost part of India	6. According to Hinduism, the actions of a person's life that affect her or him in the next life 7. Birth name of the founder of Buddhism 8. State of complete happiness and peace in Buddhism 9. Two of the three gods of the Hindu trinity 10. Meaning of the title Buddha	6. Dynasty that replaced the Zhou dynasty and gave China its name 7. Dynasty founded by the general Liu Bang in 202 B.C.E. that lasted for over 400 years 8. People killed by the hundreds by the first emperor 9. Original social status of the first Han emperor 10. People who were forced to leave their homes and live in the empire's capital city	6. Needle-based medical treatment developed by Han era physicians 7. Steering mechanism for ships invented by Han sailors 8. Caravan trading route from China across central Asia to the Mediterranean area 9. The foundation of Chinese society 10. Institution that Confucius hoped to reform

15

12. River of central India

13. First ruler of the Gupta Empire

14. Founder, in 321 B.C.E., of the first great Indian empire

15. Asoka's adviser, who wrote a hard-headed handbook on how to rule

16. Site of renowned Buddhist monastery-university

---

11. People largely responsible for spreading Buddhism

12. Characteristic of the earth proved by Indian astronomers

13. Two of three essential advances in mathematics invented in India

14. Way to protect people against communicable disease, perfected by early Indian physicians

15. Central focus of Indian life

---

11. Area to the northeast colonized by Han China

12. Area to the south colonized by Han China

13. Cause of peasant revolts

14. People hired as government officials during the Han era

15. Policy toward conquered people promoted by the Han government

---

11. Founder of the philosophy of Daoism

12. Religion introduced to China during the Han dynasty

13. How a ruler should govern, according to Confucius

14. A son or daughter's most important duty, according to Confucius

15. Goal of Daoists

20

17. Maurya and Gupta capital city

18. Dynasty that ruled central India in between the Maurya and Gupta empires

19. Greek ambassador who wrote detailed descriptions of Chandra Gupta's capital

20. Fierce invaders who threatened northern India late in the Gupta era

21. Indian playwright of the Gupta era

---

16. Sacred mounds said to contain remains of the Buddha

17. Group that opposed Buddhism in India

18. The road to enlightenment, according to the Buddha

19. Basic essence that permeates everything in the world, according to Hinduism

20. One of the two major schools that Buddhism split into

---

16. Emperor Liu Bang's honorable title

17. Han "Warrior Emperor" who greatly expanded the empire

18. Female ruler of the Han dynasty

19. "First Emperor"; he unified China

20. People who threatened China from the north

---

16. Written collection of the sayings of Confucius

17. Belief that a ruler should enforce strict laws with harsh punishments

18. Book that set out the philosophy of Daoism

19. Indescribable force that governs the universe, according to Laozi

20. China's "Grand Historian"

NOTES

13 Kingdoms, Empires, and States of Africa

	Geography of Africa	Culture and Trade	People	Places and Politics
5	1. Vast desert that separates northern and southern Africa 2. Dry grasslands of Africa 3. Term for Africa south of the Sahara 4. Sea that borders northern Africa 5. Body of water that borders western Africa 6. Densely wooded region that receives enormous amounts of rain	1. Precious metal mined in western Africa's forested regions 2. Commodity that Arab merchants brought to the African kingdoms from the Sahara 3. Religion brought to Africa by Arab traders 4. Family members venerated by most traditional African societies 5. Trade item derived from elephants that was much in demand	1. Original inhabitants of North Africa, fiercely independent desert dwellers 2. West African farmers and herders who spread widely south and east between 500 B.C.E. and C.E. 1500 3. Great Mali ruler who gave away vast amounts of gold on his hajj to Mecca 4. Muslim rulers of East African city-states 5. Mali's first great ruler, who ousted the ruler who had killed all his brothers	1. Region south of Egypt along the upper Nile River 2. Ancient kingdom of Nubia, which conquered Egypt 3. Mali trading city, center of Muslim learning 4. This kingdom's Red Sea port city was Adulis. 5. Present-day state where the ancient kingdom of Nubia was located
10	7. Inhospitable environment that makes up about 40 percent of the African continent 8. Location of earliest, and great, civilization of Africa 9. Region of Africa between the Sahara and the tropical rain forest 10. Desert of southern Africa 11. Major river of western Africa	6. Pack animals that made cross-Sahara caravans possible 7. Widespread activity that created a rich mix of cultures in Africa 8. The language of trade and business in western Africa 9. Bantu language with many Arabic words 10. Rock buildings carved in Ethiopia in the early 1200s 11. Widespread African religious belief centered around spirits in daily life	6. North African traveler and historian who wrote in detail about his journeys through Islamic Africa in the 1300s 7. People who developed city-states with clay-walled capital cities 8. People who called their ruler ghana, or war chief 9. City-state dwellers whose chiefs all traced their descent from the first ruler of Ife 10. First great ruler of Songhai, who established the empire	6. Nation ruled by Nubians at times 7. North African country that conquered the Songhai Empire 8. Earliest kingdom of the western Sudan, it flourished from the 700s to the mid-1000s. 9. Kingdom that controlled much of western African from the 1200s until about 1500 10. Capital of Morocco under Berber Muslim dynasties

15

12. Major river of central Africa
13. Mali trading city, center of Muslim learning
14. Ocean that borders eastern Africa
15. Enormous lake named by Europeans for a British monarch
16. Eastern boundary of the Sahara Desert

12. Basis of the Nubian written language
13. Religion of the ancient kingdom of Aksum and of modern-day Ethiopia
14. Group of families that claimed a common ancestor
15. Beautiful multicolored fabric worn by Ashanti kings and chiefs
16. Common African currency that came from the sea

11. Second great ruler of Songhai, a Muslim who ruled during the 1500s
12. Spanish Muslim architect who introduced Arabic styles to Mali
13. Powerful king of Aksum who conquered Kush and converted to Christianity
14. King of Kush who founded Egypt's twenty-fifth dynasty
15. People who lived in a stateless society from the ninth through the nineteenth centuries

11. Kingdom that flourished around 1500 in present-day Zaire
12. Impressive 60-acre stone city in southern Africa abandoned by 1450
13. Ancient city in West Africa near the Niger River, at least as old as 250 B.C.E.
14. West African empire that flourished in the 1400s and 1500s, overthrown by Moroccans in 1591
15. Rain-forest kingdom of the Guinea coast that was flourishing when the Portuguese arrived in 1483

20

17. Long, deep gash in the earth in eastern Africa where the first humans appeared
18. Major river of southern Africa
19. Lake on the eastern edge of western Africa
20. Large, elongated lake in eastern Africa
21. Savanna region that borders the southern edge of the Sahara Desert

17. Art form that was a specialty of Benin artists
18. West African storytellers who passed on a society's oral history
19. Ancient culture of northern Nigeria that smelted iron and produced a distinctive sculpture
20. Term for the continuing spread of the Sahara
21. Unique language of Aksum

16. Queen of the Hausa city-state of Zazzau (Zaria) renowned for her military conquests
17. Ethiopian king who had Christian churches carved downward into mountains
18. Muslim scholar known in the West as Leo Africanus
19. One of two groups of North African Berber Muslim reformers who established dynasties in the eleventh and twelfth centuries

16. Beautiful, wealthiest, and most powerful city-state of East Africa from the 1200s to the 1400s
17. Saharan village where houses were made from salt blocks
18. Prosperous capital city of the kingdom of Songhai
19. Capital of wealthy kingdom of Ghana in the mid-1000s
20. Second capital of Kush, an iron-making center

NOTES

14 The Americas

	Geography of the Americas	Early Mesoamerica	North American Cultures	Mayas, Aztecs, and Incas
5	1. South American river with a huge rain-forested basin 2. The first inhabitants of the Americas migrated from this continent. 3. Era when people first migrated to the Americas over a temporary land bridge 4. Ocean that forms the western border of North and South America 5. Great river of North America, one of the world's three longest	1. Most important food crop of Mesoamerica 2. Chianampas, used by early farmers to grow crops in shallow lakes 3. Unique and colossal Olmec monuments 4. Time-tracking device developed by several early Mesoamerican cultures 5. Body of water whose shoreline formed a boundary of the Olmec lands	1. Cone-shaped tents of the Plains Indians 2. Besides hunting, a major pastime of the Plains Indians 3. Animal that was the basis of Plains Indians' existence 4. American Indians of what is now the southwestern United States, whose name was based on their adobe dwelling centers 5. Basis of the Pueblo economy	1. People of the Yucatán, southern Mexico, and northern Central America 2. Wandering warriors who settled in central Mexico 3. People who destroyed the Aztec and Inca empires 4. People of the Andes Mountains who created an empire 5. Important and deadly aspect of the Aztec religion 6. Basis of the Mayan economy
10	6. Geographic area that lies between North America and South America 7. Present-day nation where the Mayan and Aztec states were centered 8. Mexican peninsula, home to the Mayan civilization 9. Great mountain range of western North America 10. South American mountains that were home to the Incas	6. People who developed Mesoamerica's first known civilization 7. Writing system developed by the Zapotec people 8. Typical terrain of Peru's coastal plain 9. Teotihuacán's giant structure, larger than Egypt's Great Pyramid 10. Warlike people of central Mexico who ruled an empire based on conquest from 900 to the early 1200s	6. Basis of the Plains Indian economy 7. Late migrants from Siberia who settled in the Arctic 8. Basis of northwestern American Indian economy 9. Great wooden carvings that symbolized tribal history for northwestern American Indians 10. Purpose of the mounds constructed by certain American Indians	7. What conquered peoples were required to do for the Aztecs 8. Basis of Incan religion 9. Type of communication unknown to the Incas 10. Cause of the Incan empire's decline 11. Now-ruined Incan city, isolated atop a high mountain 12. Capital city of the Incas

15	11. Human migrants came to the Americas when a land bridge replaced part of this body of water 12. Narrow land bridge that connects Central and South America 13. One of the two present-day nations where the Inca state existed 14. The southern tip of South America	11. Culture that flourished on Peru's north coast from about 100 to 700 12. City-state that was the first major civilization of central Mexico, centered around a monumental city 13. First civilization of the Andes Mountains 14. People of Peru who created huge drawings that can only be seen from the air 15. People whose civilization flourished in southern Mexico's Oaxaca Valley from about 500 B.C.E. to C.E. 600	11. Type of Anasazi canyon housing found at southwestern sites such as Mesa Verde 12. Organization formed by five eastern American Indian tribes 13. Elaborate feasting and gift-giving ceremony of northwestern tribes 14. Large underground chamber used by southwestern peoples for religious ceremonies 15. Midwestern and southern American Indians who practiced a unique building style	13. Renowned Mayan city with huge buildings located on the Yucatán Peninsula, much visited by tourists today 14. Aztec capital city in Lake Texcoco 15. Advanced feature of Mayan mathematics 16. Type of temples built by Mayans 17. Largest Mayan city, located in present-day Guatemala 18. Transportation network of 14,000 miles built by the Incas
20	15. Mountain basin 7,000 feet above sea level, in central Mexico 16. Name for the temporary land bridge that formed in prehistory between Siberia and Alaska 17. Site in Chile with evidence of human life in 10,500 B.C.E. 18. Great mountain range of Mexico	16. The Feathered Serpent, a snake-bird god common to various Mesoamerican cultures 17. Site of important Olmec remains 18. The first large urban center in the Americas, developed by the Zapotec 19. Toltec capital city	16. Great center of the Mississippian people in Illinois, featuring at least 60 mounds 17. People of the southwest who built large stone and adobe villages later called *pueblos* 18. "Vanished" farmers of the desert southwest who lived in today's Arizona 19. One of the legendary founders of the Iroquois alliance	19. Deity from whom the Inca ruler descended 20. Chief Aztec deity, the sun god 21. Incan ruler who created the empire in the 1400s 22. Knotted, colored strings used by Incans to keep records 23. Structures that recorded important events in Mayan history

NOTES

15 East Asia: Empires and Kingdoms

	China: People, Places, and Politics	China: Culture and Society	Korea and Southeast Asia	Japanese Civilization
5	1. Region of China often invaded by nomadic outsiders 2. Dynasty of 618 to 907 that greatly expanded the empire 3. Waterway that linked the Hwang He and Yangtze rivers 4. Dynasty that lost control of northern China 5. Mongol emperor who ruled all of China	1. New strains of this staple produced two crops per year instead of just one. 2. A mix of saltpeter, sulfur, and charcoal used first for fireworks in Tang China 3. New type of currency issued by the Song government 4. China's largest social class 5. Test for becoming a Tang or Song government official	1. Religion(s) brought to Southeast Asia from India 2. Southeast Asian country controlled by China for 1,000 years 3. Korea's northern neighbor 4. Main characteristic of Korea's terrain 5. Country from which Korea borrowed many ideas and customs 6. Religion that missionaries brought to Korea from China	1. Main characteristic of Japan's terrain 2. Supreme military commander 3. Religion brought to Japan from China around 550 4. Warriors pledged to serve their local lord 5. Country from which early Japan borrowed many ideas and customs 6. Long novel by Lady Murasaki Shikibu that told the story of Prince Genji
10	6. Dynasty that replaced the Mongols 7. Italian merchant who served at Kublai Khan's court for many years 8. Brief dynasty that reunited northern and southern China 9. First great Tang emperor 10. Two neighboring lands that became tributary states to China	6. New product from Southeast Asia that Chinese soon drank, produced, and exported 7. Common causes of peasant revolts 8. China's wealthy, powerful upper class 9. Body of knowledge that formed the basis of the Chinese civil service examination 10. Class of people considered inferior by Confucian standards	7. Strait that connects the Indian Ocean and the South China Sea 8. Empire that was Southeast Asia's main power from 800 to the 1200s 9. Huge city-and-temple complex built by the Khmer in the 1100s 10. Capital city of Vietnam's Ly Dynasty 11. River that forms part of Korea's northern border	7. Warrior lords who pledged to support the shogun 8. Largest island of Japan 9. Large northern island of Japan 10. Large southern island of Japan 11. Ancient religion of Japan 12. People whose naval invasion the Japanese defeated in 1274 and 1281

15	11. Tang-era ruler who was China's only female emperor 12. China's Mongol dynasty 13. Muslim admiral who led an enormous Chinese fleet on seven extensive voyages 14. People who won control of western Chinese lands by winning the Battle of Talus in 751 15. First emperor of the Sui dynasty	11. Painful procedure that resulted in the highly desirable "lily foot" 12. Artistic writing skill mastered by the scholar-gentry class 13. Shiny, hard, white pottery prized as the world's finest ceramic 14. Floating magnetized needle used by Chinese sailors 15. Palace complex of 9,000 rooms built by a Ming emperor	12. Harsh people who occupied and ruled Korea from 1231 until the 1350s 13. Body of water that forms Korea's eastern boundary 14. Body of water that forms Korea's western boundary 15. Island location of the Sailendra kingdom 16. Island where the capital city of the Srivijaya Empire was located	13. Second Japanese imperial capital 14. Social and political system in Japan from about 800 to 1600 15. Ritual suicide practiced by samurai 16. Asian country invaded by Japan in 1592 17. Term for an island chain like Japan 18. Type of writing introduced into Japan from Korea around 405
20	16. Tang capital city 17. New Song capital city in the south 18. Scholarly general who founded the Song dynasty 19. Peasant leader who founded the Ming dynasty 20. Empire established by Manchurian people in northern China in the early 1100s	16. Improved time-telling device invented during the Tang era 17. Individual characters arranged in frames that allowed for multiple prints 18. Graceful temple form with multiple stories and upcurved eaves 19. New food crop(s) introduced to China from the Americas 20. Type of literature produced by Li Bo and Du Fu	17. First Korean dynasty; it united the Korean peninsula 18. Dynasty from which the modern name Korea developed 19. Unique Korean pottery famous for its milky green glaze 20. Third Korean dynasty; it ruled from 1392 to 1910 21. Capital city of Korea's Koryo dynasty	19. Military dynasty founded by Minamoto that ruled during the 1200s 20. Line of shoguns who ruled from 1603 to 1868 21. Violent era of disorder, from the mid-1400s to the mid-1500s 22. First Japanese imperial capital 23. Samurai code of honor

NOTES

16 Europe: Feudalism, the Church, and the Crusades

	Feudal Life	Feudal People	The Medieval Church	The Crusades
5	1. Medieval farming estate, including a village 2. Noble's home and fortress made of stone 3. Body of water that protected some castles 4. Heavy door of a castle that could be raised or lowered 5. Code of conduct developed for medieval knights 6. Popular board game played by nobles and ladies	1. Person who granted land in exchange for military services 2. Class of people who were lords and vassals 3. People who farmed the land and provided services for nobles 4. Peasants who were bound to the land 5. Noble warrior on horseback	1. Organization that provided the only stable central authority in medieval Europe 2. Local Church official 3. Official language of the Church 4. Spiritual head of the Church in western Europe 5. Religious communities of nuns 6. Religious communities of monks	1. Land conquered by the Arabs that the crusaders sought to recapture 2. Religion of the Arabs 3. Muslim people who took over the Holy Land from the Arabs 4. Empire that appealed to the pope for protection from the Turks 5. Holy city recaptured by the crusaders in 1099
10	7. Below-ground area where prisoners were kept in a castle 8. Political condition that favored the development of feudalism 9. Major obligation of a vassal to a lord 10. Payment owed by a vassal if the lord was captured in battle 11. Mock battles, the great sport of feudal knights	6. Weak rulers who granted land from royal estates to powerful lords 7. Class of medieval religious leaders 8. Lesser lord who held land in return for a pledge of services and loyalty 9. Legal possession and use of land passed to this person when a lord or vassal died. 10. Peasants who rented land from the lord	7. Skills possessed by Church officials and very few other members of medieval society 8. Large church headed by a bishop 9. Ultimate punishment for heresy 10. Banishment from the Church 11. Head of a monastery 12. Religious order dedicated to reform, whose members preached among the people	6. Tragic crusade of 1212 7. Pope who called on the feudal lords to wage a holy war—a crusade—to regain the Holy Land 8. War cry of the crusaders 9. Emblem of the crusaders, sewn onto their tunics 10. Two of the things a crusader would be forgiven for or declared free from

15

12. A fight between two armored knights on horseback
13. Floor covering for a medieval manor house or castle
14. Castle room where everyone lived and ate
15. Grant of land
16. Body of vassals that decided legal cases

11. First stage of learning to be a knight, beginning at the age of seven
12. A knight's assistant
13. The last strong king in Europe before feudalism developed
14. Poet-musicians at feudal castles who sang about romantic love
15. Wandering musical entertainers

13. Responsibility taken over by the Church that benefited the less fortunate
14. The laws of the Church
15. The search for heresy by the Spanish Church
16. False doctrines or denial of the truth of dogma
17. Contribution of 10 percent of one's income to the Church

11. Crusade led by nobles that was successful
12. What the crusaders did when they recaptured the holy city
13. Two of the three kings who conducted the Third Crusade
14. Muslim leader who recaptured Jerusalem in 1187
15. Main political effect of the crusades

20

17. Wooden building built to provide protection to everyone on the lord's manor
18. High wooden fence that surrounded a noble's house
19. Tall, strong tower of a castle
20. Payment given by a bride's family to the husband-to-be
21. Condition of a field left unplanted every third year

16. Group of nonfarming freemen necessary to the village economy
17. Manor official who made sure the peasants worked hard in the fields
18. Head of a medieval university
19. Manor people that the lord's lady was obligated to care for
20. Person who kept one third of the manor's land for himself

18. First pope to become a powerful earthly ruler
19. Set of standards to regulate lives of monks, developed around 530
20. Pope who attempted to rid the Church of control by kings and feudal lords
21. Agreement of 1122 giving both the pope and the king a part in selecting bishops
22. The buying and selling of Church positions

16. Site of Church council where the pope pleaded for a crusade
17. Crusade led by Louis VII of France and the Holy Emperor Conrad III; begun in 1147
18. Term for the Third Crusade, 1189–1192
19. Pope who called for a Fourth Crusade in 1198
20. City looted by crusaders in 1204

NOTES

17 The High and Late Middle Ages in Europe

	Towns and Trade	Medieval Culture in the Towns	France and Germany Emerge From Feudalism	England Emerges From Feudalism
5	1. European country where trade first began to revive 2. Demand developed in Europe for luxury goods from this region 3. The first large trading centers of the Middle Ages developed at these locations 4. Sea that connected western Europe with the Near East 5. New class of people who provided financial services	1. Language of scholars and clergy 2. Popular poet who wrote one of the first books in English 3. Chaucer's series of stories written in English 4. Guilds of teachers and students 5. Legendary king, subject of a popular English national epic	1. Political subdivisions of France 2. Assembly of French nobles, clergy, and townspeople that advised the king 3. Long war between England and France that began in 1337 4. New weapon used by English archers against the French 5. New weapon that made castles obsolete for defense	1. Duke of Normandy who became king of England 2. Battle in which the French forces defeated the English in 1066 3. Term for the people who took over England in 1066 4. Language brought to England by the conquerors of 1066 5. Nickname for the crusading King Richard I
10	6. Associations of merchants and artisans 7. Epidemic that swept through Europe in the 1300s 8. Important Italian trading port on the Adriatic 9. Important trading center on the Black Sea 10. Type of trading route that connected northern Italy with northern Europe	6. Languages of the common people 7. Popular medieval dramas 8. Famed poet who wrote in Italian 9. Dante's greatest work, a poem in Italian 10. Attempt to change base metals to gold; forerunner of the science of chemistry 11. Style of church architecture using round arches, domes, thick walls, and small windows	6. French heroine of the Hundred Years' War 7. French king chosen by an assembly of nobles in 987 8. Line of French kings established by Hugh Capet 9. King who took back much French land from the English 10. French king who formed the Estates-General and collected taxes regularly	6. Population survey ordered by William the Conqueror 7. Clergyman who opposed King Henry II's plan to subject Church officials to royal control 8. Traveling judges who brought the king's law to all parts of England 9. King who caused a revolt among the nobles 10. Document that lessened the king's power and strengthened nobles' rights

15	11. Events that stimulated demand for Eastern goods 12. People who determined the value of coins from different regions 13. New settlements that grew up at locations important for trade 14. System that town dwellers did not fit into 15. Person in training for a trade	12. Style of church architecture using pointed arches, high spires, and large stained-glass windows 13. Rows of supporting ribs outside the walls of Gothic churches 14. Site of great university that specialized in theology and the liberal arts 15. Attempt of medieval scholars to reconcile faith and reason 16. Medieval scholar who taught in Paris and stressed reason	11. French king known for honesty, just dealings, and support of the Church 12. Large new state that consisted of Germany and northern Italy 13. Powerful German ruler who became king in 936 and seized territory in northern Italy 14. King of Germany who disobeyed the pope and continued to appoint bishops 15. German emperor defeated by the Italian city-states in 1176	11. Representative body that included members of the middle class as well as nobles and clergy 12. Upper house of Parliament, for nobles and bishops 13. Lower house of Parliament, for knights and townspeople 14. Groups that presented judges with names of people suspected of crimes 15. English king defeated by William the Conqueror
20	16. Skilled worker who worked for a master for daily wages 17. New class made up of merchants, master craftsmen, and skilled workers 18. Living conditions in medieval towns 19. Area on the northwest coast of Europe that became the earliest Atlantic trading center 20. Product of Flanders in great demand throughout Europe	17. Dominican scholar-monk who stressed both faith and reason 18. French national epic about a brave member of Charlemagne's army 19. Hero who starred in the German epic the *Nibelungenlied* 20. Site of great university that specialized in law 21. Site of great university that specialized in medicine	16. German emperor who was mostly interested in Italy 17. Important battle in which the English defeated the French during their century-long war 18. French king who owed his crown to Joan of Arc 19. Meaning of "Barbarossa" 20. League of Italian city-states formed to fight the Germans	16. Book that recorded results of the population survey 17. French wife of Henry II 18. King who wanted Church officials to be tried in royal, not Church, courts 19. Body of important clergy and nobles that advised the king 20. Law based on judges' decisions rather than statutes

NOTES

18 Southwestern and Central Asia

	The Mongol Empire	The Mughal Empire	The Seljuk and Safavid Empires	The Ottoman Empire
5	1. Dry grassland of Central Asia 2. Way of life of the Mongols of the grasslands 3. Term for a Mongol clan leader 4. The Great Khan 5. Far eastern country conquered by the Great Khan 6. Important psychological weapon employed by Genghis Khan	1. English meaning of the Persian word *Mughal* 2. Area of India that often split into warring local kingdoms 3. People who were second-class citizens under some Muslim rulers 4. Stunning tomb built for Mumtaz Mahal 5. Religion of the Mughals 6. Cause of popular revolts against the Mughal rulers in the 1600s	1. Land where the Safavid Empire was located 2. Powerful empire to the east of the Safavid Empire 3. Powerful empire to the west of the Safavid Empire 4. Native language of the Safavids and Seljuks 5. Western attacks against the Seljuks in Palestine	1. New weapon the Ottomans used to capture walled cities 2. Basis of the Ottoman soldiers' military success 3. Native language of the Ottomans 4. Land where the Ottomans originated 5. Area that the Ottomans migrated into that became the core of the empire 6. Original way of life of the Ottomans
10	7. New weapons and technology Genghis Khan adopted from his enemies 8. Important Russian city destroyed by the Mongols 9. Grandson of Genghis Khan, who ruled China 10. Colorful term for the Mongol armies 11. Modern name of the Mongol capital city in China	7. Language of India's common people, a mixture of Persian and a local language 8. People whose invasion of India in 711 went no farther than the Indus Valley 9. Widespread destruction of monasteries caused a drastic decline in this religion in India. 10. Chief builder of the Mughal empire, the founder's grandson, called "the Great" 11. Ruler who was deeply interested in the arts and built a magnificent tomb for his wife	6. Branch of Islam to which the Safavids belonged 7. Branch of Islam to which the Seljuks converted 8. Ancient Persian title for king adopted by Safavid and Seljuk rulers 9. Most outstanding Safavid ruler 10. Persian trade item much in demand in the West 11. Persian city the Seljuks took in 1055	7. Religion of the Ottomans 8. Ottoman ruler and military leader who captured Constantinople in 1453 9. New Ottoman name for the city of Constantinople 10. West European city besieged by Ottomans in 1529 and 1683 11. Ottoman sultan called "the Lawgiver" and "the Magnificent" 12. Elite troops of slaves who were former Christians

15	12. Country to the east of China that Kublai Khan's naval fleet attacked twice 13. Genghis Khan's policy toward people once he had conquered their lands 14. Things other than trade goods that moved along the Eurasian trade routes 15. What "Genghis Khan" translates into in English 16. Genghis Khan's birth name	12. What most Mughal rulers did to secure their throne 13. Akbar's policy toward non-Muslims 14. Warrior leader from Central Asia whose army destroyed Delhi in 1398 15. Capital of the sultanate that ruled much of northern India from 1206 to 1526 16. New "soldiers' language," a blend of Persian, Arabic, and Hindi	12. Body of water that formed the southern boundary of the Safavid Empire 13. Empire that the Seljuks defeated in the Battle of Manzikeet in 1071 14. Famous Persian poet patronized by the Seljuk sultan 15. Invaders who crushed the remnants of the Seljuk Empire 16. Kurdish leader of the Seljuk military who recaptured Jerusalem in 1187	13. Term for an Ottoman ruler, meaning "overlord" or "one with power" 14. European area captured by the Ottomans 15. Architectural masterpiece of Suleiman's reign 16. Magnificent Christian church in Constantinople that became a magnificent mosque 17. Ruler who gave his name to the Ottomans
20	17. Period of stability and law and order across Eurasia under Mongol rule 18. Country in the southwestern area of the empire ruled by the Ilkhanate 19. Name of the Mongol dynasty in China 20. Country in the northwestern area of the empire ruled by the Khanate of the Golden Horde 21. Region where Kublai Khan's armies and navies suffered many defeats	17. Members of a religious group that organized into anti-Mughal military forces 18. Real ruler of India during her husband Jahangir's reign 19. Turkish sultan whose armies invaded India about 1000 20. The last strong Mughal ruler, who had to fight many rebellions 21. Founder of the Mughal Empire in 1526	17. Most famous Seljuk sultan 18. Title of the Seljuk ruler's prime minister 19. Persian city that was the capital of both the Seljuk and Safavid Empires 20. Teenage ruler who established the Safavid Empire 21. Muslim empire that the Seljuks migrated into around 970	18. Royal architect under Suleiman 19. Brutal Ottoman ruler who took Mecca, Medina, and Cairo 20. Non-Muslim religious communities 21. Council that advised the Ottoman rulers 22. Nations who destroyed the Turkish fleet at the Battle of Lepanto in 1571

NOTES

19 The Renaissance and the Reformation

	Renaissance Origins in Italy	The Northern Renaissance	The Protestant Reformation	English and Catholic Reformations
5	1. Main philosophy of the Renaissance, focused on people 2. Focus of Renaissance interest 3. Renaissance artist, architect, and mathematician; he painted the *Mona Lisa* (*La Gioconda*) 4. Painter and sculptor noted for large works, such as the statue of David and the ceiling of the Sistine Chapel 5. Country where the Renaissance began	1. New machine that allowed books to be produced quickly and more cheaply 2. Wealthy Flemish people who were patrons of the arts 3. Author of masterpieces of English poetic drama genre 4. Fictional young lovers of Verona, subjects of Shakespeare tragedy 5. Form of literature and entertainment especially favored by the English people	1. German monk who started the Protestant Reformation 2. Church practice that Martin Luther especially objected to 3. Name for people who protested the decision to condemn Luther 4. The only true guide to religious truth, according to Luther 5. Luther's list of statements about his position	1. Leader of the Church reformation in England 2. Why Henry VIII wanted to end his marriage to his first wife 3. First wife of Henry VIII 4. Language of the Church reaffirmed by the Council 5. Second wife of Henry VIII and mother of the future queen
10	6. Early knowledge studied by Renaissance scholars 7. Italian painter noted for his madonnas 8. Two of the three most important city-states of the Italian Renaissance 9. Notable characteristic of Renaissance art 10. New way of showing objects in art as they appeared at different distances	6. The English Renaissance reached its height during her reign. 7. New type of painting pioneered and perfected by Flemish painters 8. Region where the Renaissance began in northern Europe 9. German who first printed books from movable type 10. Noted Spanish Renaissance author of plays, short stories, and novels, including *Don Quixote*	6. Religious faith chosen by most northern German rulers 7. Religious faith chosen by most southern German rulers 8. French-born leader of the Protestant movement in Switzerland 9. Swiss city that was a center of Protestantism 10. Calvinist leader of Scotland	6. Protestant queen who ended the pope's authority in the English Church 7. Religious faith of Queen Mary (Mary Tudor) 8. National church established by Henry VIII and Elizabeth I 9. The movement of reform within the Catholic Church 10. Spanish noble who devoted himself to Church reform

15	11. Author of *The Prince*, a book advising rulers on how to keep power, by whatever means necessary 12. Ruling family of Florence 13. Ruler of Florence called "the Magnificent" 14. Venetian artist noted for his rich colors 15. Florentine poet and story writer, author of *The Decameron*	11. German artist known for his engravings and woodcuts 12. Book by English humanist Thomas More that described an ideal society 13. German portrait painter of the 1500s known for his photographic-like realism 14. Great Flemish painter of the 1500s whose favorite subjects were the countryside and peasants	11. Calvinist church in Scotland 12. French Calvinists 13. Economic reasons for rulers to oppose the Church and support Luther 14. Calvin's belief about human fate; the opposite of free will 15. Government ruled by clergy acting in God's name, as in Geneva	11. Body that examined people who disagreed with Church officials 12. New religious order founded by Loyola, or its members 13. Primary aim of the Jesuits 14. What Henry wanted the pope to do about Henry's marriage to his first wife 15. Meeting of Church leaders that ended some of the Church abuses
20	16. "Father of humanism," Italian poet and classical scholar 17. Italian who wrote a handbook on correct behavior titled *The Courtier* 18. Sculptor who carved natural postures and revealing individual expressions 19. Artist who created the sculpted bronze door panels of Florence's baptistery	15. Flemish oil painters who were brothers 16. French writer whose comic adventure *Gargantua* and *Pantagruel* satirized outdated customs and ideas 17. Dutch scholar who translated the New Testament into Greek and wrote the satire *In Praise of Folly* 18. Spanish city that was a center for Renaissance artists and poets 19. Flemish painter known for his large, lush style	16. The way to gain salvation, according to Luther 17. Bohemian priest burned as a heretic in 1415 18. English priest who declared the Bible was the authority, not the Church 19. Dominican monk who energetically sold indulgences in Germany 20. Meeting that condemned Luther	16. How to achieve salvation, according to the Council of Trent 17. The two true guides to religious truth, according to the Church 18. Who or what is qualified to interpret the Bible, according to the Church 19. List of books the Church forbade Catholics to read

NOTES

20 The Age of Exploration

	Early Exploration and the Portuguese	Encounters in Asia and Africa	Spain in the Americas	The Struggle for North America
5	1. Navigation instrument with a magnetized needle 2. Western country that controlled Europe's trade with the Far East 3. Exotic foodstuffs that inspired European voyages to the East 4. Continent whose west coast the Portuguese explored in the 1400s 5. Disease caused by lack of vitamin C, common among early European sailors	1. Portuguese name for the southern tip of Africa 2. Explorer who opened India to Portuguese trade 3. Portuguese navigator who led a fleet on an around-the-world voyage for Spain 4. Principal export from Africa via European traders 5. Portuguese explorer who first sailed around Africa's southern tip	1. Italian explorer who sailed west from Europe to find the Spice Islands 2. Name given to the New World natives by Columbus, because he thought he had reached the East Indies 3. Term for Spanish conquerors in the New World 4. Metal sought by the Spanish conquerors 5. Name given by Magellan to Balboa's ocean	1. Main interest of the French in North America 2. Explorer for the Netherlands who gave his name to a bay, a river, and a strait 3. Most destructive "weapon" that Europeans brought to the Americas 4. A Spanish explorer was the first European to find this great North American river. 5. Pathway through North America to the Far East that explorers tried to find
10	6. Term for mapmakers 7. Brother of the king of Portugal who promoted exploration 8. Type of school started by Prince Henry 9. Religious reason for European exploration 10. Europeans' name for the Moluccas, islands rich in cloves and nutmeg	6. First Europeans to trade with Japan 7. Country that established trading forts along the west coast of Africa in the 1400s 8. Asian island group claimed by Spain and named for the Spanish king 9. The Portuguese expelled Arab traders from this section of the African coast. 10. Term for the voyage of enslaved Africans to the Americas	6. Sea that Columbus explored in the New World 7. Present-day central American area taken by Cortés 8. Spanish explorer who invaded and conquered central America 9. Central American empire conquered by Cortés 10. Two Spanish tactical advantages previously unknown to the Native Americans	6. First permanent English settlement in North America 7. Second permanent English settlement in North America 8. Italian explorer who established English claims in North America 9. Italian who explored the Atlantic coast for France 10. English explorer who founded a colony at Roanoke

15

11. Feature of the caravel that made it sail more effectively
12. Merchants who brought Asian goods to Mediterranean ports
13. Feature of European ships that allowed them to capture coastal trading posts
14. Navigation instrument, perfected by the Arabs, used to measure the angle of stars and planets
15. Portuguese explorer who accidentally landed in Brazil

11. Early European traders' term for the islands of present-day Indonesia
12. Far Eastern nation where the Dutch were allowed to trade once or twice a year
13. Europeans who established a colony at Cape Town on Africa's southern tip
14. Portuguese trading post in China, near Canton
15. Island off the coast of India that was the base of Portuguese trade

11. Spanish explorer who conquered the Indian empire of South America
12. South American Indians conquered by Pizarro
13. Spanish explorer who led an expedition through much of today's U.S. southwest
14. First European to sight the Pacific Ocean
15. Spanish explorer who found the Mississippi River

11. Bitter rival European nations who jockeyed for power in North America
12. People who established the Massachusetts Bay Colony
13. Great northern river explored by the French and the English
14. First permanent French settlement in North America, founded by Samuel de Champlain
15. Capital of Dutch settlement in North America

20

16. Countries that divided all the new Atlantic lands between themselves
17. Navigational tool used to determine latitude; it replaced the astrolabe
18. Imaginary line drawn by the pope that divided the new Atlantic lands
19. Port from which many Portuguese explorers sailed

16. Port town that the Portuguese seized, giving them control of the strait with the same name
17. Great spice port of India where da Gama landed and traded
18. Far Eastern island that was the trading headquarters of the Dutch
19. Commercial group that set up trading posts in India
20. Company that controlled Dutch trade in the Far East

16. Spaniard who explored Florida
17. Places that imported most African slaves sent to the Americas
18. Leader of the South American Indian empire
19. Today's name for the islands Columbus arrived at
20. Leader of the central American Indian empire

16. Western region of North America claimed by France
17. French explorer of North America who found a gulf and a great river
18. Explorer who claimed the entire Mississippi River valley for France
19. Two Frenchmen who explored the Mississippi Valley in 1673
20. War led by Native American leader Metacomet in Massachusetts

NOTES

21 The Rise of Monarchies

	Spain	France	Austria, Prussia, and Russia	England
5	1. Muslim conquerors driven out of Spain by the Reconquista 2. Monarchs who united Spanish kingdoms 3. Two groups of Spaniards ordered to convert to Catholicism 4. Source of Spain's precious-metal wealth 5. Huge Spanish invasion fleet destroyed by a storm in 1588	1. Result of French religious conflicts 2. Lavish palace built by the French king outside Paris 3. European language of diplomacy and nobility 4. Alliances against France aimed to preserve this in Europe 5. French Protestants	1. Ruling family of Austria 2. Prussia was noted for this well-organized body. 3. "Empire" whose title was entirely meaningless 4. Russian family that came to power in 1613 and ruled for three centuries 5. Tsar Peter the Great's goal for a changed Russian society	1. Popular ruling family 2. Unpopular ruling family 3. Leader of the Puritans, who ruled as Lord Protector 4. Fate of King Charles I 5. What the Restoration restored, politically
10	6. Church court that punished people suspected of heresy 7. Hapsburg ruler of Spain, a native of Flanders, who was also the Holy Roman emperor 8. Native Spanish Hapsburg ruler, hardworking and devout 9. How Philip strengthened Spanish government 10. Northern European country Philip tried to invade and conquer 11. Type of rule established by Ferdinand and Isabella	6. King who ended the fighting between Protestants and Catholics 7. Representative body that did not meet from 1614 to 1789 8. Family that began to rule France in 1589 9. Chief minister, churchman, actual ruler of France from 1624 to 1642 10. Social class weakened by Richelieu and Louis XIV	6. War of 1618–1648 in Germany, fought for religious and then political reasons 7. War of 1756–1763 that involved almost all of Europe 8. First important Russian ruler 9. Tsar Peter the Great ordered his nobles to remove these. 10. Russian port built as Russia's "window to Europe," named for Peter the Great	6. Popular form of entertainment that the Restoration restored 7. Document that established many basic rights of the English people 8. The last Tudor monarch 9. The first Stuart monarch 10. Type of ruler Cromwell was, essentially

15	12. Result of expelling non-Catholics from Spain 13. Religion promoted by Ferdinand and Isabella 14. Term for Philip's branch of the ruling family 15. Capital established by Philip 16. Kingdom seized by Spain in 1580	11. "Sun King" who reportedly claimed "I am the state." 12. Major drains on the French treasury under Louis XIV 13. War fought to determine the king of Spain, from which France lost territory 14. Result of Louis XIV's revocation of the Huguenots' religious freedom 15. Decree that granted French Protestants freedom of worship	11. German princess who ruled Russia from 1762 to 1796 12. Country partitioned out of existence by Russia, Prussia, and Austria 13. "The Great Fritz," Frederick II of Prussia 14. Country devastated by the Thirty Years' War 15. Most powerful and important state within the Holy Roman Empire	11. English Protestants who wanted to "purify" the Anglican Church 12. The second Stuart monarch, who dissolved Parliament in 1629 13. James I firmly believed in this theory of a monarch's power 14. Civil war began in 1642 when Charles I led troops against this body. 15. Country that the first Stuart monarch also ruled
20	17. Protestant northern European area that successfully fought for independence from Spain 18. Economic problem caused by the flood of gold and silver into Spain 19. Empire that lost a fierce naval battle to Spain at Lepanto in 1571 20. Greek artist in Spain who painted figures with very long bodies 21. Brilliant court painter to Philip IV	16. Queen who allowed Catholics to attack Protestants 17. King who let his chief minister run France 18. Louis's chief minister, a believer in mercantilism 19. Long war from which France gained much power 20. Terrible anti-Huguenot event of 1572	16. Religion of Austria 17. Religion of Prussia 18. All Hohenzollern possessions in northern Germany 19. Skillful Austrian ruler who gained her title through her husband 20. Enduring Russian foreign policy goal set by Peter the Great	16. Successor to the Cromwells 17. Reason why the English monarch had to consult Parliament 18. Term for the bloodless overthrow of King James II 19. New joint rulers of England in 1688 20. Type of monarchy Great Britain became in the 1700s
NOTES				

22 Commerce, Science, and Enlightenment

	The Commercial Revolution	The Scientific Revolution	Ideas of the Enlightenment	Enlightened Politics
5	1. European region that became the new focus of trade 2. Steady rise in prices linked to a sharp increase in the amount of money available 3. Standard that allowed the use of money throughout Europe 4. Social group that the bankers and capitalists belonged to 5. Money paid in return for a loan	1. Outstanding scientist, and artist, of the Renaissance 2. Instrument invented by Galileo to confirm his ideas 3. Newton's theory explaining the force that holds the universe together 4. Systematic way of investigating a problem in science 5. U.S. scientist famed for his electrical experiment involving lightning and a kite	1. What thinkers sought to be enlightened about 2. Another term for the Enlightenment 3. Law that governed human nature, to Enlightenment thinkers 4. International language of the Enlightenment 5. Scotsman who studied the source of nations' wealth	1. Agreement between the people and their chosen leader 2. Rights no one could justifiably take from the people 3. Two of Locke's "natural rights" 4. Two freedoms advocated by Voltaire 5. Revolutions of the 1700s influenced by Enlightenment ideas
10	6. Italian port that declined in importance as global trade spread 7. Northern European port that increased in importance as global trade grew 8. Term for the economic developments of this first age of global trade 9. Person who owned an interest in a company 10. Profit paid out for each share of stock	6. Polish astronomer of the 1500s who revived the sun-centered model of the universe 7. Italian astronomer who showed that the sun-centered theory was correct 8. Internal body system first described accurately by British physician William Harvey 9. New life-forms discovered by van Leeuwenhoek, a Dutch scientist 10. Airlike substances discovered by Joseph Black	6. Enlightenment thinkers favored these over human justice. 7. The belief that logical thinking would discover the truth 8. Major focus of medieval thought that the Enlightenment turned away from 9. The source of human corruption, according to Rousseau 10. Monumental summary of French Enlightenment ideas compiled by Diderot	6. Key U.S document heavily influenced by Enlightenment ideas 7. French writer whose ideas inspired the French revolutionaries 8. English political thinker who justified the overthrow of Britain's king 9. English philosopher who first proposed a "social contract" 10. Primary concern of Enlightenment political thinkers

15	11. Wealth earned, saved, and invested to produce profits 12. Taxes on imports 13. Term for the new global exchange of people, plants, animals, ideas, etc. 14. Territories important to mercantilism 15. Trade goods that colonies were to export to their parent country	11. Basic element of air discovered by both Lavoisier and Priestly 12. Dutch eyeglass-maker's new instrument that revealed the existence of "invisible" things 13. Fahrenheit and Celsius both developed a scale for reading this new temperature-measuring instrument. 14. Method developed by British physician Edward Jenner to prevent smallpox 15. Great English scientist who studied the laws of motion	11. Source of natural wealth, according to the Physiocrats 12. "Hands-off" economic system promoted by Adam Smith 13. Educational subject favored by Enlightenment thinkers 14. English poet who was a strong advocate of the Enlightenment 15. Term for French thinkers of the Enlightenment	11. Condition in which people lived before organizing society 12. The most nearly perfect existing government, according to Montesquieu 13. Division among government branches admired by Montesquieu 14. Limitations created by division of governmental powers 15. Development of this type of monarchy was influenced by Montesquieu.
20	16. Trade goods colonies were to import from the parent country 17. Banking service that developed as a safeguard for merchants 18. Nationality that replaced the Italians as the bankers of Europe 19. Economic policy based on the concept that a country's power depends mainly on its wealth 20. Company in which people pooled large amounts of money to carry out a business venture	16. English "father of modern chemistry" 17. System of identifying and naming living things developed by Linnaeus 18. Pioneer in the study of anatomy 19. Theory that the sun was the center of the universe 20. French physician who developed improved treatment to prevent infection	16. Condition of the newborn mind, according to Locke 17. Fashionable French gatherings for intellectual conversation 18. French thinker who stressed logic and reason to achieve scientific knowledge 19. British thinker who stressed experiments and observation to achieve scientific knowledge	16. Supreme power in politics, according to Rousseau 17. Free choice of the people in government 18. Term for rulers who supported the Enlightenment 19. French document of 1789 strongly influenced by Enlightenment ideas

NOTES

23 Revolution in North America

	Steps to Revolution	Revolutionary People	Revolutionary Places	Elements and Results of the Revolution
5	1. Elected legislative body in each colony 2. Passed in 1764, it placed a tax on sweet goods brought into the colonies. 3. Mob action that dumped tea into Boston Harbor 4. Slogan about taxes, a rallying cry for colonists 5. English law-making body	1. Commander of the colonial army 2. Main author of the Declaration of Independence 3. King of England during the American Revolution 4. Boston silversmith who made a famous "midnight ride" 5. Slang term for a British soldier 6. Colonial soldiers who could be ready to fight quickly	1. Site of the Continental Congresses 2. Winter headquarters of Washington's army in 1777–78 3. Site of famed battle in Boston 4. New York fort that Benedict Arnold planned to turn over to the British 5. Colony that took the lead in disobeying British laws 6. Ocean separating England and the colonies	1. Document that explained why the colonies had to separate from England 2. The new nation formed by the colonies 3. Document that created a new form of government in 1789 4. Type of government like ancient Rome's that the U.S. Constitution established 5. The first 10 amendments to the U.S. Constitution
10	6. Rights the colonists insisted they had 7. War that the British paid for by raising the colonists' taxes 8. Peace agreement that greatly expanded British control of North America 9. 1765 law requiring a tax on all written documents 10. Refusal by the colonists to buy British or taxed goods	7. German soldiers paid to fight for the English 8. People who opposed the split with England 9. People who favored the split with England 10. First man to sign the Declaration of Independence 11. Frenchman who was Washington's trusted aide	7. Colonial harbor closed by the British 8. Britain gained all territory east of this river from France. 9. Massachusetts towns where colonial troops first fired on British troops 10. The British planned to cut the colonies in two along this river. 11. Site of a major American victory in New York in 1777 12. Site of final American victory in 1781	6. British strength lay in the size and power of these forces. 7. U.S. system of government, with powers divided between the central government and individual states 8. Group that met in 1775 and voted to declare independence 9. Condition of all men, according to the Declaration 10. Power the Continental Congress did not have but needed

15	11. Riot in which British scldiers shot some Boston colonists 12. Trading company given the sole right to bring tea into the colonies 13. Harsh laws passed to punish the Massachusetts Colony 14. Philadelphia meeting of delegates from 12 colonies in 1774 15. Two of the three types of the 13 British colonies	12. Prussian officer who trained American troops 13. Patriot author of *Common Sense* 14. British general who surrendered his army to end the war 15. American ambassador to France during the war 16. Man who said, "Give me liberty or give me death."	13. City where the peace treaty was negotiated 14. Bodies of water on the new northern boundary of the United States 15. Spanish territory that marked the new southern boundary of the United States 16. English settlers in this territory gained rights after the war 17. The two self-governing colonies	11. Major European power that became an American ally in 1778 12. Agreement establishing the first postwar government 13. Fighting force of each state or colony 14. Under the Articles, the United States had none of these courts. 15. Americans' preferred way of fighting
20	16. Economic theory that colonies existed for the benefit of the mother country 17. Laws that restricted colonial trade to English merchants and ships (1651–1750) 18. Act restating Parliament's right to pass laws on all colonial matters 19. Series of laws taxing colonial trade, starting in 1767 20. Laws that protected the rights of French Catholics and extended Canadian boundaries	17. Important author of the Constitution and fourth U.S. president 18. Leader of the Sons of Liberty in Massachusetts 19. One of two outstanding Polish officers who served in the American army 20. Two of the three men who represented America at the peace conference 21. Colonial lawyer and Patriot who defended British soldiers after the Boston killings	18. The two Canadian cities the colonists tried to seize in 1775 19. City evacuated by the British in 1776 after a colonial siege 20. City where the American army was almost trapped 21. City where the British army spent the winter of 1777–78 22. State that did not take part in the Constitutional Convention	16. Two negative characteristics of the American army 17. Peace agreement that settled the war in 1783 18. British act dividing Canada into two provinces, one mostly British and one mostly French 19. European countries that had claims on the North American continent in 1783

NOTES

24 The French Revolution and Napoleon

	Steps to Revolution	Revolutionary Events	Napoleon's Rise and Empire	Napoleon's Decline and Fall
5	1. Name for the three classes of French society 2. Clergy and nobles did not pay these 3. Class of people most in favor of change 4. Wife of the French king, charming and irresponsible 5. Members of the First Estate 6. Members of the Second Estate	1. Parisian fort taken by a mob on July 14, 1789 2. Slogan of the Revolution 3. Source of government authority, according to the Declaration 4. The wave of killing from 1793 to 1794 5. Instrument used for execution 6. Fate of Louis XVI and his wife	1. Type of ruler Napoleon was from 1799 to 1814 2. This body had no power under Napoleon. 3. Napoleon concentrated authority to create this type of government. 4. Napoleon's new title from 1804 on 5. People Napoleon often placed on the thrones of conquered states 6. Island where Napoleon was born	1. Napoleon's conquests spread the ideas of this movement throughout Europe. 2. Widespread activity that violated Napoleon's blockade 3. Huge eastern European country Napoleon invaded in 1812 4. Island off Italy that Napoleon was exiled to 5. Napoleon's final defeat
10	7. Members of the Third Estate 8. The people had none of these before the Revolution 9. Foreign event that strongly influenced French thinking 10. Foreign war that drained the French treasury in the 1770s 11. Body called to meet for the first time in 175 years	7. Government of five directors under the third constitution 8. Leader of extreme radicals, assassinated in his bath 9. The two leaders of the radical Jacobins 10. Two countries that invaded France in 1792 11. The three different groups in the Legislative Assembly	7. Napoleon fought British forces in this African country. 8. Alliances formed against France 9. New, uniform system of French civil laws 10. The two revolutionary rights Napoleon took away from the people 11. Paris landmark where Napoleon was crowned	6. Napoleon's conquests promoted the growth of this feeling. 7. Drafting of these people weakened Napoleon's army. 8. Southern European countries that drove out the French in 1812–13 9. Natural phenomenon that helped defeat Napoleon in Russia 10. Napoleon's most severe military disaster, 1812–13

15

12. French king before and during the Revolution
13. Lack of this caused the king to call on the assembly
14. Number of votes each estate had in the Estates-General
15. Site of the costly French court
16. The three subdivisions of the Third Estate

12. Type of government set up by the Constitution of 1791
13. The National Assembly took away this institution's land
14. The royal family and National Assembly moved to this city
15. Document that stated the Revolution's principles
16. French flag of three colors adopted in 1789

12. Method of getting soldiers for the army
13. Two countries that made peace with Napoleon in 1801 and 1802
14. Vast territory that Napoleon sold in 1803 to raise money for his army
15. British admiral killed in 1805 in a sea battle against France
16. Napoleon's title from 1799 to 1804

11. Island off Africa where Napoleon died
12. British commander who defeated Napoleon in the final battle
13. Napoleon inspired desire for national unity in these two areas.
14. Important difference between Napoleon's army and earlier armies
15. The war on the Iberian Peninsula

20

17. The traditional political and social system of France before the Revolution
18. Intellectual movement that strongly influenced French thinking about reform
19. How the Third Estate insisted the Estates must meet
20. What the Third Estate declared themselves to be in 1789
21. Pledge taken by the Third Estate to write a constitution

17. The two reforms passed by the National Assembly in August 1789
18. City government of Paris set up by radicals
19. Elected group that governed France from 1792 to 1795
20. Radical court that tried enemies of the Revolution
21. Committee that directed the army

17. Napoleon expressed contempt for the British by calling them this.
18. Term for Napoleon's blockade of the British Isle
19. Empire abolished by Napoleon
20. Union of German states organized by Napoleon
21. Austrian town where Napoleon defeated Russian and Austrian forces in 1805

16. Term for the Spaniards' style of fighting
17. Napoleon's defeat in 1813
18. Ruling family restored to the French Throne in 1814
19. Napoleon's successor as ruler of France
20. Period of Napoleon's final rule in 1815

NOTES

25 The Industrial Revolution

Points	Agriculture and Manufacturing	Transportation and Communication	Conditions and Effects	Reform
5	1. Industry where the Industrial Revolution began 2. Where workers made cloth before the Industrial Revolution 3. Factories were located next to these. 4. Where workers worked, after the Industrial Revolution began 5. Cotton-cleaning machine that dramatically increased cotton production 6. Weaving machine invented in 1733 that doubled a weaver's daily output	1. Type of power that replaced wind on ships 2. American developer of the first successful steamboat 3. Waterways built to connect cities and rivers 4. Flat-bottomed boats used on canals 5. The Industrial Revolution's chief means of land transportation 6. Morse's system of dots and dashes	1. Class that increased and gained political power during the Industrial Revolution 2. Class created by the Industrial Revolution 3. Group of society that had to work along with adults 4. Centers of population that grew rapidly during the Industrial Revolution 5. Working-class children had no time for either of these two activities. 6. Increase in the number of people	1. Type of labor limited by early reform laws 2. Workers' associations allowed in England after 1824 3. Refusals to work in order to gain demands 4. Famous English novelist who described the terrible working conditions 5. New, shorter workday for textile mills 6. Negotiating by unions and management
10	7. Spinning machine of 1764 named after the inventor's daughter 8. Scottish engineer who improved the steam engine 9. This replaced water as a major source of power. 10. American inventor of the cotton-cleaning machine 11. Manufacture of standard goods in large quantities 12. Parts that fit any example of a particular product	7. American who developed the telegraph 8. Improved roads developed by the Scot John McAdam 9. Devices that control the level of water in canals 10. Fulton's famous steamboat 11. Invention that sent electrical impulses over wire 12. Heavily insulated communications wires laid underwater	7. Working conditions in factories 8. Workers who were paid lower wages 9. What the proletariat had to sell in order to live 10. Type of worker that decreased 11. New groups that ran the factories, neither owners nor laborers	7. Living standards improved when these became available to workers. 8. Social class that supported factory workers against owners 9. System in which the public owned the means of production 10. Socialists who designed model communities 11. Welsh socialist who established a utopian community for his factory workers

15	13. Englishman who found how to make steel from iron 14. Material that replaced iron in machines 15. Material that replaced charcoal for smelting iron 16. American inventor of the mechanical reaper 17. Fencing off of formerly common land in England	13. Improved transportation was necessary to move these items. 14. Chief means of land transportation before the Industrial Revolution 15. Steam engines on wheels that ran on rails 16. New form of personal transportation that first hit the roads in the late 1800s 17. Steamboat that crossed the Atlantic in 1838	12. Workers often had to do this to be near the factories. 13. Type of labor most in demand at factories 14. Great fear of urban factory workers 15. Condition of air and water in cities 16. Social class that lost power as the Industrial Revolution continued	12. Developer of "scientific socialism" 13. Marx's famous pamphlet 14. Groups that were in opposition under capitalism, according to Marx 15. Economic theory meaning "let do" favored by business owners 16. Englishman who wrote about increasing population
20	18. Inventor of the weaving machine 19. Inventor of the spinning machine 20. English engineer who developed the first practical steam engine 21. English inventor of the water frame for spinning 22. Weaving machine invented by Edmund Cartwright in 1785	18. English engineer who won a locomotive-building contest 19. Speedy locomotive that started an English railroad-building boom 20. Italian who built the first electric battery 21. American responsible for laying the trans-Atlantic cable 22. Englishman who produced electricity with a magnet	17. Cities grew around these. 18. Average length of the industrial working day 19. Normal length of the industrial working week 20. Buildings that housed many people 21. People who owned the means of production	17. English businessman who wrote that working-class poverty was unavoidable 18. English philosopher who wrote that a government should promote social welfare 19. Owen's utopian factory community in Scotland 20. Marx's co-author 21. Marx's study of capitalism

NOTES

26 Latin America and the Struggle for Freedom

	Colonial Times	Revolution in Mexico, Central America, and the Islands	Brazil	Revolution in Spanish South America
5	1. Region from Mexico to the southern tip of South America 2. South American country almost as large as the United States 3. Native peoples enslaved by the Europeans 4. Main products of Latin American mining 5. Creoles were barred from these positions. 6. The Latin American colonies had to buy these from Spain.	1. Peoples of Mexico who revolted 2. Type of government established in Mexico after the emperor 3. The countries of this part of Latin America were briefly part of Mexico 4. Country Mexico won its independence from 5. U.S. policy that protected independent Latin America from European interference	1. Valuable wood that spurred colonial settlement 2. Slaves were imported from this continent. 3. Brazil won independence without this. 4. Brazil's major river 5. People who were sent to Brazil to work off their sentences 6. Religion of Brazil	1. The "George Washington of South America" 2. Nation that most countries in South America won independence from 3. Vast mountains the creole armies had to cross 4. Capital of Peru 5. Republic named for Bolívar 6. Bolívar's native country, which gained independence in 1821
10	7. The Latin American colonies supplied Spain with these. 8. Two major Indian groups conquered by the Spanish 9. Rolling, grassy plains of South America 10. In 1550, the largest Spanish-speaking city in the world 11. Ruler of each Spanish colonial division	6. Island nation that gained independence in 1804 7. Former slave who led the revolt in Haiti 8. European event that weakened the Spanish government 9. Former Aztec city of Tenochtitlán, in Mexico 10. Three of the five countries just south of Mexico 11. Spanish colony that shared Haiti's island	7. Brazil's "mother country" 8. Primary crop of Brazilian plantations in the 1600s 9. The two most valuable products of Brazilian mining 10. Family that fled to Brazil in 1808 11. Language spoken in Brazil 12. Brazil's center of government	7. Bolívar's birthplace; Venezuela's capital 8. Class that wanted to rid itself of Spanish control 9. Union of cities and towns in La Plata 10. Argentine leader who helped free Chile 11. Chilean patriot who led a revolt 12. The "Protector of Peru"

15	12. Highest class in Spanish Latin-American society 13. Europeans of Spanish descent born in the colonies 14. People of mixed white and Indian blood 15. Religious institution which was an important force in Latin American society 16. People of mixed African and European blood	12. Country Haiti won its independence from 13. Dictator who lost a third of Mexico's land to the United States 14. First Indian to rule Mexico since the Aztecs 15. Two reforms promised in Mexico by Hidalgo 16. Island that Haiti was part of	13. The two major exports of Brazil in the 1800s 14. Pedro II encouraged this to help Brazil's economy. 15. European emperor who invaded Brazil's "mother country" and drove out the royal family 16. King who returned to Portugal in 1821 17. Son of the Portuguese king; he became Brazil's ruler	13. "The Liberator" 14. Bolívar dreamed of this, but it didn't happen 15. Native American who led a revolt in 1780 16. Later name for the union in La Plata 17. States bordering Argentina on the east; part of La Plata
20	17. Latin American colonies could not trade with this northern neighbor. 18. Flat, treeless plains of South America 19. Viceroyalty of North and Central America 20. The three viceroyalties of South America 21. Fees imposed by the Church	17. Union of countries to the south of Mexico 18. Catholic priest who led the first Mexican revolt in 1810 19. Priest who led a second Mexican revolt 20. Mexico's liberating general who became emperor 21. Former slave who was the second leader of the revolt in Haiti	18. Type of government established for the independent Brazil 19. Well-educated ruler who brought peace and good government to Brazil 20. Ruler of Brazil appointed by the king 21. Brazil borrowed money from this country for building projects. 22. Territorial strips in colonial Brazil	18. Seat of government in La Plata 19. Viceroyalty on the west coast freed in 1821 20. Country formed from the southern part of the viceroyalty of Peru 21. Nation of northern South America ruled by Bolívar 22. Three of the present-day countries that were part of Bolívar's nation

NOTES

27 Conflict and Democracy in the English-Speaking World

	Great Britain Becomes a Democracy	Canada, New Zealand, and Australia	Growth of the United States	Civil War and Reunion in the United States
5	1. Chief reform concern of the middle class and workers 2. Imprisonment for this was abolished in the 1830s 3. Queen of England from 1837 to 1901 4. Period of the English queen's reign 5. Famine occurred in Ireland when this failed 6. Members of the House of Commons finally earned this in 1911	1. Longest unfortified boundary between nations in the world 2. What Britain used Australia for at first 3. Australia is both of these, geographically speaking. 4. The original inhabitants of Australia 5. The discovery of this brought a flood of immigrants to Australia.	1. Two of the first three U.S. presidents 2. Where Native Americans were forced to resettle 3. Flood of migrants to the West Coast in search of quick riches 4. Settlers crossed this mountain range to reach the West Coast. 5. Nations that bordered the United States to the north and south 6. Famous mission that was the site of a battle in the Mexican war	1. Economic base of the northern United States 2. Economic base of the southern United States 3. Large southern farms 4. The largest single issue dividing the U.S. sections 5. Leader of the North during the war 6. The major military leader of the South
10	7. Party that favored reforms in the 1820s 8. New name of the Whig party 9. New name of the Tory party 10. Repeal of the Corn Laws allowed this to be imported free of tax 11. Witty and shrewd Conservative party leader 12. Formal, cautious Liberal party leader	6. Two major groups of settlers in Canada 7. This event resulted in the formation of the Yukon Territory. 8. Huge area Canada bought from the Hudson's Bay Company 9. Status of Canada after union 10. Australian policy that restricted immigration 11. Four of the six Australian states	7. Characteristic of U.S. government that provided stability 8. By the mid-1800s, almost all of these people could vote. 9. Purchase of this area doubled the size of the United States. 10. Southern state sold by Spain 11. The United States went to war with this country in 1846.	7. Northern general who received the Confederate surrender 8. The president's declaration that freed many slaves 9. The two major crops of the South 10. People who wanted slavery to end everywhere in the United States 11. To withdraw from the Union, as the Southern states did

15

13. Reform demanded by the Irish
14. New political party founded by Fabian socialists and union members
15. Type of legislation passed by both Liberals and Conservatives in the 1800s
16. Election districts with little or no population
17. Election districts controlled by nobles

12. Native inhabitants of New Zealand
13. First European country to discover Australia and New Zealand
14. Englishman who rediscovered Australia and New Zealand
15. Problem addressed by dividing Canada into two provinces in 1791
16. Opened in 1885, this linked eastern and western Canada.

12. Country that sold the Louisiana Territory to the United States
13. The United States gained this West Coast state (plus others) after the Mexican war.
14. The Louisiana Territory stretched from this river to these mountains.
15. Southwestern territory that triggered the Mexican war
16. Important city of Louisiana that came with the Purchase

12. Political party that pledged to stop the spread of slavery
13. Northern politicians who went to the South after the Civil War
14. The new southern nation
15. President of the new southern nation
16. The South's term for the Civil War

20

18. First law that made some voting reforms
19. Group that proposed voting reforms in the 1830s and 1840s
20. The Second Reform Bill gave the vote to these people.
21. The Third Reform Bill gave the vote to these people.
22. Act that ended the lords' power to veto tax and spending bills

17. Report that said the two Canadas should become one
18. Law joining Upper and Lower Canada
19. The British North America Act created this in Canada in 1867.
20. Number of provinces in Canada by 1898
21. New Zealand was the first country to adopt this, in 1893.

17. Two aspects of the United States that increased tremendously during the 1800s
18. American settlers in Mexican territory set up this independent republic
19. The United States gained this territory from Britain in 1846.
20. Two of the three states formed from the Oregon Territory
21. Purchase of land from Mexico in 1853

17. The South lacked these two things it needed to supply its armies.
18. Period when the seceded states were reestablished as part of the Union
19. First state to withdraw from the Union
20. The major North-South clash about slavery focused on this.
21. European country that supported the South for its cotton

NOTES

28 Reaction and Revolution in Europe

	The Congress of Vienna	Alliances and the Age of Metternich	France: Empire, War, and Republic	Revolt and Revolution
5	1. Meeting that determined how to reorganize Europe after Napoleon's defeat 2. Austrian representative who was chairman of the Congress 3. Chief French representative at the Congress 4. Form of government preferred by the Congress 5. Britain gained these kinds of territories from the French, Danes, and Dutch. 6. Nation that lost much of its territory after the Congress	1. Major benefit to Europe established by the Congress of Vienna for almost forty years 2. Statesman who dominated Europe for thirty years after the Congress of Vienna 3. Suppression of this was the allies' main concern 4. Equal strength among nations; aim of the Congress System 5. The condition of things as they are; aim of the Congress System	1. Louis Napoleon's position after being president 2. Louis Napoleon's official name as emperor 3. Waterway in the Near East built by French engineers 4. Napoleon installed an emperor in this American country. 5. France's war against the German states	1. Monarchs granted their people these rules of government because of the revolts. 2. English romantic poet who died in the Greek revolt in 1824 3. Center of riots in the French revolution of 1848 4. A revolt in this country in 1820 challenged King Ferdinand's power. 5. A revolt broke out in this area of southern Italy in 1820.
10	7. The four powers that defeated France and Napoleon 8. Russia's representative at the Congress 9. Nation that was divided between Russia and Prussia 10. Neutral alpine nation allowed to keep a constitutional republican government 11. Term for the political system set up by the Congress	6. Spy system set up by Metternich to suppress revolutionaries 7. Form of rule reestablished in Spain (and northern Italy) 8. Coalition of Great Britain, Austria, Russia, and Prussia after Napoleon 9. One of the three rulers who refused to sign the Holy Alliance 10. The European alliance after France joined it	6. Two opposed groups of society that supported Louis Napoleon 7. Two democratic features of the French empire 8. Two nondemocratic features of the French empire 9. France fought with England in this war against Russia. 10. Napoleon strengthened French rule over this North African country.	6. This neighbor of Spain experienced a revolt in 1820. 7. People who rebelled against their harsh rulers in 1821 8. Brutal rulers of the Balkan states and Greece 9. Balkan people who gained some self-government in the 1820s 10. Country that won independence from the Dutch (Holland) in 1831 11. Country where liberal reforms occurred without revolution

15	12. Control of northern states in this nation was given to Austria 13. Ally of Napoleon that lost its possession of Norway 14. Nation that was given to Sweden 15. Principle that favored restoration to their thrones of all the former ruling families 16. Great Britain's representative at the Congress	11. Ruling family of France, Spain, and Italy 12. Ruling family of Austria and northern Italy 13. How Great Britain's government differed from its allies' governments 14. Metternich's way of handling liberal ideas 15. Desire to return to the conditions of an earlier time	11. Napoleon established French control over this Indochinese country. 12. Emperor installed in America by Napoleon 13. Leader who ended the French empire in America 14. Revolutionary council of Paris set up in 1871 15. The failure of this canal-building company in the 1890s caused a financial scandal.	12. Social class that supported the French revolt of 1830 13. Voting rights gained by French in 1848 14. Two Central European nations that had unsuccessful revolutions in 1848 15. First president of the new French republic 16. Powerful force for both unity and disunity in 1800s Europe
20	17. Prussia's representative at the Congress 18. Restored Bourbon king of France 19. Two nations that were combined into the single Kingdom of the Netherlands 20. Prussia gained most of this former kingdom. 21. Payment by the aggressor for damages inflicted on other nations	16. Agreement of European rulers to rule as Christian princes 17. Ruler who formed the Holy Alliance 18. Term for the governing of Europe by international agreement during this period 19. Nation that withdrew from the Alliance in 1822 20. Metternich's official government position	16. Main reason for the instability of government in the French republic 17. Napoleon Bonaparte's relationship to Louis Napoleon 18. Government established by Louis Napoleon to succeed the republic 19. France protected these people in the Ottoman Empire. 20. Napoleon's fate in the war against Prussia	17. French king overthrown in July 1830 18. King elected by the leaders of the French revolt of 1830 19. Government set up by the French revolution of 1848 20. People who revolted against Russian rule in Warsaw in 1830 21. Elected German assembly that met in 1848 to write a constitution
NOTES				

29 Unification and Nationalism

	A United Germany	A United Italy	Central Europe	Russia
5	1. Prime minister of Prussia from 1862 to 1890 2. Basis of Prussian strength 3. Bismarck's official position 4. Title of the German emperor 5. Dominant state in the new German union of 1867 6. Major rival of Prussia for German leadership	1. Italian states ruled by the pope 2. Large island at the southern end of Italy 3. City ruled by the pope until 1870 4. Economic base of northern Italy 5. Economic base of southern Italy 6. Secret society formed by local strong men in Sicily	1. Dominant power of Central Europe 2. Ruling family of Austria 3. Region that joined equally with Austria in 1867 4. The Dual Monarchy 5. Feeling of loyalty and patriotism toward a country, strong in Central Europe	1. Russian form of government under the tsars 2. Institution abolished by the tsar in 1861 3. Freedom from serfdom (or slavery) 4. Cause of Alexander's death 5. Radicals who favored bombings and political killings
10	7. Capital of the German Empire (and of Prussia) 8. France's war against Prussia in 1870 9. Foundation of Germany's strong economy 10. Reformers strongly opposed by Bismarck 11. Event engineered by Bismarck to make the southern German states allies of the north 12. Northern country Prussia and Austria fought in 1864	7. The self-proclaimed "prisoner of the Vatican" 8. Capital of the kingdom of Italy 9. Leader who liberated southern Italy 10. Kingdom of the lower half of Italy 11. Garibaldi's army 12. Southern capital seized by Garibaldi and his army	6. Majority population and language of Hungary 7. Dominant nationality and language of Austria 8. Dominant power in the Balkans in the 1860s 9. Nickname for the Ottoman Empire 10. The Ottoman type of government 11. Country that defeated the Ottoman Empire in 1878	6. Russia wanted access to this sea. 7. Program that forced non-Russians to adopt Russian culture and customs 8. Policy that favored the union of all Slavic peoples 9. War Russia fought against France, Great Britain, and the Ottoman Empire in 1855–56 10. Body of water that bordered the Crimea 11. The only real benefit of the Crimean War

15

13. Bismarck's nickname, from his statement that he would unite Germany by "blood and iron"
14. Union of German states after the Congress of Vienna
15. Prussia's brief 1866 war against Austria
16. New union of German states established in 1867
17. King of Prussia from 1861 to 1868 and German emperor as of 1871
18. Conservative aristocratic landowners

13. King of Sardinia and of Italy
14. French ruler who allied his nation with Sardinia
15. Prime minister of Sardinia who worked for Italian unity
16. Ally of Sardinia in its war with Austria
17. Major power that dominated a divided Italy
18. Leader of Italian unification movements before 1850

12. International conference that rewrote the Russian-Ottoman treaty
13. Ruler of the Ottoman Empire
14. Ally of the Balkan people
15. Major ally of the Ottoman Empire
16. Emperor of Austria from 1848 to 1916 and King of Hungary as of 1867

12. Tsar who allowed a number of liberal reforms
13. Moderate reformers who became more and more radical
14. Type of language shared by Russians, Bulgarians, and Serbs
15. Strongly nationalistic European people who were part of the Russian Empire
16. New class that supported freedom for the serfs

20

19. Customs union that promoted free trade among German states
20. Two small northern states Austria and Prussia fought Denmark for
21. Realistic, tough-minded politics pursued by Bismarck
22. Message from the Prussian king released by Bismarck to anger the French people
23. The two houses of the German legislative branch

19. The Italian nationalistic movement; Italian for "resurgence"
20. Northern Italian state Sardinia gained after the brief war with Austria
21. Secret Italian nationalist society of the early 1800s
22. New youthful Italian nationalist movement of the 1830s
23. State added to Italy after the Austro-Prussian War in 1866

17. Conflict in which Austria lost territory to both Prussia and Italy
18. Three of the major peoples of the Balkans
19. Treaty between Russia and the Ottoman Empire in 1878
20. Mediterranean island gained by Great Britain from the Turks in 1878
21. Balkan state that gained self-rule in 1878 and independence in 1908

17. Russian naval base under siege for 11 months
18. Radical activists who wanted to abolish all political and social structures in Russia
19. Radicals who urged land reform and a better life for the peasants
20. Violent, often fatal, mob attacks, especially against Jews
21. Russia claimed to be the protector of these peoples within the Ottoman Empire

NOTES

30 Latin America, the Pacific Islands, and Imperialism

	All About Imperialism	The Pacific Islands	Spain Yields to the United States	The United States Steps Into Latin America
5	1. Extending a nation's power by acquiring or gaining control over new territories 2. Goods needed to feed industrial production 3. People of industrial nations wanted these kinds of foods. 4. Mass production created a need for these. 5. Pride in one's country; a spur to imperialism	1. New source of power for western ships 2. Pacific island group closest to the United States 3. Type of native government in Hawaii 4. Plantations were established on Hawaii to grow these crops. 5. Group on Hawaii that persuaded the United States to annex the islands	1. Memorable U.S. battleship blown up in a Cuban harbor 2. Americans sympathized with Cubans' desire for this. 3. Popular U.S. volunteer in the Spanish-American War who became vice president 4. Theodore Roosevelt's dashing group of volunteer cavalrymen 5. Status of Cuba after the war 6. These publications stirred up U.S. sentiment against Spain.	1. Latin America's new ruling class lacked this. 2. Strategic need for a Central American canal 3. Central American canal 4. Insect carrier of the deadly disease of Central America 5. Disease whose defeat allowed the canal to be built
10	6. Missionary motive of imperialism 7. An area, with its people, totally controlled by a foreign nation 8. Taxes on goods brought into a country 9. Factory owners needed new ways to invest this. 10. Colonies provided this important resource for armies.	6. U.S.-controlled islands of Samoa 7. Fuel needed by ocean-going ships 8. Islands halfway across the Pacific occupied by the United States 9. Arm of the U.S. government that controlled Samoa 10. Status of the Hawaiian islands after U.S. annexation	7. Island that was the main cause of tension between the United States and Spain 8. Cuban harbor where a U.S. battleship exploded 9. U.S. president during the war with Spain 10. The war of 1898 11. Islands southeast of the United States ceded by Spain	6. Two bodies of water connected by the Central American canal 7. Mexican bandit who raided New Mexico 8. U.S. policy that foreign nations must not take any new Latin American colonies 9. Theodore Roosevelt's addition to the Monroe Doctrine 10. Strip of land the Central American canal crossed

15	11. Colonies provided this important resource for navies. 12. So-called duty of western nations toward "backward" people 13. Colonial rivalries were an underlying cause of this global conflict. 14. Country controlled by one foreign power and "protected" from other foreign nations 15. Ports opened by treaty to foreign nations	11. Last queen of Hawaii 12. Island chain of Alaska acquired by the United States 13. English explorer who sailed to many small Pacific islands 14. Samoan harbor and site of a U.S. naval base 15. Central Pacific Island acquired by the United States	12. Islands of the Pacific ceded by Spain to the United States 13. Harbor and capital of the Philippines 14. Islands promised eventual independence when the United States took control 15. Head of the Philippine and Puerto Rican governments 16. Sea that surrounds Cuba	11. Chief financial reason for U.S. intervention in many Latin American countries 12. Country protected by the United States against expansion of British Guiana 13. The United States helped Panama gain its freedom from this country. 14. Island nation occupied by U.S. marines from 1916 to 1924 15. Former French island colony where U.S. marines landed in 1915
20	16. Early economic theory that colonies added a lot to a nation's wealth 17. Imperialism carried on for the sake of profit 18. Imperialism carried on to improve a nation's power and status 19. Region where one foreign nation had special privileges recognized by other nations 20. Social theory that people who were wealthy and powerful were superior to poorer and less powerful people	16. German-controlled islands of Samoa 17. Two of the early French island territories in the Pacific 18. Two of Great Britain's four island territories 19. Two of the German island territories 20. Islands jointly controlled from 1889 to 1899 by Germany, Great Britain, and the United States	17. Amendment to the Cuban constitution that gave the United States the right to intervene in Cuban affairs 18. The one remaining U.S. naval station in Cuba 19. Small island east of the Philippines that became an important American naval base 20. Major island that was the site of the Philippine capital 21. Leader of Filipino resistance to U.S. occupation	16. Caribbean islands the United States bought from Denmark 17. Central American country occupied by U.S. marines off and on from 1912 to 1933 18. International conference to promote peaceful cooperation 19. President Roosevelt claimed this power for the United States in Latin America. 20. Mexican port occupied by U.S. marines in 1914
NOTES				

31 Asia and Imperialism

	India	Southeast Asia	China	Japan
5	1. People who were barred from important British positions 2. The two rival religious groups 3. The Empress of India 4. How the British saw themselves as compared with Indians 5. The British policy of divide and rule worked well because India had so many of these. 6. Ruling British government official of India	1. Peninsula east of India and south of China 2. Large Asian country that strongly influenced Southeast Asia 3. What the first European traders came looking for 4. Two beverage products Southeast Asia became an important source of 5. Asian nation that once dominated eastern Southeast Asia 6. System of native work in the Dutch colony	1. Basic foreign policy of the ruling dynasty 2. Drug that the British introduced to China 3. Manchu capital 4. China's giant neighbor to the north 5. Type of government established in China by the revolution of 1912	1. Foreign policy of Japan before imperialism 2. Japan refused to help these people in distress. 3. Purpose of the first European treaties with Japan 4. Japan developed a surplus of this as it industrialized. 5. Japan had to import these important items.
10	7. European country with a near-monopoly on Indian trade in the 1500s 8. Trading company that controlled most of India 9. Small jail cell where British prisoners died overnight 10. Important state, site of Calcutta, conquered by the British 11. Two major factors that prevented Indian unity 12. The minority religious group in India	7. Ocean to the southwest of Southeast Asia 8. Early European traders along the Southeast Asian coast 9. Country that took control of Burma 10. Island at the southern tip of the Southeast Asian peninsula 11. The only independent state (a kingdom) of Southeast Asia 12. Today's name for Siam	6. Ruling dynasty from 1644 until 1911 7. War that opened China to increased British rule 8. Island granted to the British in 1842 9. Peninsular country east of China 10. Nation that defeated China in a war of 1894–95 11. Northern area Russia wanted control of	6. All Japanese became literate because of this. 7. U.S. naval officer who arranged for a treaty 8. Japan's response to Western contact 9. Japan's form of government after 1889 10. Country that Japan fought for control of Korea

15	13. This encouraged Indian ideas about nationalism, democracy, and socialism. 14. Parliament transferred rule of India to this entity in 1858. 15. Reformer and scholar often called the founder of Indian nationalism 16. Group formed to protect the interests of its religious followers 17. Military officer who expanded British control	13. European nation that took control of eastern Southeast Asia 14. Term for the French-controlled nations of Southeast Asia 15. Trading company that governed the Netherlands' island possessions 16. The Dutch colony of Southeast Asia 17. Kingdom on the eastern border of India	12. U.S.-backed policy of giving all nations equal trading rights in China 13. Movement to drive all foreigners out of China 14. Leader of the revolution against the Manchus 15. Chinese term for treaties China was forced to sign 16. Rebellion that weakened the Manchus	11. Excellent harbor taken from China by Russia, then Japan 12. Island colony acquired by Japan from China in 1894 13. Man who arranged the peace between Russia and Japan 14. Japan and Russia divided this area into two spheres of influence 15. Japan annexed this country in 1910, renaming it Chosen.
20	18. Native Indian troops 19. Mutiny (revolt) of the native troops in 1857 20. Group that favored Indian self-rule 21. Important French trading base on India's southeast coast taken by the British in 1761 22. Important British trading base on India's southeast coast	18. Peninsula that jutted out at the southern end of Southeast Asia 19. Britain controlled the northern part of this large island. 20. Britain controlled the southeastern part of this large island. 21. Sea that bordered Southeast Asia on the east 22. Three of the major islands of the Dutch colony	17. Russian naval base near Manchuria 18. Dowager empress who blocked most modernization reforms 19. The young emperor Guang Xu launched a hundred days of this. 20. The Nationalist People's Party 21. Sea between China and Korea	16. Only Japanese port open to foreign trade until the mid-1800s 17. The reign of "enlightened rule" 18. Emperor who established the reign of "enlightened rule" 19. Peninsula on Manchuria's southern coast fought over by China, Russia, and Japan 20. Treaty ending the Russo-Japanese war was signed here.

NOTES

32 Africa and Imperialism

	North Africa	West Africa	East Africa	Southern Africa
5	1. North African coast that was home to pirates 2. Sea that borders North Africa 3. European country that gained control of most of western North Africa 4. Canal built in Egypt 5. Dry region that was the southern boundary of North Africa 6. Rich country occupied by France in 1830	1. Term for Africa south of the Sahara 2. Collective name of France's territories in West Africa 3. Area east of the Cote d'Ivoire known for its gold mines 4. Belgium's large colony in west-central Africa 5. West Africa's only independent nation 6. Body of water that borders West Africa	1. Scottish missionary and renowned explorer 2. Journalist sent to find Livingstone 3. Stanley's famous greeting 4. Germany's protectorate in East Africa 5. Britain's large coastal protectorate in East Africa 6. Italian desert land on the Indian Ocean	1. Dutch settlers in southern Africa 2. Man largely responsible for expansion of British power in southern Africa 3. Gems found in Cape Colony 4. Discovery of this caused a rush of people to the Transvaal 5. Territory named for Rhodes 6. Seaport established by the Dutch in 1652
10	7. Country on the western end of North Africa 8. Native, warlike peoples of North Africa 9. Original owner of almost half the stock of the Suez Canal company 10. Seas connected by the Suez Canal 11. Country that gained control of the Suez Canal in 1875 12. Italy's new name for its North African colony	7. Large French territory from the Congo to the north 8. Largest British colony in West Africa 9. British journalist and explorer of the Congo River basin 10. Person who was the first European "owner" of the Congo basin area 11. Capital named after President James Monroe 12. Portugal's colony on western Africa's coast	7. Ocean bordering Africa's east coast 8. Sea bordering Egypt and the Sudan 9. Interior region invaded by Italy 10. Eastern region just south of Egypt 11. French toehold on the Red Sea 12. The only independent nation of eastern Africa	7. War between the British and the Dutch settlers 8. Language of the Boers 9. Union of English colonies and Boer states 10. Portugal's colony to the north and east of South Africa 11. German territory to the north and west of South Africa 12. Oldest colony in Africa, a Portuguese possession

15

13. Religion of North Africa before colonization
14. Country that acquired a small northern strip of Morocco
15. Country that included the site of ancient Carthage
16. Empire that controlled most of North Africa in the 1800s
17. Mountains of Morocco

13. Port city of Nigeria
14. Two of four French settlements along the coast of western Africa's "bulge"
15. Ancient city of the western Sudan region
16. The French worked inland from the western coast along this river.
17. Coastal area south of the "bulge" claimed by France

13. European powers that vied for possession of the Sudan
14. Major river that flows through the Sudan
15. Large lake bordering Uganda
16. Name for the Sudan under British and Egyptian control
17. African uprising in German East Africa

13. Spectacular falls in Zimbabwe
14. Dutch colony seized by Great Britain in the early 1800s
15. The two independent Boer republics
16. Rhodes's dream for Africa
17. Region west of the Transvaal controlled by Great Britain

20

18. Conference held to settle rivalry over Morocco
19. Frenchman who led the Egyptian canal-building company
20. Egyptian city bombarded by a British fleet
21. Muslim "savior" whose followers fought fiercely against the British in the Sudan
22. Turkish ruler of a North African state

18. Major river basin of central Africa; site of Brazzaville
19. Confederation of native tribes in the Gold Coast region
20. Leader of anti-French resistance in West Africa for 16 years
21. Germany's possessions in West Africa
22. Spanish colonies on western Africa's coast

18. Large island claimed by France
19. Rich inland territory gained by the British from Germany
20. Italian desert land along the Red Sea
21. Sudanese city besieged by rebelling natives for 10 months
22. Ethiopian emperor whose army crushed the invading Italians

18. Colonies united to form the British dominion of South Africa
19. Natives of German Southwest Africa who rebelled
20. River of Mozambique and Rhodesia explored by Livingstone
21. Renowned Zulu warrior and chief of the early 1800s
22. Another name for Mozambique

NOTES

33 The Growth of Science and Technology in the Nineteenth Century

	The Physical Sciences	The Biological Sciences	The Social Sciences and Psychology	Industrial Advances
5	1. Sciences that deal with the nonliving parts of nature 2. Two of the physical sciences 3. Theory that all matter in the universe is made up of atoms 4. The relative weight of an atom 5. Radioactive element discovered by the Curies 6. Particles inside atoms	1. Sciences that deal with the living parts of nature 2. Center of cells, discovered by a British botanist 3. British naturalist who argued that life forms on the earth developed over a long period of time 4. Darwin's idea about changes in natural forms 5. Age of the earth, according to early evolutionists	1. Sciences that deal with people as members of society 2. The objective study of law and government 3. The study of people's relationships with their fellow people 4. The study of the human mind and behavior 5. The study of the production, distribution, and consumption of goods and services 6. Social science improved by the search for old written records	1. New power source that replaced steam 2. Outstanding U.S. inventor involved with electricity 3. These replaced gas lamps. 4. Power generated by use of water 5. American teacher of the deaf who patented the telephone
10	7. Scientists of this ancient nation first thought of the atomic theory. 8. A way to describe chemical compounds 9. Table that classifies the elements 10. The science of the physical history and characteristics of the earth 11. The science of matter and energy 12. The science of the makeup of all substances and the changes they undergo	6. Prehistoric creatures whose existence was first discovered in the nineteenth century 7. German biologists announced this theory of cells. 8. Darwin's famous book outlining his theory 9. Survival of creatures that are best adapted to the existing conditions 10. The study of ways in which inborn characteristics are passed on to descendants	7. This field saw dramatic discoveries of ancient remains and ruins such as Troy 8. Pavlov's experimental subjects 9. Authors of *The Communist Manifesto* 10. Economic system in which major industries are owned by the public 11. The study of people's culture	6. Natural resources used to run electric generators 7. Engine that used a portable supply of gasoline or oil 8. German engineer who invented an economical oil-burning engine for heavy vehicles 9. Improved material that allowed skyscrapers to be built 10. The Bell Telephone Co. was formed to create this.

15	13. Roentgen's discovery 14. Tiny subatomic particle with a negative electrical charge, discovered by Thomson 15. Release of energy by disintegrating atoms, discovered by Bacquerel 16. French scientists who experimented with radiation 17. The father of modern atomic theory	11. Austrian monk, founder of the science of genetics 12. Mendel used these vegetables as the subjects of his experiments. 13. Threadlike bodies in cells that divide to form new cells, first observed by Fleming 14. Virchow found that outside agents destroyed or changed cells to cause this. 15. The process of passing changed forms by inheritance; basis of Lamarck's theory	12. Term for application of Darwin's theory to human society 13. Perfect living places promoted by factory owner Robert Owen 14. The two warring classes, according to *The Communist Manifesto* 15. Russian biologist who studied animal behavior 16. Outstanding British historian of the period	11. Marconi's invention, a way to send messages through space without wires 12. Edison invented the first practical model of this sound machine. 13. Important centers of scientific study 14. Industry that set up the first U.S. research labs 15. The two German pioneers of self-propelled vehicles; they gave their names to a major car company.
20	18. Russian chemist who designed the table of elements 19. German physicist who discovered penetrating but invisible radiation 20. American astronomer who discovered a new comet in 1847 21. Planet discovered in 1846 by Johann Galle, from predictions of others 22. The study of this phenomenon led scientists to think about atomic motion.	16. First organizations to employ scientists 17. British botanist who studied living plant cells 18. The pre-Darwin explanation of the variety of living things 19. French biologist who suggested living beings changed form in response to environment 20. German biologist who first described cell division	17. Frenchman who started the science of sociology 18. Englishman who extended Darwin's ideas to society 19. Type of behavior demonstrated by Pavlov's experiments 20. "Hands-off" economic doctrine based on "natural laws" 21. Use of this method made study of social subjects objective and factual.	16. Brothers credited with inventing the first successful gas-powered automobile in the United States in1893 17. The modern chemical industry began when Perkins accidentally produced this. 18. Country that took the lead in the production of synthetic chemical materials 19. American who perfected the simple camera 20. Machine that transformed mechanical power into electrical energy
NOTES				

34 Western Culture in the Nineteenth Century

	Public Health and Medicine	The Life of the People	Literature and Philosophy	The Fine Arts
5	1. Of every three children born in the nineteenth century, this many died while very young. 2. Leading cause of death during most of the 1800s 3. Pasteur showed that these caused disease. 4. Pasteur developed a vaccine against this disease passed by animal bites. 5. Scientific advances, not a rising birthrate, caused the rapid growth of this. 6. Medical technique that greatly advanced when it became less painful	1. Population shifted away from this region in the 1800s. 2. The use of cold to keep food from spoiling 3. People began moving out of inner cities to these areas in the late 1800s. 4. Children legally belonged to this parent during most of the 1800s. 5. One reason people lived longer after 1850 was that there was more of this basic staple available.	1. English romantic poet who died in the Greek struggle for independence 2. Growing sentiment that led authors to write about their own countries 3. Germans who collected their country's fairy tales 4. American author of the fantastic, supernatural, and mysterious 5. Tolstoy's monumental novel detailing the realities of war 6. U.S. author who depicted Mississippi River life	1. Artistic emphasis on feeling, emotion, and imagination 2. Artistic emphasis on showing the world as it is 3. School of painting that explored light and color effects 4. Center for artists from many lands 5. German who wrote emotional, expressive symphonies
10	7. Person who established professional nursing care for wounded soldiers 8. English doctor who developed inoculation 9. The first European vaccine prevented this disease. 10. French chemist who studied bacteria and disease 11. Disease similar to smallpox used to make a vaccine for smallpox 12. One of the pain-relieving drugs discovered for medical use in the 1840s	6. Widespread condition of being unable to read or write 7. Number, in millions, of people who left Europe for the United States between 1870 and 1900 8. Two major reasons for emigration 9. Railroad cars designed to transport meat, fruit, and vegetables 10. Parts of public life from which women were barred	7. English poet who wrote "The Rime of the Ancient Mariner" 8. Two major English romantic poets known for their odes 9. Scottish novelist who wrote about the days of knighthood 10. Giant of German literature, noted for being a poet, novelist, and playwright 11. U.S. novelist who idealized American Indians and the frontier 12. Realistic Norwegian dramatist	6. Polish composer of romantic piano pieces 7. Russian composer of melodic, emotional works such as the *Nutcracker Suite* 8. Great Italian composer of *Aïda* and other operas 9. Opera composer whose plots often came from German myths 10. Great German romantic composer of the "Lullaby" 11. The two best-known French Impressionists

15

13. In the mid-1800s, patients who survived surgery often died of this.
14. Natural process made much safer by the use of antiseptics in hospitals
15. Measures such as water purification that greatly reduced disease
16. Antiseptics greatly reduced infection in these effects of war.
17. Process of heating liquids to kill bacteria

11. These eighteenth-century French and U.S. events made it seem important for all citizens to be educated.
12. Type of schooling first offered to U.S. and French citizens
13. Level of government that controlled school systems in the United States
14. Level of government that controlled school systems in Western Europe
15. Women first gained some independence because of these.

13. Noble English poet who expressed Victorian values
14. English naturalistic author of *The Return of the Native*
15. Young woman who wrote the famous gothic horror novel *Frankenstein*
16. Three English sisters who published novels under male pseudonyms
17. Alexandre Dumas's three swashbuckling heroes

12. French sculptor who broke with classical traditions
13. French artist who painted colorful, flat Tahitian scenes
14. Dutch painter noted for intense emotions and swirling brush strokes
15. Country whose artists dominated painting and sculpture in the 1800s
16. German composer famous for his songs

20

18. Country where inoculation was practiced in the 400s
19. Drugs that allowed great advances in surgery
20. English surgeon who developed a method of reducing bacterial infections
21. Chemicals used to kill germs that caused infection
22. German who isolated the germs that cause tuberculosis and cholera

16. Reform laws limited the working hours of these people.
17. Mass publication of reading materials was made possible by this.
18. U.S. state that allowed women the vote in 1869
19. Country that allowed women the vote in 1893
20. After 1870 education became this, by law.

18. Extremely popular British author whose novels were often published in installments
19. Realistic portrayals of everyday life in different parts of the United States
20. Realistic writers who wrote objectively about ugly and sordid aspects of life
21. French leader of the frank and objective school of writing
22. French novelist who wrote about a medieval hunchback

17. New musical instrument of the 1800s
18. Hungarian composer of rhapsodies based on native folk songs and dances
19. Two outstanding romantic English landscape painters
20. French postimpressionist artist who emphasized planes of color
21. Countries whose artists dominated music in the 1800s

NOTES

35 World War I

	The Stage Is Set	Conflict Begins	The Fighting	The Peace and Its Aftermath
5	1. Desire to unite all people with a common language, race, and culture under a single government 2. The move to establish overseas empires; this resulted in increased rivalries 3. Glorification of and reliance on armed strength 4. Officials who exercised influence over civilian politicians 5. Financial result of the race to build military strength	1. Site of the 1914 assassination that triggered the war 2. The assassin was a nationalist of this ethnic group 3. Country whose heir to the throne was assassinated 4. Germany's response to Russian troop mobilization 5. Nation that wanted to create a Slavic state 6. Slavic nation, a major power, that supported Serbia's Pan-Slavism	1. New rapid-fire weapon 2. New armored vehicle 3. New airborne weapon 4. New oceangoing weapon 5. New form of chemical warfare 6. Soldiers protected themselves from machine-gun fire and artillery in these.	1. American president who led the United States at the peace conference 2. Agreement to stop fighting until a treaty could be written 3. Site of the peace conference 4. Germany lost all of these possessions under the treaty. 5. Group that suffered almost as much loss of life as the armed forces during the war
10	6. Hidden, nonpublic agreements among nations to help each other 7. Overseas territories where European nations competed 8. Ordering of reserve military forces into active service 9. European nations engaged in this race to build their strength. 10. Formal agreements among countries to help each other if attacked	7. Leader assassinated in 1914 8. The final terms offered for a settlement, presented by Austria to Serbia 9. Russia's action to prepare to defend Serbia 10. Neutral country invaded by Germany 11. Event that brought Great Britain into the war	7. Result each side expected in the summer of 1914 8. Germany and its allies 9. Britain and its partners in the war 10. How the armies of World War I were different from earlier European armies 11. Sea blockaded by the British to cut off Germany 12. British passenger liner sunk by German submarines	6. Woodrow Wilson's statement of Allied aims for the war 7. The Big Four of the peace conference 8. The Big Four became the Big Three when this country left the peace conference angry 9. Germany had to agree to these payments for war damages. 10. By signing the treaty, Germany admitted this.

15

11. Members of the Triple Alliance
12. Members of the Triple Entente
13. A friendly agreement or understanding among nations
14. "The powder keg of Europe"
15. Route Germany proposed to build through the Balkans

12. Far East nation that declared war as Britain's ally
13. Triple Alliance member that remained neutral at first
14. Empire that joined Germany and Austria in November 1914
15. Nation that presented Serbia with an ultimatum
16. Germany's new leader in the 1890s

13. German policy that drew the United States into the war
14. Why the United States entered the war, according to Woodrow Wilson
15. Event that caused Russia to drop out of the war
16. Two uses for airplanes in the war
17. Battle that ended Germany's hope of a quick victory

11. The Dual Monarchy split to become these two separate nations.
12. Nation that lost more territory than Germany did
13. International organization created by the peace treaties
14. Major country that never joined the League
15. Financial problem facing countries that fought the war

20

16. Two main strengths of the Triple Alliance
17. Two main strengths of the Triple Entente
18. Two main weaknesses of the Triple Alliance
19. Two main weaknesses of the Triple Entente
20. Three areas in which Germany challenged Great Britain

17. Germany's reason for invading a neutral country
18. Name of the Serb assassin at Sarajevo
19. Balkan nation that entered the war as Germany's ally in 1915
20. The Turks kept Russia's southern fleet bottled up in this sea
21. Austrian territory Serbia wanted; where the assassination took place

18. The war's only large naval battle
19. Site of deadly but inconclusive monthlong fight in France
20. Secret message that outraged Americans
21. The battle to open up the Dardanelles Strait
22. Forest battle that forced the Germans back to their border

16. The two countries with especially severe property damage
17. The new international court
18. Three empires that had fallen by 1919
19. Two entirely new nations created out of the old Dual Monarchy
20. The two main aims of the League, according to its covenant

NOTES

36 The Russian Revolution

	Steps to Revolution	Revolution and Civil War	The Lenin Years	The Stalin Years
5	1. Russia's ruler from 1894 until 1917 2. Work stoppages that forced the tsar to make some changes 3. Important strategic body that remained loyal to the tsar in 1905 4. Russia had very little of this kind of development. 5. One of the three groups who protested their discontent 6. Russian people who lived in poverty after being freed	1. Local revolutionary councils of workers and soldiers 2. The radical Marxists 3. Leader of the Bolsheviks 4. Class, very small in Russia, that Marx expected would revolt 5. Symbolic revolutionary color adopted by the communists 6. Temporary government set up in March 1917	1. New communist capital of the U.S.S.R. 2. Old, precommunist capital of Russia 3. Guiding economic system of the U.S.S.R. 4. Fate of the tsar and his family 5. Agriculture declined so badly, city people faced this. 6. Owner of the major industries	1. Secretary general of the Communist Party and Lenin's successor 2. Type of state established by Stalin 3. Type of economy Stalin established 4. These were sharply reduced while heavy industry was vastly expanded. 5. People who fiercely resisted Stalin's agricultural policy 6. English translation of the Russian word *stalin*
10	7. Russia's form of government before the revolution 8. Violent event of 1905 when soldiers shot peaceful marchers 9. World War I Russian soldiers lacked these necessities. 10. Capital of tsarist Russia 11. The Russian people were promised these in 1905 but never got them.	7. The moderate Marxists 8. Groups that rivaled the temporary government for power 9. Vladimir Ilyich Ulyanov 10. Lenin modified this socialistic-communistic philosophy. 11. Where Lenin had lived before his return to Russia 12. The seizure of power in November 1917	7. Alternative name for the U.S.S.R. 8. Russia's official new name 9. Tsar and tsarina who were the last ruling monarchs of Russia 10. Separate government entities joined together in the federal union 11. Lenin's modified version of Marxist theory 12. Lenin decided the U.S.S.R. had to take this before it could take "two steps forward."	7. Main rivals for post-Lenin leadership 8. Where the revolution had to take place, according to Marx, in order to be successful 9. Where the revolution should stay for the time being, according to Stalin 10. Master plans of Soviet growth 11. All farms, under Stalin 12. Organization that lost its property

15

12. Russia had few of these two essentials of transportation.
13. Two kinds of events that broke out in 1917
14. Members of this key group deserted the government and joined the rioters.
15. Defeat in a war against this small country in 1904–05 exposed the Russian government's weakness.
16. Uprising that forced some temporary reforms

13. New name for the Bolsheviks as of 1918
14. After the second revolution, Russia suffered through three years of this.
15. The military forces of the new government
16. Russian family whose rule ended in 1917
17. Country that arranged for Lenin's return to Russia from exile

13. Outside source of funds welcomed for development
14. Group whose needs were met first during the war
15. Lack of this made it difficult to build a Marxist society.
16. People who carried out the revolution instead of the workers
17. Organization that ruled the Soviet Union under Lenin

13. Belief taught to children in place of religion
14. Artistic style required under Stalin
15. Arm of the Communist Party that held most power
16. Stalin's "purification," or removal of everyone not loyal to him
17. Stalin's native republic
18. Lev Bronstein, brilliant party organizer

20

17. Parliament created after the 1905 uprising
18. These were enormous for Russia in World War I.
19. Decree of 1905 that promised individual liberties and limited elections
20. The tsar's reaction to the legislature's demands for reform
21. The Romanov monarchy ended in March 1917 when the tsar did this.

18. Lenin's slogan
19. World War II participants with whom Russia signed peace treaties in 1918
20. Russians who fought the communists from 1917 to 1920
21. Western nations that helped the Whites with money, arms, and troops
22. The uprising that ousted the tsar

18. Marx based his "scientific socialism" on this form of economic development.
19. Lenin's economic policy, which was not pure Marxism
20. Lenin's economic policy allowed some of this.
21. Wave of executions similar to the French Reign of Terror
22. Huge representative body that had little real power

19. Outcome of the power struggle for Trotsky
20. Trotsky's final fate
21. The parliament under Stalin
22. Organization that agitated for the overthrow of capitalist governments
23. Small ruling committee of the parliament

NOTES

37 Nationalism and Communism in Asia and Africa

	China	Japan	India	Africa and the Middle East
5	1. Political party founded by Mao and other revolutionaries 2. Leader of the Chinese Communists 3. Class of people whom Mao sought as his party's base of support 4. Chaotic condition of China from 1916 through the 1940s 5. "Father of Modern China" who was (briefly) the first president of the Chinese republic	1. Japanese head of state who wielded no real power 2. In the 1920s, Japan agreed to limit the size of this part of its military forces. 3. Element of Japanese society that controlled the government by the 1930s 4. Need for these fueled Japan's desire to expand. 5. Growth of this fueled Japan's desire to expand.	1. Indian nationalist leader 2. Indians' name for Ghandhi, meaning "saintly one" or "Great Soul" 3. Imperialist country that ruled India as its colony 4. The way to respond to British shootings and beatings, according to Gandhi 5. Hindu social system that Ghandhi opposed	1. Middle Eastern land promised to both Jews and Arabs by Great Britain 2. Surname adopted by Turkish leader, meaning "Father of the Turks" 3. New name of Persia as of 1935 4. System of racial segregation and discrimination set up in South Africa 5. Two rival peoples in Palestine
10	6. Nationalist leader in China after Sun Yixian's death 7. Nation that sent advisers to help China 8. Nations that ignored the Nationalists' requests for help 9. The 6,000-mile trip of the communists to northwest China 10. Supporters of China's left wing, ejected from the Nationalist party	6. Neighboring country that Japan invaded in the 1930s 7. Important source of Japanese wealth, disrupted by the Great Depression 8. Man who reigned on Japan's throne from 1926 to 1989 9. Increased characteristic of Japanese government during the 1920s 10. Term for extreme nationalists	6. Britain promised more self-government if Indians fought in this war. 7. British-made item that Indians boycotted widely 8. Peaceful protest led by Gandhi to defy the British laws about salt 9. Deliberate and public refusal to obey an unjust law 10. Gandhi's profession, which he practiced in South Africa	6. Revolutionary leader who was the first president of Turkey 7. People the Arabs fought in return for British support of an Arab state 8. Policy of modernization followed in Turkey and Iran by Atatürk and Reza Shah 9. North African nation that gained independence in 1922 but was still controlled by Britain 10. Nationalist movement built on the shared heritage of Arabs

Points	Card 1	Card 2	Card 3	Card 4
15	11. Class of people who supported the Nationalists 12. Nickname of Mao's fighting forces 13. Nation that invaded and took over eastern China in 1937 14. New base of the Chinese Communists after their year-long trek 15. Political party that tried to establish a Chinese republic	11. Northern Chinese province that Japan seized in 1931 12. By signing the Kellogg-Briand Pact, Japan pledged to renounce this "as an instrument of national policy." 13. Japan put pressure on this neighbor with the Twenty-one Demands in 1915. 14. Zaibatsu, people who strongly influenced politics in the 1920s	11. Non-Hindu Indian independence group 12. Gandhi's policy of peaceful resistance through refusing to cooperate with the government 13. India's leading political party 14. Indian province where the Amritsa massacre took place in 1919 15. Reforms allowed by the Government of India Act of 1935	11. Movement that focused on the unity of all Africans 12. New Islamic nation founded by Abd al-Aziz Ibn Saud 13. Territories in the Middle East governed by European nations, set up at the end of World War I 14. Empire that the Turkish revolution ended 15. Oil-rich kingdom that gained independence in 1930
20	16. China's last dynasty, overthrown in 1912 17. Reform movement sparked by student protests in 1919 18. China's industrial northern province, invaded by Japan in 1931 19. Soviet leader whom Mao and his fellow communists admired 20. Capital city of both the Nationalists and occupying Japan	15. Name of the Japanese Parliament 16. Values vigorously promoted by the military-dominated government 17. Japan's name for its puppet state in Manchuria 18. International body that Japan withdrew from in 1933 because of its condemnation of Japanese aggression	16. Leader of the Muslim League beginning in the 1930s 17. New goal of the Muslim League under Jinnah 18. Social injustice that Gandhi worked against in South Africa 19. Garment adopted by Gandhi in place of western clothing	16. British statement that "viewed with favor" a Jewish "national home" 17. Army officer who overthrew Iran's shah and set up his own Pahlavi dynasty 18. West African movement that promoted pride in African roots 19. Jamaican native who promoted the message "Africa for Africans"

NOTES

38 The Western World Before and Between the Wars

	THE AMERICAS	ECONOMIC CONDITIONS	EUROPE	THE RISE OF FASCISM
5	1. U.S. president who dealt with the Great Depression 2. Young U.S. women who embraced shocking new freedoms of dress and behavior 3. Nickname for the boom years of the 1920s in the United States 4. Movement of people that the United States limited after World War I 5. Popular, hard-riding rebel from northern Mexico	1. Institution that took more control of economics after the war 2. Condition of many countries because of wartime borrowing 3. Source of government revenue, very high in many postwar countries 4. Drastic business collapse of the 1930s 5. Many of these financial institutions failed in the 1930s.	1. Average life span of a French government cabinet 2. British workers who inspired a general strike 3. British working-class party that gained power in 1924 4. Irish force that fought British troops 5. Portion of Ireland that stayed part of the United Kingdom 6. Line of defenses built along the French-German frontier	1. Italy had few industries because it lacked these. 2. Italy's dictator 3. Germany's dictator 4. Ethnic group Hitler especially despised 5. Hitler's book, the "Bible" of the Nazi movement 6. Hitler's secret police force
10	6. Business-oriented political party that dominated U.S. national government during the 1920s 7. Term for the years during which manufacture or sale of alcoholic beverages was prohibited in the United States 8. U.S. president who said that prosperity was "just around the corner." 9. Mexican artist famed for his bold, bright murals inspired by folk art	6. Condition of 30 million workers in 1932 7. Condition caused by demobilizing (disbanding) the armed forces 8. Common postwar condition of rising prices 9. Widespread walls that blocked free trade among nations 10. Investment arena that collapsed in October 1929	7. German coal and iron valley that French troops attempted to occupy 8. British prime minister elected with working-class support 9. The Irish nationalist uprising of 1916, named for a holiday 10. The independent southern portion of Ireland 11. Main characteristic of Eastern European economies 12. Union with Germany, desired by many Austrians	7. Name of Hitler's regime, meaning "Third Empire" 8. Hitler's title, meaning "the leader" 9. Mussolini's title, meaning "the leader" 10. Mussolini's political philosophy 11. Bavarian capital briefly taken over by communists 12. Germany's lower legislative house; site of a fire in 1933

15	10. Latin American nations that benefited from oil reserves 11. Indian from southern Mexico who led a peasant revolt 12. Caribbean island nation occupied by U.S. marines for years 13. U.S. fright stirred up by fear of communists and radicals in 1919-20 14. Country in which Augusto César Sandino led a guerrilla movement against U.S. troops	11. The program of relief and reform in the United States 12. Law that gave U.S. workers unemployment and old-age benefits for the first time 13. Group that pressured governments to help with workers' problems 14. Work stoppage by laborers in many areas of the economy 15. U.S. farm prices fell because of this.	13. Form of Hungarian government under Admiral Horthy 14. Form of government in Poland after the constitutional democracy failed 15. Owners of most land in Eastern Europe 16. Because France had so many political parties, it had this type of government 17. European nations' agreement to settle future disputes peacefully	13. Italy didn't have enough food because of these two conditions. 14. General term for government system that controlled almost every part of people's lives 15. Fascism promoted this feeling toward one's country. 16. Government in which the leader used armed forces and police to crush opposition 17. The Italian and German fascist parties were violently opposed to this.
20	15. Political party that dominated Mexican politics from 1929 through the 1990s 16. Term for female soldiers in the Mexican revolution 17. FDR's new policy toward Latin America 18. "Giant" nickname given the United States by distrustful Latin American nations	16. The International Monetary Conference of 1933 tried to promote this among nations. 17. Government programs that provided employment for workers 18. Global activity that dropped by 65 percent in the 1930s 19. Policy of improving a nation's economy without regard for other countries 20. Practice of buying stock with only a small cash down payment	18. French coalition government of socialists and communists 19. French socialist premier 20. Hungarian communist who seized power in 1919 21. One of the Eastern European nations that maintained democratic government 22. Paris treaty that condemned war as a way of settling disputes	18. The National Socialist German Workers' Party 19. Basic principle of fascism 20. Classes fascism appealed to 21. Mussolini's fascist supporters 22. The German federal republic 23. The Nazis' private army
NOTES				

39 World War II

	The Road to War	Conflict Begins	The War in Europe and North Africa	The War in Asia
5	1. Independent African country invaded by Italy 2. Northern Chinese province occupied by Japan 3. Spanish fascist leader 4. Conference that now symbolizes appeasement and surrender 5. Territory on the French side of the Rhine River invaded by Hitler 6. Response of Britain and France to Hitler's aggressive moves in 1936 and 1938	1. The three major Axis Powers 2. English statesman elected to replace Chamberlain 3. Major Allied country taken by Hitler in June 1940 4. Leader of the French fighters 5. Germany signed a nonaggression treaty with this country in 1939. 6. Strip of Polish territory that cut through Germany	1. Official policy of the United States toward the war until 1941 2. Vast country Germany invaded in 1941 in violation of 1939 treaty 3. The three leading Allied statesmen who met often during the war years 4. Term for Hitler's war against the Jews 5. European beaches where the Allies landed in 1944	1. When Japan bombed this naval base, the United States entered the war. 2. Island continent threatened by the Japanese 3. Large ships that were seagoing air bases 4. U.S. commander in the Pacific 5. Terrifying new weapon first used on August 6, 1945 6. First Japanese city hit by the new bomb
10	7. How the League of Nations reacted to Japanese aggression 8. Japan went to war with this country in 1937. 9. Emperor of Ethiopia who asked for League protection 10. Nations that withdrew from the League in the 1930s 11. Official policy of the Western democracies toward the Spanish civil war 12. Nation joined to Germany in 1938 by *Anschluss*	7. Hitler's attack on this country started World War II. 8. Hitler's tactic of "lightning war" 9. The four major Allies 10. Two Scandinavian countries invaded by Hitler in April 1940 11. The three Low Countries taken by Hitler in May 1940 12. Allied troops withdrew from this French seaport to England, by all boats available.	6. The period of heaviest German bombing of Great Britain 7. Fighting unit that successfully defended Great Britain 8. Germany's general in North Africa, the "Desert Fox" 9. Chief British general in North Africa 10. Supreme commander of the Allied forces in Europe 11. Soviet city; site of tremendous six-month battle	7. Suicide attacks by bomb-laden Japanese planes 8. Second Japanese city hit by the new bomb 9. The day Japan signed surrender documents 10. Island group secured for the Allies by the Battle of Leyte Gulf 11. Allied strategy of capturing some islands and skipping others

15	13. German area of Czechoslovakia 14. British prime minister who gave in to Hitler's demands 15. Nation that disappeared from the map in 1939 16. *Lebensraum*, Germany's excuse for expanding its borders 17. The German-Italian alliance	13. The French group that continued to fight the Germans 14. Two Western nations that were defensive allies of Poland 15. Free city on the Baltic Sea open to Poland, desired by Germany 16. Germany's line of defense in the Rhineland 17. Country that disappeared when the Soviet Union moved into it in 1939	12. New tracking device using sound waves that located submarines 13. New electronic tracking system that detected incoming aircraft 14. Term for the day of the Allied landings in France 15. Term for the day of victory in Europe 16. Hitler committed suicide during the battle for this city.	12. Southern island of the Solomons, site of an airfield and fierce fighting 13. Alaskan islands where Japan landed 14. Crucial battle near Hawaii that turned back the Japanese 15. Sea battle that stopped the Japanese thrust toward Australia 16. One of two American island outposts captured by Japan in 1941–42
20	18. International treaty rejecting war as a way to settle disputes 19. The League's reaction to Italy's aggression in Africa 20. Treaty that Germans deeply resented 21. The two opposing sides in Spain's civil war 22. "Hands-off" foreign policy favored by many Americans in the 1930s	18. The only country to be expelled from the League of Nations for aggression 19. Term for the nearly actionless early days of the war 20. Term for the countries of Estonia, Latvia, and Lithuania taken by the Soviets in 1940 21. The U.S.S.R. was expelled from the League of Nations for invading this Scandinavian country. 22. The French government under Hitler	17. Hitler's plan to invade and conquer the British Isles 18. U.S. policy of supplying Britain with war materials on credit 19. Egyptian site where the British stopped the German advance 20. Germany's final counterattack against the Allies in Europe 21. Axis power that was invaded from the south; it surrendered in 1943	17. Region north of China taken from Japan by the Soviet Union in 1945 18. Japan's slogan to keep Asia out of Western control 19. Dutch island colony taken by Japan 20. French colony that became a Japanese protectorate 21. Japan's great naval strategist

NOTES

40 The Cold War and Postwar Europe

	Postwar Settlements	Cold War Politics	Economic Recovery	The Eastern Bloc
5	1. Units that controlled the German occupation zones 2. Type of government established in postwar Italy 3. Defeated nations had to return these. 4. Former Nazis were put on trial, accused of being this. 5. Postwar leader of France	1. The two strongest nations of the postwar world 2. War fought by politics and economics, not weapons 3. How Great Britain and the United States sent supplies to Berlin 4. Massive construction between East and West Berlin 5. Descriptive name of the nonphysical wall between Western and Eastern Europe	1. German transportation industry that became a strong competitor of its American counterpart 2. Great Britain's moderate socialist party 3. State like Great Britain where government took main responsibility for its citizens' welfare 4. Discontented French workers caused these to spread rapidly in 1968. 5. The European Recovery Program; it provided U.S. aid to Europe	1. The leader of Yugoslavia 2. Term for the East European countries dependent on and subordinate to the U.S.S.R. 3. Communist country that split with the U.S.S.R. to act independently 4. Soviet leader, Stalin's successor, who visited the United States in 1959 5. Term for satellite independence; named for Yugoslavia's leader
10	6. Main characteristic of France's postwar foreign policy 7. International forum that tried Nazi leaders for war crimes 8. Systematic killing of an entire people, practiced by Hitler 9. Nation that objected violently to German reindustrialization 10. Loss of territory to other nations caused a flood of these into Germany.	6. British leader who coined the term "Iron Curtain" 7. Country that surrounded Berlin 8. U.S. policy that aimed at restricting the spread of communism 9. European country that received U.S. aid in 1947 to put down a communist-supported rebellion 10. The Soviet attempt to keep any supplies from reaching West Berlin 11. The Berlin Wall was built to stop the flow of these.	6. The most stable currency in postwar Europe 7. What happened to British railroads, coal mines, and utilities 8. EEC, the economic and trade union of Western Europe 9. Common name of the European economic union 10. Trade barriers the Western European nations gradually dropped	6. Soviet troops changed from an army of liberation in Eastern Europe to this 7. Countries that took all of East Prussia 8. Authority that set up communist governments in Romania, Bulgaria, and Hungary 9. The new communist government of East Germany 10. Country that briefly deposed its Soviet-controlled government in 1956

15	11. Payments to nations that had been invaded 12. Wartime meeting near Berlin where the Allies agreed how the peace treaties would be written up 13. Wartime meeting in the southern Soviet Union where the Allies agreed to divide Germany into occupation zones 14. Number of zones Germany and Berlin were each divided into 15. City/territory disputed by Italy and Yugoslavia 16. It took 10 years for a peace treaty to be signed with this country.	12. The mutual defense pact of the Western nations 13. The East European military alliance 14. Soviet term for harmony between East and West 15. Meetings of the leaders of the major world powers 16. Country where the Cold War became hot in 1950	11. Major European nation that remained outside the EEC for 15 years 12. The U.S. Trade Expansion Act allowed the president to cut these. 13. Many newly independent nations of this continent joined the EEC as associate members in the 1960s. 14. U.S. official who suggested the policy of massive aid to Europe 15. The EEC members had the most trouble agreeing on this policy.	11. Country that gained a small amount of domestic independence in 1956 12. Four of the six Soviet satellites 13. Class of people in East Germany who revolted in 1953 14. Germany lost a lot of territory to this country after World War II. 15. Country that ejected the Sudetan Germans
20	17. West German chancellor in the 1950s and 1960s 18. New French government established in 1958 19. Britain's postwar leader 20. The new democratic government of West Germany 21. A council of these government officials wrote up the postwar peace treaties.	17. Gradual relaxation of tensions between the United States and U.S.S.R. 18. The Communist Information Bureau; its goal was to stir up dissent and revolution 19. U.S. statement that it would help countries threatened by communism 20. Stated 1950s U.S. policy of willingness to go to the verge of war 21. Event that doomed a U.S.–Soviet conference in 1960	16. The East European nations' common market 17. Country that vetoed British membership in the EEC 18. Union of Western Europe's coal and steel industries, ECSC 19. Term for the amazingly rapid economic recovery of Germany 20. UNRRA, the organization that gave emergency relief aid to war-torn countries	16. Northern states annexed by the U.S.S.R. in 1940 17. Two of the three northern (Baltic) states annexed by the U.S.S.R. in 1940 18. Local communists set up governments in these two countries. 19. Central European country whose democratic government was replaced by a communist government in 1948 20. A workers' revolt in this country was put down by Soviet forces in 1953.

NOTES

41 Revolution in Asia

	China and Korea	The Indian Subcontinent	The Island Nations	Southeast Asia
5	1. China's first Communist ruler 2. Huge farming communities in which Chinese peasants had to live 3. South Korean capital; site of the 1988 Summer Olympics 4. Most powerful Chinese leader of the 1980s and 1990s 5. The Korea that emerged as an economic powerhouse in the 1990s 6. Chinese student movement of 1989	1. The subcontinent was divided along these lines. 2. Major stumbling block to economic improvement 3. Natural phenomena that periodically devastate Bangladesh 4. Nehru's daughter, India's prime minister, assassinated in 1984 5. Controversial items tested by Indian and Pakistan in 1998	1. Asia's leading industrial power in the later twentieth century 2. Japan's leading trading partner 3. Japan's economy depended on these. 4. Philippine dictator ousted in 1986 5. The United States struggled to keep these strategic posts in the Philippines.	1. Communist leader of North Vietnam 2. The communist guerrillas in South Vietnam 3. U.S. president who greatly expanded U.S. involvement in Vietnam 4. Capital of Vietnam 5. Capital of South Vietnam; fell to the communists in 1975 6. Refugees from Southeast Asia who attempted to emigrate by sea
10	7. Island home of the Chinese Nationalists 8. Official name of communist China 9. Chinese premier, Mao's second in command 10. American president who visited China in 1972, opening relations 11. China's domestic upheaval in the 1960s	6. Predominant population of Pakistan 7. Predominant population of India 8. India's first prime minister from 1950 to 1964 9. Major stumbling block to Indian unity, besides religion and caste 10. Current name of former East Pakistan 11. Indian minority responsible for Indira Gandhi's assassination	6. Japanese emperor who died in 1989 7. Natural disasters that often rock Japan 8. Name of Ceylon as of 1972 9. Type of government established in Japan in 1947 10. Island nation expelled from the United Nations in 1971 11. Nation given independence by the United States on July 4, 1946	7. Large drain on Thailand's economy 8. Collective term for the countries that border the Pacific Ocean 9. New name of Saigon 10. Neighbor of Vietnam invaded by U.S. troops 11. U.S. president who first sent aid to Vietnam

15

12. Radical semimilitary groups of students and young people during China's Cultural Revolution
13. International body that China joined in 1971
14. North Korea's basic foreign policy principle
15. North Korea's leader from 1948 to 1994
16. Site of Beijing's 1989 student demonstrations and massacre

12. Indira Gandhi's successor, also assassinated
13. Nations that fought each other following a civil war between East and West Pakistan
14. Former president's daughter, elected prime minister of Pakistan in 1988
15. Tibetan leader who fled to India in 1959
16. River valley of West Pakistan
17. River delta of East Pakistan (now Bangladesh)

12. Military rule, imposed on the Philippines by Marcos in 1972
13. The U.S.–Asian mutual defense organization
14. Rebels who fought a continuing battle against the Philippine government
15. Prosperous independent city-state at the tip of the Malay Peninsula
16. Filipino democratic leader, successor of Marcos
17. New name for the Netherlands East Indies

12. The communist forces of Cambodia who established a brutal rule in the 1970s
13. Country that invaded Cambodia in 1979 and took control for a decade
14. Cambodia's ruler from 1941 through 1970, who remained active in exile
15. Site of crushing French army defeat by the Vietnamese
16. Communist-led group of Laos

20

17. Neutral zone between North and South Korea
18. Thriving business center and British colony that reverted to China in 1997
19. China allowed a limited amount of this in its economy in the 1980s.
20. Dividing line between North and South Korea
21. Army that fought North Korean troops from 1950 to 1953

18. Northern Indian state, claimed by both India and Pakistan, site of many clashes
19. India's dominant political party
20. Pakistani dictator killed in 1988 plane crash
21. Site of disastrous poison gas leak in India, December 1984
22. Afghanistan's strict Islamic rulers in the 1990s

18. Two of the five largest islands of Indonesia
19. General who ruled Indonesia from 1968 through 1998
20. Guerrillas of Sri Lanka who wage a bloody campaign for an independent homeland
21. New nation that included Malaya, Sabah, and Sarawak
22. Indonesia's first president

17. The one nation of Southeast Asia that never was a European colony
18. Nation to the east of India; it gained independence in 1948
19. New name given Burma by its military leaders
20. The three countries formed out of French Indochina
21. Burmese woman who won the Nobel Prize in 1991 while under house arrest

NOTES

42 Independent Africa

	Independence Politics	Former British Africa	Leaders	Former Non-British Africa
5	1. Workers' organizations that gave Africans political experience 2. Usual number of political parties in an African country 3. People who have carried out many coups since the mid-1960s 4. Most common government and economic system in Africa 5. Type of workers in short supply 6. Common state of African economies	1. First independent British Commonwealth colony; it gained its independence in 1957 2. The former British colonies all joined this British group 3. Terrorist Kikuyu movement in Kenya 4. Country that included the kingdom of Buganda	1. Kenya's nationalist leader and first president 2. South African nationalist leader jailed for 27 years and elected president in 1994 3. South African bishop; 1984 Nobel Peace Prize winner 4. French government leader who supported colonies' independence 5. Uganda's notorious dictator; forced from office in 1978 6. Emperor of Ethiopia; deposed in 1974	1. How the French people decided on the colonies' independence 2. France outlawed this kind of labor in its colonies in 1946. 3. First and last European colonial power 4. The Portuguese who rebelled and ended the colonial wars
10	7. South Africa's policy of "apartness," or separation of the races 8. Organization of all the continent's independent states, established in 1963 9. All African states broke relations with this nation by 1974. 10. Many African nations became associate members of this European economic organization. 11. The OAU granted observer status to this Arab organization by 1973.	5. Country with the first African government in colonial Africa 6. Landless Kenyan people who fought a guerrilla war against whites 7. Countries that united to form Tanzania 8. Nigeria's most valuable export 9. South African police fired on an unarmed crowd here in 1960.	7. Ghana's nationalist leader and first president 8. Senegalese leader and noted poet 9. Guinea's first president elected in 1958; a nationalist leader 10. First premier of the Democratic Republic of the Congo who was forced from office and killed in 1961 11. First president of both Tanganyika and Tanzania	5. Two of the three Portuguese colonies that fought wars of independence 6. New name of Portuguese Guinea in 1974 7. French colony with the earliest mass political involvement 8. Former South West Africa; became independent in 1990 9. Cameroon, Gabon, the Republic of the Congo, Chad, and the Central African Republic used to form this territory.

15

12. Continued control of former colonies' economies by colonial powers
13. Main stumbling block to African unity
14. British colonies where the earliest nationalist parties grew
15. Most African economies had a poor balance between these two elements at independence.
16. The Pan-African movement started with these people.

10. Black town near Johannesburg; site of 1976 riots
11. Britain opposed this colony's independence, declared by the white minority.
12. Ghana's former name
13. Site of 1976 Israeli commando raid on a hijacked airliner in Uganda
14. These were outlawed by South Africa's Immorality Act of 1950.

12. Uganda's nationalist leader
13. Prime minister of Rhodesia who declared independence in 1965
14. First Zambian president, a nationalist leader
15. Leader who became Cote d'Ivoire's first president in 1960
16. African nationalist leader of Southern Rhodesia

10. Eastern country whose starvation and anarchy caught the world's attention in the early 1990s
11. A force from this organization was sent to the Democratic Republic of Congo in 1960.
12. Country that experienced tragic conflict between its Tutsi and Hutu peoples
13. Mining center in the Democratic Republic of the Congo that declared independence in 1960
14. A West African peace-keeping force intervened in this country in 1990.

20

17. Meeting open to all black people, not just African governments
18. Agreement of 1975 that linked both ex-British and ex-French colonies with the EEC
19. A U.N. body for Africa established in 1958
20. The single most important influence on the rise of African nationalism
21. Meeting of 1944 to determine the common future of France and its African colonies

15. In this country, much of the north is Muslim, and much of the south Christian.
16. The 1953 union of Malawi, Zambia, and Southern Rhodesia
17. Homelands for South African blacks
18. Rhodesia's new name under African rule
19. One of the two South African opposition parties banned in 1960

17. South African leader who urged nonviolence; 1961 Nobel Peace Prize winner
18. Apartheid leader assassinated in parliament in 1966
19. Former U.S. professor, founder of modern Mozambique nationalism; assassinated in 1969
20. Longtime leader who changed his country's name from Congo to Zaire
21. South African president who began the dismantling of apartheid laws

15. Area that became federated with Ethiopia in 1952
16. The former French Somali Coast
17. Formerly Upper Volta, renamed in 1984
18. Former Portuguese colony plagued by a 16-year civil war
19. New name for Dahomey

NOTES

43 North Africa and the Middle East: Tensions and Conflict

	North Africa	Arab-Israeli Conflict	The Middle Eastern States	The Saudi Peninsula and the Politics of Oil
5	1. Predominant religion of North Africa 2. Leader of Libya who took power in 1969 3. Basis of Libya's economy 4. The U.S. government has often accused Libya of promoting this. 5. Algeria represented this country in 1980 hostage negotiations. 6. Morocco's form of government	1. Ancient name of the land disputed by Jews and Arabs 2. Reaction of Arabs to Israel's independence 3. Arab group that seeks to establish an Arab state in Palestine 4. Longtime leader of the PLO 5. Status of most Arabs who left Israeli Palestine after its 1948 independence	1. Israeli collective farm 2. Scarce Middle East natural resource 3. Opposing groups in Lebanon's civil war 4. Iran's fundamentalist government leader; died in 1989 5. Capital of Lebanon, largely destroyed by the civil war 6. Leader of Iraq who began ruling in 1979	1. The association of oil-producing countries 2. OPEC's policy during the 1970s 3. Country that has one fifth of the world's oil reserves 4. Body of water where oil shipping is concentrated 5. Iranian pilgrims rioted in this holy city in the 1980s
10	7. Morocco's ruler from 1961 to 1999 8. Egypt's first democratically elected leader 9. Gigantic dam built to increase Egyptian farmland 10. Waterway nationalized by Nasser 11. North African country bombed by the United States in 1986 12. Nasser's successor in Egypt	6. Coastal area seized from Egypt by Israel in a 1956 invasion 7. Egyptian territory between Israel and the Suez Canal 8. Organization that divided Palestine into Arab and Jewish states 9. Term for the Palestinian uprising in Israeli-occupied territories 10. Waterway Egypt closed to Israel 11. Short Arab-Israeli war of 1967	7. Country that sent troops into Lebanon to help restore order 8. Country that experienced an Islamic revolution in 1979 9. Countries that started an eight-year war in 1980 10. Many U.S. marines were killed in Lebanon by this kind of attack in 1983. 11. Ruling party of Iraq 12. Union to promote Arab cooperation	6. The United States protected tankers in this body of water in the 1980s. 7. War waged in 1991 by a U.N.-backed coalition 8. Country invaded by Iraq in 1990 9. One of the four countries that has one tenth of the world's oil reserves 10. Saudi king assassinated in 1975

15

13. Sadat's fate
14. Two European nations that invaded Egypt in the Canal crisis of 1956
15. Leader who became an Arab hero during the Canal crisis
16. Libya's form of government from independence until 1969
17. North African country; site of guerrilla war against France

---

12. Arab residents of this Israeli-held territory began angry demonstrations in 1987.
13. War that broke out on the Jewish high holy day in 1973
14. Egyptian and Israeli leaders who agreed to peace
15. U.S. president who brought Egyptian and Israeli leaders together
16. Hard-line Israeli prime minister who took office in 2001
17. Eastern (Arab) Palestine became part of this country.

---

13. Warfare broke out between this group and the Jordanian government in 1970.
14. Jordan's king from 1952 to 1999
15. Israel's prime minister from 1969 to 1974
16. Ethnic group in northern Iraq, target of government attacks
17. Moderate Iranian president elected in 1997
18. Arab states that gained independence in the 1940s

---

11. Country that sold antiaircraft missiles to Saudi Arabia
12. Body of water that borders the southeastern end of the Arabian Peninsula
13. Gulf at the southern end of the Persian Gulf
14. Three of the seven Arab members of OPEC
15. Pro-Western Saudi leader; he became king in 1982

20

18. Extremist French group that resisted Algerian independence
19. One of Algeria's three "B" post-independence leaders
20. Union of Egypt and Syria
21. The first U.S. president to visit Egypt
22. Sadat's successor in Egypt
23. Ethiopia's last emperor

---

18. High land in Syria seized by Israel in 1967
19. The Arab-Israeli Oslo agreement of 1993 allowed some of this.
20. Term for the Egypt-Israel peace agreements
21. Israel invaded this country in 1982 to wipe out PLO bases.
22. Country that abandoned its ties with West Bank Palestinians in 1988
23. Joint winners of the 1994 Nobel Peace Prize

---

19. Israel's first president
20. Israel's first prime minister
21. He became Syria's president in 1971.
22. Iraq's type of government when it became independent
23. One of Israel's four major party leaders between 1992 and 2001
24. Middle Eastern leaders who turned away from westernization and to the Sharia (Muslim laws)

---

16. Independent sheikdom consisting of a group of islands in the Persian Gulf
17. Thousand-mile-long country ruled by a sultan
18. Country, ruled by a sheik, that occupies a small Persian Gulf peninsula
19. Loose federation of sheikdoms
20. New nation formed in 1990 when two states that shared the same name merged

NOTES

44 The Western Democracies Since 1960

	Western Europe	The United States Abroad	The United States at Home	Canada, Australia, and New Zealand
5	1. Spain's chief of state until 1975 2. Former U.N. secretary-general elected president of Austria in 1986 3. New German capital, moved from Bonn in 1991 4. Underwater vehicle route that links France and Britain 5. Conservative British prime minister from 1979 to 1990	1. President Kennedy's "army" of overseas volunteers 2. Confrontation between the United States and U.S.S.R. in the Caribbean in 1962 3. The U.S. war in Southeast Asia in the 1960s and 1970s 4. U.S.-led war in the Mideast in 1991 5. Revolutionaries of this nation took U.S. embassy workers hostage.	1. The economic slowdowns of the 1950s and early 1970s 2. The main domestic concern of the mid- and late 1960s 3. Black leader and Nobel Peace Prize winner killed in 1968 4. Violence that broke out in U.S. cities in 1967, and in Los Angeles in 1992 5. Widespread protests among these people started at Berkeley in 1964. 6. *Brown v. Board of Education* banned this practice.	1. Loose organization of former British colonies 2. Canadian province with a strong separatist movement 3. Official language of Quebec province from 1974 to 1979 4. This civic duty is compulsory in Australia at age 18 5. U.S.-Canadian 2,400-mile waterway from the Great Lakes to the Atlantic Ocean
10	6. A shaky peace plan of the 1990s aimed to end "the troubles" in this country. 7. French leader who challenged the U.S. role in Western Europe 8. Until 1990, "One Nation, Two States" 9. German chancellor who moved toward closer relations with the Eastern bloc in the 1970s 10. West Germany granted automatic citizenship to the citizens of this country.	6. Iranian leader supported by the United States 7. Nixon became the first U.S. president to visit these two nations in 1972. 8. The United States attacked this Taliban-led country in 2001 in response to a massive terrorist attack inside the United States 9. Failed U.S.-backed attempt by Cuban refugees to invade their homeland in 1961 10. President Carter worked to solve a dispute with this Central American country over a waterway.	7. Father-and-son U.S. presidents 8. Black leader shot to death in Harlem in 1965 9. U.S. president impeached by the House in 1998 10. Frightening events at places like Columbine High School 11. The United States set up a homeland security office in 2001 in response to this threat. 12. Man who was elected president by a landslide in 1980	6. The main advantage of belonging to the Commonwealth 7. Canada's two territories 8. French-Canadian prime minister from 1968 to 1979 and 1980 to 1984 9. The British Parliament no longer has to approve any Canadian changes in this. 10. Different party that won the Canadian elections of 1984 11. Liberal prime minister of Canada elected in 1993

15

11. Labour Party leader elected British prime minister in 1997
12. French socialists' program for major industries
13. Spain's new ruler as of 1975
14. Spanish separatists who repeatedly demanded self-rule
15. Britain fought this country for the Falkland Islands in 1982.

11. President who established normal diplomatic relations with China in 1979
12. President Carter arranged peace meetings between these warring Middle East nations.
13. The United States supported rebels in this Central American country in the 1980s.
14. The United States supported this Central American government against rebels in the 1980s.
15. Central American country invaded by the United States in 1989

13. President Johnson's domestic program
14. Person who got the most popular votes for U.S. president in 2000
15. Buildings destroyed in New York City terrorist attack on September 11, 2001
16. U.S. presidential candidate slain in 1968
17. The major political scandal of the 1970s
18. The worst episode of domestic terrorism, in 1995

12. Governing Australian party from 1983 to 1996
13. Port calls of these U.S. ships sparked a U.S.–New Zealand crisis.
14. New Zealand party that held office from 1984 to 1990
15. Self-governing homeland of Canada's Inuit, created in 1999
16. Act of 1931 that recognized Canada, Australia, New Zealand, and South Africa as completely independent

20

16. Treaty for European unification signed in 1991
17. Socialists defeated the Gaullists to elect this president in 1981.
18. Portugal's dictator from 1932 to 1968
19. Belgium suffers from divisions between these two groups.
20. Socialist leader of Sweden shot on the street in 1986
21. Economic union of Belgium, the Netherlands, and Luxembourg

16. President Johnson sent U.S. marines to this island nation in 1965.
17. Site of captured U.S. embassy in the Middle East
18. U.S. policy of aid to Mideast countries, announced in 1957
19. Terrorist bombs killed Americans at military posts in this country in 1995.
20. The United States fought troops of this country in Grenada in 1983.

19. New voting age set by the 26th Amendment in 1971
20. Man who became U.S. president in 1974 without having been elected to the post
21. The only two Democrats elected president from 1968 through 1992
22. The only U.S. president to resign from office
23. U.S. senator who claimed to find communist conspiracies everywhere

17. Number of Canadian provinces
18. Number of Australian states
19. Title of Australia's official head of state
20. Alliance of the United States, Australia, and New Zealand
21. Agreement recognizing Quebec as a "distinct society" that failed in 1990

NOTES

45 Changes in the Communist World

	The Soviet Union at Home	The Soviet Union Abroad	The Eastern "Bloc"	The Soviet Empire Collapses
5	1. The Soviet secret police force 2. Youngest Soviet leader since Stalin 3. Nuclear plant; site of 1986 disaster 4. Soviet citizens faced continuing shortages of this. 5. New 1977 constitution gave dominance to this political party. 6. Food was imported from the West when these failed.	1. Khrushchev had to remove missiles from this country in 1962. 2. The United States often brought up this domestic Soviet issue. 3. Direct teletype connection between the United States and U.S.S.R. 4. A split developed between the Soviet Union and this neighboring communist country in 1961. 5. The U.S.S.R. was mired in a war with this country from 1979 to 1989.	1. Polish organization of trade unions 2. Founder of the Polish workers' union 3. Polish workers' strikes began in these workplaces. 4. East Germany established formal relations with this country in 1974. 5. East Germany periodically challenged Western access to this city.	1. First popularly elected leader in Russian history 2. Gorbachev survived this in August 1991. 3. Military alliance that dissolved in 1991 4. Pieces of this historic German structure became souvenirs when it was torn down in 1989. 5. Country that East Germany united with in 1990 6. East European country that broke apart and erupted into war in 1991
10	7. Strong Russian leader of the 1960s and 1970s 8. Soviet foreign minister for 28 years; he became president in 1985 9. Region that suffered a devastating earthquake in 1988 10. Soviet citizens who protested government violations of the people's rights 11. Khrushchev's attack on Stalinist policies	6. Soviet leader who met with U.S. President Nixon 7. Two "northern" nations the U.S.S.R. supported in their wars with southern neighbors 8. The United States led a boycott against this Moscow event of 1980. 9. The United States froze exports of this commodity to the U.S.S.R. in 1980. 10. A spy plane from this country was shot down over the Soviet Union in 1960.	6. Reforming Czech leader of the 1960s 7. Country that was invaded by Soviet troops after starting reforms in 1968 8. Members of this NATO rival became discontented in the 1970s. 9. Country that established martial law in late 1981 10. Polish port city, formerly Danzig, site of workers' strikes in 1980	7. The three northwest republics of the U.S.S.R. that declared independence in 1990–91 8. Group term for the three northwest republics of the U.S.S.R. that declared independence 9. Startling type of government that started in Poland and spread rapidly through Eastern Europe in 1989 10. Country of 15 republics that dissolved in 1991 11. Severe, rising problem that plagued the newly noncommunist economies

15	12. Commodity the Soviet Union had to buy from the West in 1963 13. Some republics demanded more of this in the 1970s and 1980s. 14. Critics of the government were sometimes placed in these medical facilities. 15. Gorbachev's new policy of openness 16. Innovative feature of Russian elections beginning in 1989	11. Soviet influence expanded in this continent during the 1970s. 12. Brezhnev's policy of easing tensions with the West 13. West German firms built a pipeline to carry this from Siberia to Western Europe. 14. Airborne pollution that spread abroad from the Soviet Union in 1986	11. Many East Germans left their country in 1989 when their government did this. 12. All of these were closed in 1967 to make Albania an atheist state. 13. Romania's repressive leader from 1974 until his execution in 1989 14. Communist European country that was not a Soviet satellite when all others were 15. Term for the Czech uprising of 1968	12. Work condition previously unknown in former communist economies 13. The two new nations formed when Czechoslovakia split peacefully in 1993 14. Novel event held in most East European countries in 1990 15. The Soviet legislature passed power to these entities in 1991. 16. Breakaway Russian republic that fought for independence in the 1990s
20	17. Brezhnev's successor, former head of the KGB 18. Term for Russian Jews who were denied permission to emigrate 19. Gorbachev's new policy of economic reform 20. Gorbachev promoted a reduced government role for this organization 21. Gorbachev assumed this position only after it was given real power over policy.	15. Event in the United States boycotted by the Soviets in 1984 16. Fighting broke out with this country over a border dispute in 1969. 17. Détente developed because the Soviet Union needed these two things from the West. 18. A Soviet fighter shot down a passenger jetliner from this country in 1983.	16. East Germany's leader from 1976 to 1989 17. One of two original members that stopped cooperating with the Warsaw Pact 18. Long-time Communist party leader of Hungary 19. According to the Brezhnev Doctrine, the U.S.S.R. could do this to any East European country. 20. Central Prague site of mass protests in 1989	17. Czechoslovakia's playwright-president, elected in 1990 18. "Ethnic cleansing" was carried out by Yugoslavian Serbs against these people. 19. The two largest countries formed from the former Soviet Union 20. Thousands fled this country by boat for Italy in 1990. 21. Country where former Communists overwhelmingly won the first free elections
NOTES				

46 Postwar Latin America

	Inter-American Relations and Economies	Central America and Mexico	South America	The Caribbean Islands
5	1. The free trade agreement among Mexico, Canada, and the United States 2. Men who have often taken over Latin American governments 3. Major social and economic problem of Latin America 4. The rapid growth of this worsens social and economic problems. 5. Latin American governments faced economic disaster in the 1980s when they could not repay these.	1. Country that took over a waterway in 1999 2. Production of this boosted Mexico's economy in the 1970s. 3. Site of a disastrous Mexican earthquake in 1985 4. Area of Panama formerly controlled by the United States 5. Panama's military leader, tried in the United States for drug trafficking 6. Country invaded by U.S. forces in 1989	1. President and dictator of Argentina 2. First democratically elected Marxist leader in the Western Hemisphere 3. U.S. group accused of being involved in Allende's overthrow 4. Argentina went to war with Great Britain in 1982 over these islands. 5. Brazil moved its capital to Brasilia to help develop this area. 6. By 1970, most Brazilians lived in these areas.	1. Cuba's revolutionary leader 2. Caribbean island with a communist government 3. The U.S.S.R. removed these weapons from Cuba in 1962. 4. Cuba tried to export this throughout Latin America. 5. Center of Cuban exile settlement in the United States 6. Target city for Puerto Rican immigration into the United States
10	6. Destruction of this environment affects the entire world. 7. Common Latin American need to help build industries 8. Growing demand for these often causes violent protest. 9. Small group, often of military officers, that overthrows a democratic government 10. The United States often intervened when it feared this type of takeover in a Latin American country. 11. Common crop of one-crop countries	7. Large country with a long record of elected presidents 8. Rebels who overthrew the Nicaraguan government in 1979 9. Rebels who opposed the new, 1980s government of Nicaragua 10. Cuba and the Soviet Union supported this side in the 1980s El Salvador fighting. 11. Sandinista leader elected president of Nicaragua in 1984 and defeated in 1990	7. The army of this large country rebelled against a leftist government in 1964. 8. Country that had a Marxist president 9. Deadly disease that became an epidemic in the early 1990s 10. Either of Juan Perón's wives who helped him rule 11. First female president in the Western Hemisphere	7. Natural disasters that periodically devastate the islands 8. Cuban communist revolutionary leader; close associate of Castro 9. Cuba's close ally and aid-giver 10. Cuba took over all of these businesses in 1961. 11. Cuban coastal area invaded in 1961

15

12. Breaking up of large estates and distribution of land to peasants
13. Latin American countries had to pay much higher prices for these as of the late 1970s.
14. Commodity whose rise in price staggered many Latin American economies
15. Latin American countries received much less for these starting in the late 1970s.
16. Assembly plants along Mexico's northern border

12. Nicaraguan contras established guerrilla bases in this country.
13. First president of Mexico since 1929 not from the PRI party, elected in 2000
14. Winner of 1987 Nobel Peace Prize for his Central American peace initiative
15. Civilian leader of El Salvador's government in the 1980s
16. New name of British Honduras as of 1993

12. *Los desaparecidos* of Argentina
13. Country that connects South America with Central America
14. South American member of OPEC
15. A country terrorized by its drug lords
16. Country whose army fought the Tupamaros guerrillas

12. Self-governing U.S. territory in the Caribbean
13. Country that voted in 1967 to remain a commonwealth
14. Troops from this country landed in the Dominican Republic in 1965.
15. Haiti's president and dictator from 1957 to 1971
16. Duvalier's successor in 1971; ousted in 1986

20

17. Inter-American organization founded in 1948
18. Aid project to promote Latin American development progress
19. Class that paid few taxes
20. Where wealthy Latin Americans preferred to invest their funds
21. Inter-American agreement declaring that no state has the right to intervene in another state's affairs

17. Country that endured a thirty-year civil war that tapered off in the 1990s
18. Nicaragua's ruling family from the 1930s to 1979
19. Neutral nation with an orderly succession of democratic governments since 1974
20. Peasant rebels have caused turmoil in this southern Mexican state.
21. The United States helped to overthrow this country's liberal government in the 1950s.

17. Argentina's Spanish name for the Falklands
18. Brazilian city; major industrial center of South America
19. Military leader who succeeded Allende in Chile
20. Leftist guerrilla group of Peru
21. Paraguay's military leader from 1954 to 1989

17. Country where U.S. and U.N. troops kept order in the 1990s
18. Country invaded in 1983 by the United States and troops from six Caribbean nations
19. Dictator of Cuba before the revolution
20. Cuban troops fought in this southern African nation's civil war
21. The massive exodus of Cubans to the United States in 1980

NOTES

47 International Cooperation

	The United Nations	U.N. Peacekeeping	International Associations and Agreements	Nuclear Arms Control
5	1. Main U.N. body charged with maintaining peace and settling disputes 2. Site of the U.N. headquarters 3. Deliberative body made up of representatives of all member nations 4. The U.N.'s court, headquartered at The Hague 5. Head of the Secretariat	1. Large-scale combat forces were sent here in the early 1950s. 2. The U.N. arranged a cease-fire between these two Mideast belligerents in 1956. 3. The Security Council arranged a cease-fire in 1967 to end this Arab-Israeli war. 4. The U.N. arranged another cease-fire for this region in 1973. 5. U.N. resolutions set the terms for settlement of this brief 1991 war.	1. Association of the world's major oil-producing nations 2. Association that helps people harmed by natural disasters 3. Group that works to free political prisoners and to improve prison conditions 4. Group that uses confrontation and intervention in its quest to protect the environment 5. Free trade agreement among the United States, Mexico, and Canada	1. Series of meetings in the 1970s on limiting nuclear arms 2. U.S. demand to verify Soviet weapons reduction 3. The Soviets said inspection was really an excuse for this. 4. New frontier that is supposed to be off-limits to the arms race 5. The United States deployed medium-range missiles here in 1983.
10	6. Main task of the United Nations 7. Agency that works to improve all people's health 8. Important voting power held by each permanent member of the Security Council 9. The most frequent user of the Security Council veto power 10. Common acronym of the U.N. Educational, Scientific, and Cultural Organization	6. Small U.N. groups that supervise cease-fires or truces 7. Mideast crisis of 1956 that created a U.N. emergency force 8. The U.N. intervened when this former Communist nation in the Balkans split up. 9. Unpaid peacekeeping charges brought the U.N. close to this in the 1960s. 10. Major weakness of the League of Nations that the U.N. avoided	6. Major body that supervises international trade 7. Group that promotes Arab solidarity and common interests 8. U.S.-Latin American association formed in 1948 to promote cooperation 9. Organization of major industrial democracies that meet for annual summits 10. Common name of the International Bank for Reconstruction and Development	6. No permanent nuclear weapons are to be installed off nations' coastlines in this place. 7. Type of missiles limited by the SALT agreements 8. U.S.-Soviet agreement signed in 1979, but never approved by the U.S. Senate 9. U.S.-U.S.S.R. 1988 treaty called for dismantling of all of these in Europe 10. Neutral, demilitarized, nonnuclear continent

15

11. Agency concerned with children's health and welfare
12. The five permanent members of the Security Council
13. The clerical and administrative body of the U.N.
14. Seventh Secretary-General, the second from Africa
15. Third Secretary-General, the first from Asia

11. The U.N. worked out a cease-fire between these parties in 1949.
12. U.N. peacekeepers went to this Caribbean island in 1995.
13. Island nation that received a U.N. peacekeeping force in 1964
14. A U.N. force was sent to this Mideast nation in 1978.
15. U.N. troops tried but failed to restore order in this East African nation in the 1990s.

11. Association dedicated to achieving European cooperation and unity
12. Medical group that treats victims in war-torn areas
13. International agreement of 1975 to honor basic human rights
14. Agency that promotes stable currencies and international monetary cooperation
15. Association that promotes cooperation among Caribbean nations

11. Areas off-limits to nuclear testing, according to 1963 agreement
12. Formal name of space-based defense system planned during Reagan's presidency
13. Nickname for SDI
14. Iceland's capital; site of U.S.-Soviet summit conference
15. Soviet and U.S. leaders who signed a weapons-reduction treaty in 1987

20

16. Norwegian who was the first Secretary-General
17. Sixth Secretary-General, the first from Africa
18. American U.N. mediator between Arabs and Israelis; winner of the 1950 Nobel Peace Prize
19. The six official languages of the U.N.
20. The U.N. High Commissioner helps these people.

16. The U.N. lacks this for peacekeeping duties.
17. Conflict between these groups on Cyprus caused U.N. intervention.
18. How the U.N. pays for its special peacekeeping forces
19. The Netherlands granted this country independence in 1949 due to U.N. efforts.
20. African country that asked for U.N. troops to create stability in 1960

16. Agreement to lower trade barriers worldwide
17. Group set up in 1963 to promote cooperation among African nations
18. Cooperative association of six Southeast Asian nations formed in 1967
19. Group formed to promote trade across the Pacific Rim region

16. Focus of U.S.-Soviet arms talks after the 1987 treaty
17. U.N. body created to help regulate and reduce arms
18. Nonnuclear nations' 1968 agreement not to produce or receive nuclear weapons
19. Treaty to reduce nuclear arms, signed in 1991 after nine years of negotiating

NOTES

48 The New Global Economy and Environment

Points	Energy: Sources and Strategies	The Environment: Air and Water	The Environment: Earth	Global Business and Economics
5	1. Energy sources from the remains of prehistoric plants and animals 2. Energy created by splitting atoms 3. Energy created from the sun's rays 4. Form of energy that propels sailboats 5. The world's most widely used fossil fuel 6. The cleanest fossil fuel, often sent through pipelines	1. The killing of these sea mammals is now controlled by international agreement. 2. Polluted precipitation 3. Mixture of fog and smoke; major pollutant of many cities' air 4. Prolonged lack of rain, experienced often in Africa. 5. Tanker accidents that can devastate coastal areas 6. Site of world's largest oil spill, result of war, 1991	1. Large open area where solid waste is buried 2. Chemical products used to kill insect pests 3. Chemical products used to kill weeds 4. Having more people than a region can support 5. Process that robs farmland of topsoil	1. Levels of comfort, expected to be lower in the future 2. Complete control of a commodity, service, or market 3. International commerce without trade barriers 4. Chief reason why manufacturers locate in underdeveloped nations 5. Businesses that are natural monopolies
10	7. Energy produced by the natural rise and fall of the oceans 8. Energy created by water 9. Formerly the world's chief fuel, this provides only a small percentage of today's energy. 10. Motor fuel that's a mixture of ethanol and gasoline 11. Term for energy sources that can be rebuilt or regenerated	7. Site of devastating Alaskan oil spill in 1989, or the tanker that caused the spill 8. Layer of the atmosphere that is beginning to break down 9. Ozone in the atmosphere protects us from this. 10. Gradual warming of the earth's atmosphere 11. Centers that break down organic wastes in waste water 12. Global warming is expected to produce a rise in this.	6. Watering of land by artificial means, used on 550 million acres worldwide 7. Reprocessing of waste materials 8. Byproducts of nuclear power plants 9. Development of new high-yielding seeds for rice and wheat 10. The new high-yielding crops need heavy doses of this.	6. New, common European currency 7. Tax on imported goods to protect native products 8. Reducing the value of a nation's currency in relation to other countries' currencies 9. A corporation that produces and sells a product in two or more countries 10. The expectation of people in underdeveloped nations to have a higher standard of living

15	12. Term for energy sources that will run out eventually 13. Element commonly used in nuclear fission 14. The combining of atomic nuclei, a possible future energy source 15. Nuclear fusion does *not* produce this dangerous byproduct 16. The world's second most widely used fossil fuel	13. Major contributor to smog and carbon dioxide pollution, especially in the United States 14. Result of too much exposure to ultraviolet light 15. Dangerous radiation released from nuclear explosions 16. Organisms that increase when nitrate and phosphorous levels increase in water 17. Addition of heated water to a natural body of water	11. U.S. agency that works to cut down pollution 12. Living things in danger of becoming extinct 13. Disposal of these nonusable things is a growing problem. 14. Clearing of this Brazilian area may affect the world's climate. 15. Three most commonly recycled materials	11. Most of the world's underdeveloped countries are in this hemisphere. 12. Underdeveloped countries contain most of the world's remaining stores of these. 13. The United States changed from a creditor nation to this in the 1980s. 14. Annual meetings of world industrial leaders 15. High duties on a long list of imported goods
20	17. Mideast nation with greatest amounts of petroleum reserves 18. Two leading West European producers of crude petroleum 19. Devices that convert sunlight into electricity 20. Power generated when water contacts heated underground rocks 21. Gaseous element that may become a major future energy source	18. Manufactured particles that are damaging the upper atmosphere 19. Global network to monitor atmospheric pollution 20. Substance in the air created by burning carbon-containing fuels 21. Mechanisms on cars that remove some of the exhaust pollutants 22. Major pollutant released when coal is burned	16. Programs to reduce loss of topsoil 17. Method of controlling population growth 18. Substance that has been removed from gasoline and paints 19. Popular name for international meeting in Rio de Janeiro on the environment and development in 1992 20. Main cause of species extinction	16. Agreements reached by the United States with both Canada and Mexico in the 1980s and 1990s 17. The Four Tigers of Asia 18. Industries that multiplied in developed nations as manufacturing jobs moved to developing nations 19. Selling goods abroad at less than they sell for at home 20. Policy of setting high import duties to protect native products
NOTES				

49 Science and Technology in the Twentieth Century

Points	Technology	The Physical Sciences	The Biological and Psychological Sciences	The Space Age
5	1. Site of the first sustained, powered flight 2. Pioneers of sustained, powered flight 3. The first inexpensive, dependable, mass-produced car 4. Major communications medium from the 1950s on 5. Worldwide linkage of computer networks 6. Portable, wireless, handheld telephone	1. Famed German scientist who revolutionized physics 2. Einstein's theory about space and time 3. Center of the atom, first described by Rutherford 4. Idea that the universe began as the result of an explosion 5. Elementary particles; the opposite of ordinary particles	1. Treatment of disease with chemicals, often used for cancer patients 2. The first antibiotic 3. Units of heredity, identified around 1910 4. Vaccines were developed in the early 1950s for this dreaded childhood disease. 5. Father of psychoanalysis 6. Incurable disease of the immune system, first identified in 1979	1. The first artificial satellite sent into earth orbit, in 1957 2. The U.S. manned spacecraft designed to be reusable 3. Huge industry that designs and builds space equipment 4. A Soviet space pilot 5. Space shuttle that exploded in 1986 6. The U.S. space agency
10	7. Personal, electronic messages 8. These two sources replaced kerosene for lighting. 9. Major communications medium in the 1930s and 1940s 10. Innovative addition to motion pictures in 1927 11. Ford's method of producing cars 12. Tiny devices that control electronic signals	6. High-energy particles from outer space 7. Ability of some metals to conduct electricity with no resistance at temperatures near absolute zero 8. Tiny subatomic particle with positive charge, discovered by Rutherford 9. Einstein's famous equation 10. Study of the earth based on the principals of physics 11. Physicists found more and more of these particles after 1945.	7. Term for the use of disease-causing agents by terrorists 8. The study of inborn characteristics and their inheritance 9. Cell structures that contain genes 10. Creation of an identical copy of a living organism using DNA 11. The substance that carries genetic information 12. Drugs that fight disease-causing microbes	7. The first men on the moon 8. The moon-landing flight satellite 9. The first U.S. space laboratory 10. First man to circle the earth in a spaceship 11. First American to circle the earth in a spaceship 12. Space between the stars

15

13. Device that produces a thin, intense beam of light
14. Miniature electronic device consisting of thousands of transistors on a single chip
15. Type of engine powered by batteries
16. Most common semiconductor material; nickname of a valley in California
17. Devices that do jobs too boring, difficult, or dangerous for people

12. Glass filaments that transmit data via light pulses
13. Italian-born physicist whose team achieved the first controlled nuclear chain reaction
14. Planck's theory that energy is released in definite packages
15. Englishman who disintegrated atoms, showing they were not solid
16. Small, rapidly rotating star that emits radio waves

13. Computerized axial tomographic scanner; takes cross-sectional X rays of the body
14. Delicate surgery that uses microscopes
15. Brain disorder involving memory loss, a concern of older people
16. Surgical replacement of a diseased body organ
17. Field of medicine that focuses on genetic diseases

13. Satellite on which a crew lives for an extended period
14. Unmanned spacecraft that explore other planets
15. The first communications satellite
16. First planet to experience a satellite landing
17. Soviet space station that plunged into the Pacific Ocean in 2000
18. Orbiting astronomy tool launched in 1990

20

18. Mass production made these much more available and affordable.
19. Type of engine that replaced steam for trains and ships
20. Solid material that conducts electricity and is used to make transistors
21. Faster, smaller computers that replaced the first computers
22. Device that reduces harmful automobile emissions

17. Extremely luminous object at the center of a distant galaxy
18. Particle that may be the basic subunit of neutrons and protons
19. Billionth of a second
20. Idea that the earth's outer shell consists of rigid, moving plates
21. Device used to create high-velocity beams of subatomic particles

18. Technology that produces images of the body's internal organs
19. Altering of an organism's hereditary makeup
20. Project devoted to mapping all human genetic material (DNA)
21. The study of extremely low temperatures; used to freeze living body parts
22. Doctors who specialize in care of newborn infants

19. Radiation belt that circles the earth, discovered by satellites and probes
20. U.S. and Soviet spacecraft that linked up in 1975
21. The first animal sent into space, a Soviet dog
22. The first woman in space
23. The first U.S. space shuttle

NOTES

50 Western Culture in the Twentieth Century

	Literature, Philosophy, and Religion	Music, Poetry, and Theater	Painting and Photography	Architecture and Sculpture
5	1. Supernatural teachings and beliefs 2. U.S. author, nicknamed "Papa," known for his simple, clear style 3. U.S. author of *The Great Gatsby;* often wrote about the very rich 4. U.S. author known for his stream of consciousness technique 5. U.S. author of *The Grapes of Wrath* 6. African-American cultural flowering in 1920s New York City	1. American poets of the 1950s and 1960s who condemned middle-class life 2. New Englander who was the most popular U.S. poet of his time 3. U.S. dramatist who wrote *A Streetcar Named Desire* 4. U.S. dramatist who wrote *The Crucible* 5. Best-known U.S. center of professional theater 6. New style of music first embraced by young people in the 1950s	1. Film that can store reduced images 2. The attempt to move beyond impressionism 3. Style that used basic geometric shapes, such as cubes 4. Style that expressed highly personal, intense views 5. U.S. comic-strip style that showed common objects 6. Use of color and patterns to create optical illusions	1. Sculptural works that are actually part of nature 2. U.S. architect whose buildings harmonized with their natural settings 3. Buildings with this status may not be destroyed or significantly altered. 4. Spectacular New York City skyscraper complex with twin 110-story towers, destroyed by terrorists in 2001 5. King Kong's hangout; located in New York City, it is one of the world's tallest skyscrapers.
10	7. Mix of mysticism, belief in former lives, and personal fulfillment 8. Philosophy that individuals create themselves by the choices they make 9. American blacks who adopted the Islamic faith 10. Authors of the 1920s who wrote about disillusioned and rootless characters 11. Irish author who revolutionized modern fiction	7. U.S.-born British poet who wrote *The Waste Land* 8. Welch poet known for his stirring, passionate verse 9. First U.S. dramatist to win international recognition 10. Drama that emphasizes the illogical, like *Waiting for Godot* 11. Lively U.S. musical style developed in New Orleans, Memphis, and Chicago 12. New York theaters that emphasize very inventive plays	7. Work of artists with little or no formal training 8. American primitive painter who started painting at age 76 9. Painting that explored the unconscious mind 10. First large U.S. modern art show, in 1913 11. Nonrepresentational style known for swirling masses of lines 12. Paintings of simple shapes or objects with as little emotional content as possible	6. One of the world's tallest buildings, located in Chicago 7. Sculptural shapes found in nature 8. Sculptor known for vast reclining figures 9. U.S. center of modern architecture in the early 1900s 10. Famed German school of design, founded in 1919 11. Plain, severe architectural style with expanses of steel and glass

15

12. Flow of a character's thoughts and mental images in a novel
13. Writing on two levels of meaning
14. Where most U.S. short stories first appeared
15. Next to Christianity, the two religious faiths with the most U.S. adherents
16. Noted French existentialist writer and philosopher

13. Theater company that succeeded Britain's famed Old Vic
14. Britain's government-supported Shakespearean company
15. Formerly a popular form of stage entertainment, a combination of comedy, song, dancing, and other activities
16. The first rock opera
17. U.S. organization that makes grants to artistic groups

13. Painting that represents objects very exactly
14. Most popular U.S. painter of the mid-1900s, a realist known for *Christina's World*
15. Enormously popular U.S. artist known for his *Saturday Evening Post* covers
16. U.S. pop artist known for his paintings of Campbell's soup cans
17. Miniature 35-mm camera that revolutionized photographic equipment in 1924

12. Building material with metal rods for extra strength
13. Renowned Swiss architect of the international style
14. Chinese-American architect noted for broad, irregular geometric shapes
15. Architectural movement that rejects the international style
16. Moving sculpture form invented by Alexander Calder

20

17. Movement that seeks to unify Christians worldwide
18. Meeting of Catholic leaders that modernized the Church
19. African-American woman who won the Nobel Prize for Literature in 1993
20. Modern fiction that mixes fantastical and realistic events, as in the novels of Gabriel García Márquez
21. Push by Roman Catholic clergy in Latin America to get the Church more involved in social reform

18. This confessional woman poet committed suicide in 1963.
19. Critical Soviet poet, author of "Babi Yar"
20. German dramatist who wrote *The Threepenny Opera*
21. U.S. dramatist who wrote *A Raisin in the Sun*
22. Country with the largest state-supported theater system

18. U.S. documentary photographer of the 1930s
19. American who helped develop photography as a creative art
20. School of art that used extremely bright colors
21. Absurd school of art
22. U.S. group that painted realistic street scenes of modern life

17. Romanian sculptor of *Bird in Space*
18. American woman who assembled man-made or machine-made objects into sculptures
19. Pioneering group of modern American architects
20. German architect who emphasized functionalism
21. The master of glass and steel architecture
22. Frank Lloyd Wright's long, low buildings

NOTES

Answer Key

1 Prehistoric Times and the Concepts of History

	Historical Vocabulary	The Ages of Prehistory	Our Human Ancestors	Prehistoric Life
5	1. What is prehistory? 2. What is history? 3. What is writing? 4. What are legends? 5. What is culture? 6. What is population?	1. What was the Ice Age? 2. What does B.C. stand for? 3. What is A.D.? 4. What was the Stone Age? 5. What is "Common Era"?	1. What is Africa? 2. Who were Neanderthals? 3. Who were Cro-Magnons? 4. What was erect posture? 5. What was language?	1. What were gathering and hunting? 2. What was a tool? 3. What was animal skin? 4. What was fire? 5. What were caves? 6. What was a mammoth?
10	7. What is a historian? 8. What is geography? 9. What is a geologist? 10. What is an archaeologist? 11. What is civilization? 12. What is an artifact?	6. What is "Before the Common Era"? 7. What are glaciers? 8. What are interglacial periods? 9. What is an eon? 10. What is an era?	6. What was a large brain? 7. What was a sloping forehead, thick eyebrow ridges, heavy jaw, large nose, or receding chin? [Name one.] 8. Who was *Homo habilis*? 9. Who was *Homo erectus*? 10. Who was *Homo sapiens?*	7. What was burial? 8. What were cave paintings? 9. What were farming and herding? 10. What were villages? 11. What was pottery? 12. What was cloth?
15	13. What is a clan? 14. What is excavation? 15. What is to decipher? 16. What is research? 17. What is a theory? 18. What is to date?	11. What was the Paleolithic Age? 12. What was the Neolithic Age? 13. What is a millennium? 14. What were tree rings? 15. What is carbon-14?	11. Who was Java man? 12. Who was Peking man? 13. What was 100,000 years ago? 14. What was 40,000 years ago? 15. What was skin?	13. What was metal? 14. What was the wheel? 15. What was a loom? 16. What was straw or dung? 17. What were nomads? 18. What was obsidian?
20	19. What is a philologist? 20. What is an anthropologist? 21. What is patrilineal? 22. What is matrilineal? 23. What is a paleontologist?	16. What was the Neolithic (agricultural) Revolution? 17. What was c. 3000 B.C.E.? 18. What was c. 8000 B.C.E.? 19. What were c. 2.5 million to 8000 B.C.E.? 20. What was c. 8000 B.C.E.?	16. Who are aborigines? 17. Who was Lucy? 18. What was the Neander? 19. What is hominids?	19. What was chipping? 20. What was grinding? 21. What was life after death? 22. What was the dog? 23. What was pastoralism?

2 Mesopotamia: The Fertile Crescent

	River Valley Life	Cultural Developments	Mesopotamian Places	Mesopotamian People
5	1. What is a delta? 2. What is civilization? 3. What were floods? 4. What were cities? 5. What were classes? 6. What were river valleys?	1. What was clay (mud) brick? 2. What was clay? 3. What were roads? 4. What were coins? 5. What was a city-state? 6. What was cuneiform?	1. What was Mesopotamia? 2. What was the Tigris? 3. What was the Euphrates? 4. What was Babylon? 5. What was the Fertile Crescent?	1. Who were the Sumerians? 2. Who were the Hittites? 3. Who were the Assyrians? 4. Who was Cyrus the Great? 5. Who were scribes?
10	7. What was copper? 8. What was bronze? 9. What was iron? 10. What was irrigation? 11. What were dikes (levees)? 12. What was government?	7. What was the arch? 8. Who were priests (or priest-kings)? 9. What was the Code of Hammurabi? 10. What was an empire? 11. What was the potter's wheel? 12. What was a library?	6. What were India and China? 7. What was the Persian Gulf? 8. What is Iraq? 9. What was Sumer? 10. What was Nineveh?	6. Who were the Persians? 7. Who was Gilgamesh? 8. Who was Sargon? 9. Who was Hammurabi? 10. Who were the Chaldeans?
15	13. What was trade? 14. What was farming? 15. What were calendars? 16. What was writing? 17. What were irrigation and flood control?	13. What were provinces? 14. What were astronomy and astrology? 15. What was hereditary kingship? 16. Who was the city's god? 17. What was a ziggurat?	11. What was the Mediterranean Sea? 12. What were the Hanging Gardens of Babylon? 13. What was Persepolis? 14. What is Iran? 15. What was Egypt?	11. Who was Nebuchadnezzar? 12. Who were the Medes? 13. Who was Darius? 14. Who was Xerxes? 15. Who was Zoroaster?
20	18. What were wheeled vehicles? 19. What was division of labor? 20. What is a pictogram? 21. What is an ideogram? 22. What is a phonogram?	18. What was a number system based on 60, or algebra? [Name one.] 19. What was retribution ("an eye for an eye")? 20. What was payment of damages? 21. What was polytheism? 22. What were satrapies?	16. What was Armenia (Eastern Turkey)? 17. What was Ur? 18. What was the Indus River? 19. What was the Royal Highway (Road)? 20. What was Arabia?	16. Who were women? 17. What was warfare? 18. Who was Ashurbanipal (Assurbanipal)? 19. Who was Cambyses? 20. Who was Assur, (Ashur)?

3 Egyptian Civilization

	Geography and Sites	Religion	Government and Rulers	Culture
5	1. What is Africa? 2. What is the Nile? 3. What is the Mediterranean Sea? 4. What is the Nile Delta? 5. What was desert? 6. What was the Sphinx?	1. What was a god? 2. What were pyramids? 3. What was mummification? 4. What were temples? 5. Who was Re (Ra)? 6. Who was Osiris?	1. Who was Tutankhamen? 2. Who were priests and nobles? 3. What was a pharaoh? 4. What was brother-sister marriage? 5. What was a dynasty? 6. Who was Menes?	1. What was the hieroglyphic system? 2. What was papyrus? 3. What was the Rosetta Stone? 4. What was agriculture? 5. What was trade?
10	7. What was the Great Pyramid? 8. What was Upper Egypt? 9. What was Lower Egypt? 10. What was Thebes? 11. What are cataracts? 12. What is Giza?	7. Who was Isis? 8. Who was Aten, or Aton? 9. What was the *Book of the Dead*? 10. What were tombs cut into cliffs? 11. What was a sacred animal? 12. What was life after death?	7. Who was Ikhnaton (Akhenaton)? 8. Who was Nefertiti? 9. Who was Ramses II? 10. What was the Old Kingdom? 11. What was the Middle Kingdom? 12. What was the New Kingdom, or Empire?	6. What was medicine? 7. What were cities? 8. What was ink? 9. What was mud-brick (or reeds and mud)? 10. What was the horse?
15	13. What was Nubia? 14. What are minerals? 15. What was a dry climate? 16. What is the Red Sea? 17. What is 4,000 miles?	13. What was a scarab? 14. Who was Amon? 15. Who was Amon-Re? 16. Who was Horus? 17. What was the west bank of the Nile?	13. Who was Alexander the Great? 14. Who was the pharoah? 15. Who was Khufu (Cheops)? 16. Who was Howard Carter? 17. Who was Ahmose?	11. What was a scribe? 12. What was June? 13. What was geometry? 14. What was the 365-day calendar? 15. What was cotton?
20	18. What were Syria and Palestine? 19. What was the Isthmus of Suez? 20. What was Memphis? 21. What was Heliopolis? 22. What was Tell el Amarna (Tall al 'Amārinah)?	18. What was the Eater of the Dead? 19. What was a scale? 20. What is monotheism? 21. What is polytheism? 22. Who was Hapi or Apis?	18. Who was Hatshepsut? 19. Who was Thutmose III? 20. What was Kush? 21. Who were the Hyksos? 22. Who were the Assyrians?	16. What were ramps and levers? 17. What were estates? 18. What were granaries? 19. What were granite and limestone? 20. What was 80?

4 Civilization in Ancient India and China

	Peoples	Places	Early Indian Culture	Early Chinese Culture
5	1. Who were ancestors? 2. Who were foreigners? 3. Who were barbarians? 4. What were dynasties? 5. Who were warlords? 6. Who were elders?	1. What was the Indus? 2. What is the Huang He (Yellow River)? 3. What is the Yangtze (Chang Jiang)? 4. What is the Pacific Ocean? 5. What is the Ganges?	1. What was destroyed them? 2. What is class division, or the caste system? 3. What were dikes and dams? 4. What is the monsoon? 5. What was female? 6. What was kiln drying, or firing?	1. What are legends? 2. What were dikes? 3. What was change course? 4. What was silk? 5. What were silkworms? 6. What were dragons and/or serpents?
10	7. Who were the rich (rich, learned, and skilled)? 8. Who were the poor (farmers, peasants)? 9. Who were the Harappans? 10. Who were the Aryans? 11. What were nomads?	6. What is the Huang He (Yellow River)? 7. What is the Yellow Sea? 8. What is the Gobi? 9. What is the Khyber Pass? 10. What is the Arabian Sea?	7. What was city planning? 8. What was cotton? 9. What was a sewer system? 10. What was a citadel (fortress) or temple? 11. What were granaries? 12. What was barley?	7. What were millet, wheat, barley, and/ or rice? [Name two.] 8. What was bronze? 9. What were spirits? 10. What was iron? 11. What were family ties?
15	12. What was the Shang? 13. Who were nobles? 14. Who was Peking man? 15. Who were warriors? 16. Who were Brahmins?	11. What are the Himalayas? 12. What was Harappa or Mohenjo-Daro? [Name one.] 13. What is subcontinent? 14. What were wide deserts, high mountains, and large bodies of water? [Name one.] 15. What was the Middle Kingdom?	13. What were mounds? 14. What was in a grid, or uniform network? 15. What are seals? 16. What was the Vedic Age? 17. What was Sanskrit?	12. What was agriculture? 13. What was the lunar calendar? 14. What was clay? 15. What was the Mandate of Heaven? 16. What were the palace and temple?
20	17. What was light skin or height? [Name one.] 18. What was the Xia? 19. Who were the Zhou? 20. Who were priest-astronomers? 21. Who was Yu?	16. What is the Hindu Kush? 17. What was the Indus-Ganges plain? 18. What was Anyang? 19. What is the Si? 20. What are the Tien Shan?	18. What were the Vedas? 19. What was the Great Bath? 20. What was animism, or polytheism? [Name one.] 21. What was the tribe (or clan)? 22. What was the *Mahahbarata*?	17. What were (oracle) bones? 18. What was calligraphy? 19. What was more than 10,000? 20. What was silt (or loess)? 21. What was the gap between rich and poor?

Ancient Greece

	Origins and Geography	Politics and Society	The Era of City-States	The Hellenistic Age
5	1. Who were the Minoans? 2. What was sea trade? 3. What is the Mediterranean? 4. What were mountains? 5. What are the Alps?	1. What was the city-state? 2. What was a monarchy? 3. What was democracy? 4. Who were slaves? 5. Who were women? 6. What was military service?	1. What was Sparta? 2. What was Athens? 3. What were the Persian Wars? 4. Who was Darius? 5. Who was Xerxes?	1. Who was Philip II? 2. Who was Alexander the Great? 3. What was Persia? 4. What was Egypt? 5. What was Greek culture?
10	6. Who was Minos? 7. Who were the Myceneans? 8. What was the Trojan War? 9. What was the *Iliad*? 10. Who were the Dorians? 11. What was the Aegean?	7. What was the polis? 8. What was the acropolis? 9. What was the agora? 10. What was an aristocracy? 11. What was a constitution? 12. Who were helots?	6. Who was Pericles? 7. Who was Draco? 8. Who was Solon? 9. Who was Cleisthenes? 10. What was the Battle of Marathon?	6. Who was Demosthenes? 7. What was assassination? 8. Who was Aristotle? 9. What was India, or the Indus River? 10. What was fever? 11. What was its lighthouse, the Pharos?
15	12. What was the Adriatic? 13. What was Alexandria? 14. What was trade? 15. What was Knossos? 16. What was Macedonia?	13. What were military barracks? 14. What was being abandoned to die? 15. What was being sold into slavery? 16. What was household management? 17. Who were overseers (or ephors)? 18. What was the Assembly (or the Council of Elders)?	11. What was the Delian League? 12. What was the Peloponnesian War? 13. What was plague? 14. What was Thebes? 15. Who were tyrants?	12. What was to unite the Greek city-states, or to spread Greek culture? [Name one.] 13. What was Thebes? 14. What was unification, or the spread of Greek culture? [Name one.] 15. What was a phalanx? 16. What was the Battle of Chaeronea?
20	17. What is the Balkan Peninsula? 18. What was the Peloponnesus? 19. What was Ionia? 20. What are the Apennines? 21. What is Sicily?	19. What was the Assembly? 20. What was the Council of Four Hundred (later Five)? 21. What were iron bars? 22. What was a sound mind in a healthy body? 23. What was barbarian?	16. What was Thermopylae? 17. What was the Battle of Salamis? 18. What was the Battle of Plataea? 19. Who was Pisistratus? 20. What were triremes?	17. What was 20? 18. What was Macedonia? 19. What was Egypt (and Palestine)? 20. What was the Seleucid Empire (Persia)? 21. What was its museum?

6 Ancient Rome

	Origins and Geography	Government and Society	Leaders	Expansion, Decline, and Fall
5	1. What was seven? 2. What was the Tiber? 3. What was the Mediterranean? 4. What was a she-wolf? 5. What is the Adriatic?	1. What was a republic? 2. Who were patricians? 3. Who were plebeians? 4. What was the Pax Romana? 5. What were bathhouses? 6. What were free public games?	1. Who was Julius Caesar? 2. What was the Ides of March (March 15, 44 B.C.E.)? 3. Who was Mark Antony? 4. Who was Octavian? 5. What was Augustus?	1. Who was Hannibal? 2. What were the Alps? 3. What were elephants? 4. What was Constantinople? 5. Who were the Germans? 6. Who were the Huns?
10	6. Who were Romulus and Remus? 7. Who were the Latins? 8. Who were the Etruscans? 9. Who were the Greeks? 10. What was drainage? 11. What was the arch?	7. Who were gladiators? 8. Who were dictators? 9. Who were the consuls? 10. What was the Forum? 11. What was the legion?	6. What was emperor? 7. Who was Nero? 8. Who were Tiberius and Gaius Gracchus? 9. Who was Sulla? 10. Who was Pompey?	7. Who was Attila? 8. What was Carthage? 9. What were the Punic Wars? 10. What was North Africa? 11. Who was Scipio? 12. Who was Diocletian?
15	12. What was a monarchy? 13. What was the Rubicon? 14. What was the Atlantic Ocean? 15. What was the Sahara Desert? 16. What was Britain?	12. Who were tribunes? 13. Who were slaves? 14. Who were small farmers? 15. What were laws should be fair and laws should apply to all people equally? 16. What were aqueducts?	11. Who was Brutus or Cassius? [Name one.] 12. Who was Trajan? 13. Who was Hadrian? 14. Who was Marcus Aurelius? 15. Who was Tiberius?	13. Who was Constantine? 14. Who were the Visigoths? 15. Who was Alaric? 16. What was a lack of fixed succession? 17. What were expenses greater than revenues (and then inflation)?
20	17. What was Gaul? 18. What was the Black Sea? 19. What were the Rhine and the Danube? 20. What is the Palatine or the Capitoline hill? [Name one.] 21. What was the Greek alphabet?	17. What were paved highways? 18. What was agriculture? 19. What was adoption of heirs? 20. What were apartment buildings? 21. What was the gap between rich and poor?	16. Who was Caligula? 17. Who were the Good Emperors? 18. Who was Nerva? 19. Who was Cicero? 20. What was civil war?	18. What was moral decline/lack of patriotism? 19. What was Macedonia? 20. What were Sardinia and Corsica? 21. What was plowed salt into the fields? 22. Who were the Barracks Emperors?

7 Greek, Hellenistic, and Roman Culture

	Science and Religion	Architecture, Sculpture, and Painting	Literature and Theater	Philosophy and History
5	1. Who was Zeus or Jupiter? [Name one.] 2. Who was Hera or Juno? [Name one.] 3. Who was Athena? 4. What were the Olympic Games? 5. Who was Hippocrates?	1. What was the Colosseum? 2. What was the Acropolis? 3. What were vases? 4. What was the Parthenon?	1. What were open-air theaters (ampitheaters)? 2. What is drama? 3. What is tragedy? 4. What is comedy? 5. Who was Homer?	1. What was philosophy? 2. Who was Socrates? 3. Who was Plato? 4. Who was Aristotle? 5. What was *The Republic*?
10	6. What was the Hippocratic Oath? 7. Who was Euclid? 8. Who was Pythagoras? 9. Who was Galen? 10. Who was Ptolemy?	5. What was sculpture? 6. What was the Discus Thrower (Discobolus)? 7. What was the Pantheon? 8. What were the Baths of Caracalla? 9. What was the Circus Maximus?	6. Who was Aesop? 7. Who was Sappho? 8. Who was Aristophanes? 9. What was Latin? 10. What was the *Aeniad*?	6. What is the Socratic method? 7. Who was Tacitus? 8. Who was Cicero? 9. Who was Marcus Aurelius? 10. Who was Herodotus?
15	11. What was the earth as the center of the universe (geocentric theory)? 12. Who was Thales (of Miletus)? 13. Who was Archimedes? 14. Who was Eratosthenes? 15. Who was Aristarchus?	10. What was Pompeii? 11. What were the arch and the vaulted dome? 12. Who was Myron? 13. Who was Phidias? 14. Who was Praxiteles?	11. Who was Virgil? 12. Who was Horace? 13. Who was Ovid? 14. What was the Latin (or Roman) alphabet?	11. Who was Thucydides? 12. What was the Golden Mean? 13. What was the Academy? 14. What was the Lyceum? 15. Who was Livy?
20	16. Who was Democritus? 17. What were accurate instruments for observing and measuring? 18. What was classification? 19. What was polytheism?	15. What is neoclassical? 16. What is bas-relief? 17. What were frescoes? 18. What were mosaics?	15. Who was Aeschylus? 16. Who was Sophocles? 17. Who was Euripedes? 18. What were the Romance languages?	16. Who was Julius Caesar? 17. Who was Plutarch? 18. What were rhetoric schools? 19. What was Stoicism? 20. What was Epicureanism?

8 Near Eastern Worlds and the Rise of Christianity

	The Phoenicians	The Hebrews	Christianity	Near Eastern Places
5	1. What was sea trading? 2. What was cedar? 3. What was the city-state? 4. What were mountains? 5. What were walls? 6. What was the port?	1. What was Judaism? 2. What was one god only? 3. Who was Moses? 4. What were the Ten Commandments? 5. What was the Promised Land (Canaan)? 6. Who was Yahweh (Jehovah)?	1. Who was Jesus? 2. Who were the Jews? 3. What was crucifixion? 4. Who were the Romans? 5. Who was the Messiah? 6. Who was the pope?	1. What was Bethlehem? 2. What was Nazareth? 3. What was the Mediterranean Sea? 4. What was Phoenicia? 5. What was Egypt? 6. What was the Red Sea?
10	7. What was seafaring, trading, or shipbuilding? [Name one.] 8. Who were the Canaanites? 9. What were kings/ high priests? 10. What was purple dye? 11. What were colonies?	7. Who was Abraham? 8. What was the Exodus? 9. What was a covenant? 10. What were farming and sheepherding? 11. Who was David? 12. Who was Solomon?	7. What was love one another? 8. What is the Golden Rule? 9. What is resurrection? 10. What was the Son of God? 11. What was honoring the emperor as a god? 12. What was King of the Jews?	7. What was Jerusalem? 8. What was Palestine? 9. What were Tyre, Sidon, Byblos, and Berytus (Beirut)? [Name two.] 10. What was Carthage? 11. What was North Africa? 12. What was Canaan?
15	12. What was the alphabet? 13. What was Middle Eastern culture? 14. What was embalming? 15. What was Africa? 16. What were councils of merchants?	13. Who were the prophets? 14. Who were rabbis? 15. What is the Torah? 16. What is the Old Testament? 17. Who were the Canaanites or the Philistines? [Name one.]	13. What was the Roman Catholic Church? 14. What was the Eastern (Greek) Orthodox Church? 15. What is the New Testament? 16. What are the Gospels? 17. Who was Augustus?	13. What was Mount Sinai? 14. What was Israel? 15. What was Judah? 16. What was the Jordan? 17. What was Babylon?
20	17. What was murex? 18. Who was Dido? 19. What were minerals? 20. What were Baals? 21. What was Sicily, Sardinia, Malta, or Cyprus? [Name one.]	18. What were tribes? 19. Who were the judges? 20. Who was Saul? 21. What was social justice, or the rule of law? 22. Who were Elijah, Amos, Hosea, Isaiah, Micah, Jeremiah, and Ezekiel? [Name three.]	18. Who was Paul? 19. What was the great Roman fire of C.E. 64? 20. Who was Constantine I? 21. What was the Edict of Milan? 22. Who was Theodosius?	18. What is Lebanon or Syria? [Name one.] 19. What is Israel or Jordan? [Name one.] 20. What were the Lebanon Mountains? 21. What is Tunisia? 22. What was Ur, in Mesopotamia? 23. What was the Sinai Peninsula (or Desert)?

Early Cultures in Europe

	The Germans	The Franks	Britain and Ireland	The Vikings
5	1. What was being a warrior? 2. Who were women and slaves? 3. What was the clan (or tribe)? 4. Who were the Vandals? 5. What was the kingdom? 6. Who were the Huns?	1. What was Christianity? 2. What was the Church? 3. What is France? 4. What was Islam? 5. What is Charles the Great?	1. Who were the Celts? 2. Who were the Angles, Saxons, and Jutes? 3. Who were the Angles? 4. What were Wales, western Scotland, and Ireland? [Name one.] 5. Who was St. Patrick? 6. What was the peasant class?	1. What was Norsemen (or Northmen)? 2. What was Scandinavia? 3. What was being brutal or pitiless in fighting? 4. What was shipbuilding? 5. What was trade? 6. What was being a warrior?
10	7. What were the Dark Ages? 8. What was the Danube? 9. Who was Woden? 10. Who was Thor? 11. Who were the Ostrogoths?	6. What was the Rhine? 7. Who was Clovis? 8. What were a common religion and a common language? 9. What is France? 10. What is Germany? 11. Who was Charles Martel?	7. Who were the Picts and the Scots? 8. What was the North Sea? 9. What were monasteries? 10. Who was St. Augustine? 11. What was Canterbury? 12. Who was Alfred the Great?	7. What was opening of new trade routes, or learning shipping skills? [Name one.] 8. What were Norway, Sweden, and Denmark? 9. What were schools? 10. Who was Odin (or Wotan)? 11. Who was Thor?
15	12. Who were the Visigoths? 13. What is vandalism? 14. What was Spain? 15. What was anarchy? 16. What was the fact that they had no written language?	12. What was the Battle of Tours? 13. Who was Pepin (the Short, or III)? 14. Who was Charlemagne? 15. Who were the Lombards, Saxons, Slavs, Avars, and Arabs (Muslims)? [Name two.] 16. What was education?	13. What was Danes? 14. What was *Beowulf*? 15. What were shires? 16. Who were sheriffs? 17. What is the Irish Sea? 18. What was Northumbria?	12. What was the Baltic Sea? 13. Who was Eric the Red? 14. What were Greenland and Iceland? 15. Who was Leif Eriksson? 16. What was Vinland? 17. What was the Atlantic Ocean?
20	17. What was Valhalla? 18. Who was Alaric? 19. Who were the people? 20. Who were the Lombards? 21. Who were the Burgundians?	17. Who was Louis the Pious? 18. What was the Treaty of Verdun? 19. What was Paris? 20. What was Aix-la-Chapelle (or Aachen)? 21. Who were the Magyars?	19. What was Mercia? 20. What was Wessex? 21. Who was Gregory I? 22. Who was Ethelbert, king of Kent? 23. What was the Danelaw?	18. What were runes? 19. What were the Eddas? 20. What were sagas? 21. Who was Canute? 22. What was Normandy?

10 The Rise and Spread of Islam

	Peoples and Places of the Arab Empire	Governing the Arab Empire	Islamic Culture	Religious Beliefs
5	1. What was Arabia? 2. What is desert? 3. What was Mecca? 4. Who were the Moors? 5. What was herding?	1. Who was Muhammad? 2. What was generously, or tolerantly? 3. What was Arabic? 4. What was a caliph? 5. What was the Golden Age of Islam?	1. What was algebra? 2. What were Arabic numerals? 3. What was medicine? 4. What were living creatures?	1. Who is Allah? 2. What is the Qur'an? 3. What is a masjid (or mosque)? 4. What is a (the last and greatest) prophet? 5. What is pork? 6. What is liquor (alcoholic beverages)?
10	6. Who were the Bedouins? 7. What was Medina? 8. What was Mecca? 9. What was the Red Sea? 10. What was Africa? 11. What was Spain?	6. What was a camel driver (or caravan trader)? 7. What was by election? 8. What was by heredity? 9. What were taxes? 10. What was the Battle of Tours?	5. What was calligraphy? 6. Who were alchemists? 7. Who were astronomers? 8. Who were geographers? 9. What was *The Thousand and One Nights*, or *The Arabian Nights*?	7. What is five? 8. What is facing Mecca? 9. What is give alms (charity)? 10. What is fast? 11. Who are mullahs?
15	12. What was the Persian Empire? 13. What was the Byzantine Empire? 14. What were Palestine and Syria? 15. What was Egypt? 16. What was the Tigris?	11. Who was Fatima? 12. Who was Abu Bākr? 13. Who was Ali? 14. What was the Hijrah (Hegira)? 15. Who were the Umayyad?	10. What was Spain? 11. What were the Crusades? 12. What were minarets? 13. What was the astrolabe? 14. What was the *Canon on Medicine*?	12. Who were the Jews and Christians? 13. What is a hajj? 14. Who was the angel Gabriel? 15. What is the Ka'aba? 16. What is "submission to God"?
20	17. Who was Khadijah? 18. What was Yathrib? 19. What was Damascus? 20. What was Baghdad? 21. What was Córdoba (Córdova) or Toledo? [Name one.]	16. Who were the Shi'ites? 17. Who were the Sunnis? 18. Who were the Abbasids? 19. What was a caliphate? 20. What was the Shari'a?	15. Who was Omar Khayyám? 16. Who was al-Razi, or Avicenna? 17. What were steel swords? 18. What was the Dome of the Rock? 19. What was the House of Wisdom?	17. What is "There is no God but Allah, and Muhammad is his prophet [or messenger]"? 18. What is an imam? 19. What is Ramadan? 20. What is "one who submits"? 21. What is the Hijrah (Hegira)?

11 The Byzantine and Eastern Empires

	Byzantine Territory and People	Byzantine Culture	Important People of the Eastern Empires	Landmarks of the Eastern Empires
5	1. Who was Constantine? 2. What was Constantinople? 3. What was Byzantium? 4. What was Rome? 5. What was the Roman Empire? 6. Who was Justinian?	1. What was Christianity? 2. What were trading routes? 3. What were mosaics? 4. What were icons? 5. What was a dome?	1. Who were the Slavs? 2. Who were the Vikings (or Rus)? 3. Who were the Mongols? 4. Who was Genghis Khan? 5. What was the tsar (czar)? 6. Who were the serfs?	1. What was the Baltic Sea? 2. What was the Black Sea? 3. What were the steppes? 4. What was Eurasia? 5. What were the central Asian plains?
10	7. What was the Black Sea? 8. What was the Aegean (or Mediterranean)? 9. Who was Theodora? 10. What was Hagia Sophia? 11. What was Italy? 12. What was North Africa?	6. What was 1,000? 7. What was the Eastern (Greek) Orthodox Church? 8. What was God? 9. Who were women? 10. What was the Hippodrome?	7. Who was Rurik? 8. Who was Vladimir I? 9. Who was St. Cyril? 10. Who was Yaroslav the Wise? 11. What was khan?	6. What was dense forest? 7. What was the Volga? 8. What was the Dnieper? 9. What was the Caspian Sea? 10. What was Novgorod?
15	13. Who were Christians? 14. Who were Muslims (Arabs, Turks)? 15. What was Asia Minor? 16. What was the Bosporus? 17. Who were the Ottoman Turks?	11. What was Greek? 12. Who was the patriarch? 13. What was the Roman Catholic Church? 14. Who was the emperor? 15. Who were missionaries?	12. Who were women? 13. Who was Ivan the Great (Ivan III)? 14. Who was Ivan the Terrible (Ivan IV)? 15. Who were the cossacks? 16. Who were the Rus?	11. What was Kiev? 12. What were the Urals? 13. What was Moscow? 14. What were the Carpathians? 15. What were the Caucasus?
20	18. What is Istanbul? 19. Who was Belisarius? 20. Who was St. Cyril? 21. Who was Leo III? 22. Who were the Persians?	16. Who was the pope? 17. What was the Justinian Code? 18. What were the sea and the city's huge walls? 19. What were Greek and Roman learning and culture? 20. What was Greek fire?	17. Who was Oleg? 18. Who were the boyars? 19. Who was Princess Olga? 20. What was the Golden Horde? 21. Who was Dmitry?	16. What was Byzantium? 17. What was Poland? 18. What was Hungary? 19. What was Moscow? 20. What was the Don?

12 Empires of India and China

	Indian People, Politics, and Places	Indian Religion and Culture	Chinese Government and Politics	Chinese Thought and Culture
5	1. Who were rajahs? 2. Who was Rama and/or Sita? 3. What is the Ganges? 4. What is the Indus? 5. Who was Alexander the Great?	1. What was Hinduism? 2. What is reincarnation? 3. What is the caste system? 4. What is desire? 5. Who were the Untouchables (pariahs, outcasts)?	1. What was the Great Wall of China? 2. What was the civil service system (or civil service exams)? 3. What were books? 4. What is the Huang He (Yellow River)? 5. What is the Yangtze?	1. What was paper? 2. What was silk? 3. What was farming? 4. Who was "Confucius"? 5. What was the wheelbarrow?
10	6. What was the Maurya dynasty? 7. Who were the Gupta? 8. What was a strong central government? 9. What was the Deccan? 10. Who was Asoka? 11. Who were the Tamil?	6. What is karma? 7. What was Siddhartha Gautama? 8. What is nirvana? 9. Who are Brahma, Vishnu, and Shiva? [Name two.] 10. What is "The Enlightened One"?	6. What was the Quin dynasty? 7. What was the Han dynasty? 8. Who were Confucian scholars? 9. What was a peasant? 10. What were noble families?	6. What was acupuncture? 7. What was the rudder? 8. What was the Silk Road? 9. What was the family? 10. What was government?
15	12. What was the Narbada? 13. Who was Chandragupta? 14. Who was Chandragupta Maurya? 15. Who was Kautilya? 16. What was Nalanda?	11. Who were missionaries and/or traders? 12. What was roundness? 13. What were modern ("Arabic") numerals, the decimal system, and zero? [Name two.] 14. What was inoculation? 15. What was the family (or the village)?	11. What was Manchuria or Korea? 12. What was Vietnam? 13. What were high taxes, harsh laws, and/or forced labor? [Name one.] 14. Who were Confucian scholars? 15. What was assimilation?	11. Who was Laozi? 12. What was Buddhism? 13. What is virtuously (by good example)? 14. What is filial piety (respect for parents)? 15. What is to live in harmony with nature?
20	17. What was Pataliputra? 18. What was the Andrha dynasty? 19. Who was Megasthenes? 20. Who were the Hunas? 21. Who was Kalidasa?	16. What are stupas? 17. Who were the Brahmins? 18. What was the Eightfold Path? 19. What is brahman? 20. What was Mahayana or Theravada? [Name one.]	16. What was Gaozu? 17. Who was Wudi? 18. Who was Empress Lü? 19. Who was Shi Huangdi? 20. Who were the Xiongnu (or nomads)?	16. What was the Analects? 17. What was legalism? 18. What was The Way of Virtue? 19. What is dao? 20. Who was Sima Qian?

13 Kingdoms, Empires, and States of Africa

	Geography of Africa	Culture and Trade	People	Places and Politics
5	1. What is the Sahara? 2. What are savannas? 3. What is sub-Saharan? 4. What is the Mediterranean? 5. What is the Atlantic Ocean? 6. What is a rain forest?	1. What was gold? 2. What was salt? 3. What was Islam? 4. Who were ancestors? 5. What was ivory?	1. Who were the Berbers? 2. Who were the Bantu? 3. Who was Mansa Musa? 4. Who were sultans? 5. Who was Sundiata?	1. What was Nubia? 2. What was Kush? 3. What was Timbuktu? 4. What was Aksum? 5. What is Sudan?
10	7. What is desert? 8. What was the Nile River valley? 9. What is the Sudan? 10. What is the Kalahari? 11. What is the Niger?	6. What were camels? 7. What was trade? 8. What was Arabic? 9. What was Swahili? 10. What were churches? 11. What is animism?	6. Who was Ibn Battuta? 7. Who were the Hausa? 8. Who were the Soninke? 9. Who were the Yoruba? 10. Who was Sunni Ali?	6. What was Egypt? 7. What was Morocco? 8. What was Ghana? 9. What was Mali? 10. What was Marrakesh?
15	12. What is the Congo? 13. What was Timbuktu? 14. What is the Indian Ocean? 15. What is Lake Victoria? 16. What is the Red Sea?	12. What was an alphabet? 13. What is Christianity? 14. What was a lineage? 15. What was kente cloth? 16. What were cowrie shells?	11. Who was Askia Muhammad? 12. Who was as-Sahili? 13. Who was Ezana? 14. Who was Piankhi? 15. Who were the Igbo, Efe, San, Tiv, or Nuer? [Name one.]	11. What was Kongo? 12. What was Great Zimbabwe? 13. What was Djenné-Djeno? 14. What was Songhai? 15. What was Benin?
20	17. What is the Great Rift Valley? 18. What is the Zambezi? 19. What is Lake Chad? 20. What is Lake Tanganyika? 21. What is the Sahel?	17. What was bronze and/or brass sculpture? 18. Who were griots? 19. What was Nok? 20. What is desertification? 21. What was Geez?	16. Who was Amina? 17. Who was King Lalibela? 18. Who was Hassan ibn Muhammad? 19. Who were the Almoravids or the Almohads? [Name one.]	16. What was Kilwa? 17. What was Taghaza? 18. What was Gao? 19. What was Kumbi Saleh? 20. What was Meroë?

14 The Americas

	Geography of the Americas	Early Mesoamerica	North American Cultures	Mayas, Aztecs, and Incas
5	1. What is the Amazon? 2. What was Asia? 3. What was the Ice Age? 4. What is the Pacific Ocean? 5. What is the Mississippi?	1. What was maize (corn)? 2. What were floating gardens? 3. What were sculpted heads? 4. What was the calendar? 5. What was the Gulf of Mexico?	1. What were tepees? 2. What was fighting? 3. What was the buffalo? 4. Who were the Pueblos? 5. What was farming?	1. Who were the Maya? 2. Who were the Aztecs? 3. Who were the Spanish explorers? 4. Who were the Incas? 5. What was human sacrifice (on a massive scale)? 6. What was agriculture?
10	6. What is Central America? 7. What is Mexico? 8. What was the Yucatán Peninsula? 9. What are the Rocky Mountains? 10. What were the Andes?	6. Who were the Olmec? 7. What were hieroglyphics? 8. What is harsh desert? 9. What was the Pyramid of the Sun? 10. Who were the Toltec?	6. What was hunting? 7. Who were the Inuit? 8. What was fishing? 9. What were totem poles? 10. What were burial places?	7. What was pay tribute? 8. What was sun worship? 9. What was a written language? 10. What was civil war? 11. What was Machu Pichu? 12. What was Cuzco?
15	11. What was the Bering Strait? 12. What is the Isthmus of Panama? 13. What is Peru or Chile? [Name one.] 14. What is Tierra del Fuego?	11. Who were the Moche? 12. What was Teotihuacán? 13. What was the Chavín culture? 14. Who were the Nazca? 15. Who were the Zapotec?	11. What were cliff dwellings? 12. What was the Iroquois League? 13. What was the potlatch? 14. What was the kiva? 15. Who were the Mound Builders?	13. What is Chichén Itzá? 14. What was Tenochtitlán? 15. What was the concept of zero? 16. What were stepped pyramids? 17. What was Tikal? 18. What was the road system?
20	15. What is the Mexican Valley? 16. What was Beringia? 17. What is Monte Verde? 18. What is the Sierra Madre?	16. Who was Quetzalcoatl? 17. What was San Lorenzo or La Venta? [Name one.] 18. What was Monte Albán? 19. What was Tula?	16. What was Cahokia? 17. Who were the Anasazi? 18. Who were the Hohokams? 19. Who was Hiawatha or Deganawidah? [Name one.]	19. Who was Inti, the sun god? 20. Who was Huitzilopochtli? 21. Who was Pachacuti? 22. What were quipu? 23. What were carved stone pillars?

East Asia: Empires and Kingdoms

	China: People, Places, and Politics	China: Culture and Society	Korea and Southeast Asia	Japanese Civilization
5	1. What was northern China? 2. What was the Tang dynasty? 3. What was the Grand Canal? 4. What was the Song dynasty? 5. Who was Kublai Khan?	1. What was rice? 2. What was gunpowder? 3. What was paper money? 4. What were peasants? 5. What was a civil service examination?	1. What were Hinduism and Buddhism? 2. What was Vietnam? 3. What was China (or Manchuria)? 4. What is mountainous? 5. What was China? 6. What was Buddhism?	1. What is mountainous? 2. Who was the shogun? 3. What was Buddhism? 4. Who were the samurai? 5. What was China? 6. What was *The Tale of Genji*?
10	6. What was the Ming dynasty? 7. Who was Marco Polo? 8. What was the Sui dynasty? 9. Who was Tang Tiazong (or Li Shimin)? 10. What were Vietnam, Tibet, and Korea? [Name two.]	6. What was tea? 7. What were high taxes and/or forced labor? 8. What were gentry? 9. What was Confucian learning? 10. What were merchants?	7. What is the Strait of Malacca or the Sunda Strait? [Name one.] 8. What was the Khmer Empire? 9. What was Angkor Wat? 10. What was Hanoi? 11. What is the Yalu River?	7. Who were daimyo? 8. What is Honshu? 9. What is Hokkaido? 10. What is Kyushu or Shikoku? [Name one.] 11. What was Shinto? 12. Who were the Mongols?
15	11. Who was Wu Zhao? 12. What was the Yuan dynasty? 13. Who was Zheng He? 14. Who were the Arabs? 15. Who was Sui Wendi?	11. What was footbinding? 12. What was calligraphy? 13. What was porcelain? 14. What was the magnetic compass? 15. What was the Forbidden City?	12. Who were the Mongols? 13. What is the Sea of Japan? 14. What is the Yellow Sea? 15. What was Java? 16. What was Sumatra?	13. What was Heiankyo (or Kyoto)? 14. What was feudalism? 15. What was hara-kiri, (or seppuku)? 16. What was Korea? 17. What is archipelago? 18. What was Chinese?
20	16. What was Chang'an? 17. What was Hangzhou? 18. Who was Song Taizu (or Zhao Kuangyin)? 19. Who was Zhu Yuanzhang (or Hongwu)? 20. What was the Jin Empire?	16. What was the mechanical clock? 17. What was movable type? 18. What was the pagoda? 19. What were corn and/or sweet potatoes? 20. What was poetry?	17. What was the Shilla (or Silla) dynasty? 18. What was the Koryu (or Koryo) dynasty? 19. What was celadon? 20. What was the Choson (or Yi) dynasty? 21. What was Kaesong?	19. What was the Kamakura Shogunate? 20. What was the Tokugawa Shogunate? 21. What was the "Warring States" period? 22. What was Nara? 23. What was bushido?

16 Europe: Feudalism, the Church, and the Crusades

	Feudal Life	Feudal People	The Medieval Church	The Crusades
5	1. What was a manor? 2. What was a castle? 3. What was a moat? 4. What was a drawbridge? 5. What was the code of chivalry? 6. What was chess?	1. Who was a lord? 2. Who were nobles? 3. Who were peasants? 4. Who were serfs? 5. Who was a knight?	1. What was the Church? 2. Who was a parish priest? 3. What was Latin? 4. Who was the pope? 5. What were nunneries (or convents)? 6. What were monasteries?	1. What was Palestine (the Holy Land)? 2. What was Islam? 3. Who were the Seljuk Turks? 4. What was the Byzantine Empire? 5. What was Jerusalem?
10	7. What was a dungeon? 8. What was no strong central government (or weak kings)? 9. What was military aid and service? 10. What was ransom? 11. What were tournaments?	6. Who were kings? 7. Who were the clergy? 8. Who was a vassal? 9. Who was the oldest son? 10. Who were freemen?	7. What were reading and writing? 8. What was a cathedral? 9. What was burning at the stake? 10. What was excommunication? 11. What was an abbot? 12. What were the Franciscans or the Dominicans? [Name one.]	6. What was the Children's Crusade? 7. Who was Urban II? 8. What was "God wills it!"? 9. What was a red cross? 10. What were debts, taxes, sins, and criminal punishment? [Name two.]
15	12. What was a joust? 13. What was straw? 14. What was the great hall? 15. What was a fief? 16. What was the lord's court?	11. What was a page? 12. What was a squire? 13. Who was Charlemagne? 14. Who were troubadours? 15. Who were minstrels?	13. What was social welfare? 14. What was canon law? 15. What was the Inquisition? 16. What was heresy? 17. What was a tithe?	11. What was the First Crusade? 12. What was massacred the inhabitants? 13. Who were Richard the Lion-Hearted of England, Emperor Frederick Barbarossa of Germany, and King Philip Augustus of France? [Name two.] 14. Who was Salah al-Din (or Saladin)? 15. What was an increase in the power of kings?
20	17. What was the manor house? 18. What was a palisade? 19. What was the keep? 20. What was a dowry? 21. What was fallow?	16. Who were skilled workers (or artisans)? 17. Who was a bailiff? 18. Who was a chancellor? 19. Who were the poor and sick? 20. Who was the lord?	18. Who was Gregory I (the Great)? 19. What was the Benedictine Rule? 20. Who was Gregory VII? 21. What was the Concordat of Worms? 22. What was simony?	16. What was Clermont? 17. What was the Second Crusade? 18. What was the Crusade of Three Kings? 19. Who was Innocent III? 20. What was Constantinople?

17 The High and Late Middle Ages in Europe

	Towns and Trade	Medieval Culture in the Towns	France and Germany Emerge From Feudalism	England Emerges From Feudalism
5	1. What was Italy? 2. What was the East? 3. What were seaports? 4. What was the Mediterranean? 5. Who were bankers?	1. What was Latin? 2. Who was Geoffrey Chaucer? 3. What was *The Canterbury Tales*? 4. What were universities? 5. Who was King Arthur?	1. What were provinces? 2. What was the Estates-General? 3. What was the Hundred Years' War? 4. What was the longbow? 5. What was the cannon?	1. Who was William the Conqueror? 2. What was the Battle of Hastings? 3. Who were the Normans? 4. What was French? 5. What was Richard the Lion-Hearted?
10	6. What were guilds? 7. What was the Black Death (or bubonic plague)? 8. What was Venice? 9. What was Constantinople? 10. What was an overland route?	6. What was the vernacular (English, Italian, French, German, Spanish)? 7. What were miracle (or mystery) plays? 8. Who was Dante Alighieri? 9. What was *The Divine Comedy*? 10. What was alchemy? 11. What was Romanesque?	6. Who was Joan of Arc? 7. Who was Hugh Capet? 8. Who were the Capetians? 9. Who was Philip Augustus (Philip II)? 10. Who was Philip IV, "the Fair"?	6. What was a census? 7. Who was Thomas à Becket (the Archbishop of Canterbury)? 8. Who were circuit (or royal) judges? 9. Who was John? 10. What was the Magna Carta?
15	11. What were the Crusades? 12. Who were moneychangers? 13. What were towns? 14. What was the feudal system? 15. Who was an apprentice?	12. What was Gothic? 13. What were flying buttresses? 14. What was Paris or Oxford? [Name one.] 15. What was scholasticism? 16. Who was Peter Abelard?	11. Who was Louis IX, "Saint Louis"? 12. What was the Holy Roman Empire? 13. Who was Otto I, "the Great"? 14. Who was Henry IV? 15. Who was Frederick I, "Barbarossa"?	11. What was Parliament? 12. What was the House of Lords? 13. What was the House of Commons? 14. What were grand juries? 15. Who was Harold?
20	16. Who was a journeyman? 17. What was the middle class? 18. What was crowded and/or unsanitary? 19. What was Flanders? 20. What was woolen cloth?	17. Who was Thomas Aquinas? 18. What was *The Song of Roland*? 19. Who was Siegfried? 20. What was Bologna? 21. What was Salerno?	16. Who was Frederick II? 17. What was Crécy, Agincourt, or Poitiers? [Name one.] 18. Who was Charles VII? 19. What was "red beard"? 20. What was the Lombard League?	16. What was the Domesday Book? 17. Who was Eleanor of Aquitaine? 18. Who was Henry II? 19. What was the Great Council? 20. What was common law?

18 Southwestern and Central Asia

	The Mongol Empire	The Mughal Empire	The Seljuk and Safavid Empires	The Ottoman Empire
5	1. What was the steppe? 2. What was nomadic herding? 3. What was khan? 4. Who was Genghis Khan? 5. What was China? 6. What was terror?	1. What is Mongol? 2. What was the northern plain? 3. Who were Hindus? 4. What was the Taj Mahal? 5. What was Islam? 6. What were heavy taxes?	1. What was Persia? 2. What was the Mughal Empire? 3. What was the Ottoman Empire? 4. What was Turkish? 5. What were the Crusades?	1. What was the cannon? 2. What was gunpowder? 3. What was Turkish? 4. What was Central Asia? 5. What was Asia Minor? 6. What was nomadic?
10	7. What were catapults and gunpowder? 8. What was Kiev? 9. Who was Kublai Khan? 10. What was the Golden Horde? 11. What is Beijing?	7. What was Hindi? 8. Who were Arabs? 9. What was Buddhism? 10. Who was Akbar? 11. Who was Shah Jahan?	6. What was Shi'ite? 7. What was Sunni? 8. What was shah? 9. Who was Abbas the Great? 10. What were carpets? 11. What was Baghdad?	7. What was Islam? 8. Who was Muhammad II? 9. What was Istanbul? 10. What was Vienna? 11. Who was Suleiman? 12. Who were the janissaries?
15	12. What was Japan? 13. What was tolerance? 14. What were bubonic plague, ideas, and/or inventions? 15. What is "universal ruler"? 16. What was Temujin?	12. What was kill their rivals? 13. What was tolerance? 14. Who was Timur the Lame (or Tamerlane)? 15. What was Delhi? 16. What was Urdu?	12. What was the Persian Gulf (or Indian Ocean)? 13. What was the Ottoman Empire? 14. Who was Omar Khayyám? 15. Who were Mongols? 16. Who was Salah al-Din, or Saladin?	13. What was "sultan"? 14. What were the Balkans (or Hungary)? 15. What was the Mosque of Suleiman? 16. What was the Hagia Sophia? 17. Who was Osman?
20	17. What was the Mongol Peace? 18. What was Persia? 19. What was the Yuan dynasty? 20. What was Russia? 21. What was Southeast Asia?	17. What were the Sikhs? 18. Who was Nur Jahan? 19. Who was Mahmud? 20. Who was Aurangzeb? 21. Who was Babur?	17. Who was Malik Shah? 18. What was vizier? 19. What was Isfahan? 20. Who was Isma'il? 21. What was the Abbasid Empire?	18. Who was Sinan? 19. Who was Selim the Grim? 20. What were millets? 21. What was the divan? 22. What were Spain and Italy?

19 The Renaissance and the Reformation

	Renaissance Origins in Italy	The Northern Renaissance	The Protestant Reformation	English and Catholic Reformations
5	1. What was humanism? 2. What was the individual? 3. Who was Leonardo da Vinci? 4. Who was Michelangelo? 5. What was Italy?	1. What was the printing press? 2. Who were merchants? 3. Who was William Shakespeare? 4. Who were Romeo and Juliet? 5. What was the play (or the drama)?	1. Who was Martin Luther? 2. What was the sale of indulgences? 3. Who were Protestants? 4. What was the Bible? 5. What were the Ninety-Five Theses?	1. Who was Henry VIII? 2. What was to have a son to succeed to the throne? 3. Who was Catherine of Aragon? 4. What was Latin? 5. Who was Anne Boleyn?
10	6. What were classical (Greek and Roman) writings? 7. Who was Raphael? 8. What were Florence, Venice, and the Papal States (Rome)? [Name two.] 9. What was realism? 10. What was perspective?	6. Who was Elizabeth I? 7. What was oil painting? 8. What was Flanders? 9. Who was Johann Gutenberg? 10. Who was Cervantes?	6. What was Lutheranism? 7. What was Catholicism? 8. Who was John Calvin? 9. What was Geneva? 10. Who was John Knox?	6. Who was Elizabeth I? 7. What was Roman Catholic? 8. What was the Church of England (or Anglican Church)? 9. What was the Counter or Catholic Reformation? 10. Who was Ignatius of Loyola?
15	11. Who was Macchiavelli? 12. Who were the Medicis? 13. Who was Lorenzo de Medici? 14. Who was Titian? 15. Who was Boccaccio?	11. Who was Albrecht Dürer? 12. What was *Utopia*? 13. Who was Hans Holbein? 14. Who was Pieter Brueghel?	11. What was the Presbyterian Church? 12. Who were the Huguenots? 13. What were the opportunities to take Church lands and to stop paying taxes to Rome? 14. What was predestination? 15. What is a theocracy?	11. What was the Inquisition? 12. What was the Society of Jesus (or Jesuits)? 13. What was to check the spread of Protestantism? 14. What was to annul it? 15. What was the Council of Trent?
20	16. Who was Petrarch? 17. Who was Castiglione? 18. Who was Donatello? 19. Who was Ghiberti?	15. Who were the van Eycks (Jan and Hubert)? 16. Who was Rabelais? 17. Who was Erasmus? 18. What was Toledo? 19. Who was Peter Paul Rubens?	16. What was through faith alone? 17. Who was John Hus? 18. Who was John Wycliffe? 19. Who was Johann Tetzel? 20. What was the Diet of Worms?	16. What was through good works and faith? 17. What were the Bible and Christian tradition? 18. What is only the Church? 19. What was the Index of Prohibited Books?

20 The Age of Exploration

	Early Exploration and the Portuguese	Encounters in Asia and Africa	Spain in the Americas	The Struggle for North America
5	1. What was the (magnetic) compass? 2. What was Italy? 3. What were spices? 4. What was Africa? 5. What was scurvy?	1. What was the Cape of Good Hope (or Cape of Storms)? 2. Who was Vasco da Gama? 3. Who was Ferdinand Magellan? 4. What were slaves? 5. Who was Bartholomeu Dias?	1. Who was Christopher Columbus? 2. What was Indians? 3. What was conquistadors? 4. What was gold? 5. What was the Pacific?	1. What was the fur trade? 2. Who was Henry Hudson? 3. What was disease? 4. What was the Mississippi? 5. What was the Northwest Passage?
10	6. What was cartographer? 7. Who was Henry the Navigator? 8. What was a navigation school? 9. What was to spread Christianity? 10. What were the Spice Islands?	6. Who were the Portuguese? 7. What was the Netherlands? 8. What were the Philippines? 9. What was East Africa? 10. What was the Middle Passage?	6. What was the Caribbean? 7. What was Mexico? 8. Who was Hernando Cortés? 9. What was the Aztec Empire? 10. What were horses and guns?	6. What was Jamestown (Virginia)? 7. What was Plymouth (Massachusetts)? 8. Who was John Cabot (Giovanni Caboto)? 9. Who was Giovanni da Verrazano? 10. Who was Sir Walter Raleigh?
15	11. What were triangular sails? 12. Who were Muslim traders? 13. What were cannons? 14. What was an astrolabe? 15. Who was Pedro Alvarés Cabral?	11. What was the East Indies? 12. What was Japan? 13. Who were the Dutch? 14. What was Macao? 15. What was Goa?	11. Who was Francisco Pizarro? 12. Who were the Incas? 13. Who was Francisco Coronado? 14. Who was Vasco Núñez de Balboa? 15. Who was Hernando de Soto?	11. What were Britain and France? 12. Who were the Puritans? 13. What was the St. Lawrence River? 14. What was Quebec? 15. What was New Amsterdam?
20	16. What were Spain and Portugal? 17. What was the sextant? 18. What was the papal line of demarcation? 19. What was Lisbon?	16. What was Malacca? 17. What was Calicut? 18. What was Java? 19. What was the English East India Company? 20. What was the Dutch East India Company?	16. Who was Ponce de León? 17. What were the Caribbean islands and Brazil? 18. Who was Atahualpa? 19. What are the West Indies? 20. Who was Montezuma?	16. What was Louisiana? 17. Who was Jacques Cartier? 18. Who was Robert de la Salle? 19. Who were Father Jacques Marquette and Louis Joliet? 20. What was King Philip's War?

21 The Rise of Monarchies

	Spain	France	Austria, Prussia, and Russia	England
5	1. Who were the Moors? 2. Who were Ferdinand and Isabella? 3. Who were Jews and Moors (Muslims)? 4. What were the American colonies? 5. What was the Armada?	1. What was a civil war? 2. What was Versailles? 3. What was French? 4. What was the balance of power? 5. Who were the Huguenots?	1. Who were the Hapsburgs? 2. What was its army? 3. What was the Holy Roman Empire? 4. Who were the Romanovs? 5. What was westernization?	1. Who were the Tudors? 2. Who were the Stuarts? 3. Who was Oliver Cromwell? 4. What was to be beheaded? 5. What was the monarchy?
10	6. What was the Inquisition? 7. Who was Charles I (Charles V of the Holy Roman Empire)? 8. Who was Philip II? 9. What was a strong centralized government? 10. What was England? 11. What was an absolute monarchy?	6. Who was Henry IV (Henry of Navarre)? 7. What was the Estates-General? 8. Who were the Bourbons? 9. Who was Cardinal Richelieu? 10. Who were the nobles?	6. What was the Thirty Years' War? 7. What was the Seven Years' War? 8. Who was Peter the Great (Peter I)? 9. What were beards? 10. What was St. Petersburg?	6. What was the theater? 7. What was the Bill (Declaration) of Rights? 8. Who was Elizabeth I? 9. Who was James I? 10. What was a military dictator?
15	12. What was the destruction of the middle class? 13. What was Catholicism? 14. What were the Spanish Hapsburgs? 15. What was Madrid? 16. What was Portugal?	11. Who was Louis XIV? 12. What were years of wars and/or costs of the court? 13. What was the War of the Spanish Succession? 14. What was loss of skilled workers and businesspeople? 15. What was the Edict of Nantes?	11. Who was Catherine the Great? 12. What was Poland? 13. Who was Frederick the Great? 14. What was Germany? 15. What was Austria?	11. Who were the Puritans? 12. Who was Charles I? 13. What was the divine right of kings? 14. What was the House of Commons? 15. What was Scotland?
20	17. What was the Netherlands? 18. What was inflation? 19. What was the Ottoman Empire? 20. Who was El Greco? 21. Who was Diego Velásquez?	16. Who was Catherine de Medici? 17. Who was Louis XIII? 18. Who was Colbert? 19. What was the Thirty Years' War? 20. What was the St. Bartholomew's Day massacre?	16. What was Catholic? 17. What was Protestant? 18. What was Prussia? 19. Who was Maria Theresa? 20. What was to acquire warm-water seaports?	16. Who was Charles II? 17. What was to raise taxes? 18. What was the Glorious Revolution? 19. Who were William and Mary? 20. What was a limited constitutional monarchy?

22 Commerce, Science, and Enlightenment

	The Commercial Revolution	The Scientific Revolution	Ideas of the Enlightenment	Enlightened Politics
5	1. What was the Atlantic coast? 2. What was inflation? 3. What was fixed value? 4. What was the middle class? 5. What was interest?	1. Who was Leonardo da Vinci? 2. What was the telescope? 3. What was the law of gravity (or universal gravitation)? 4. What was the scientific method? 5. Who was Benjamin Franklin?	1. What were problems of the time? 2. What was the Age of Reason? 3. What was natural law? 4. What was French? 5. Who was Adam Smith?	1. What was a social contract? 2. What were natural rights? 3. What were the rights of life, liberty, and property? [Name two.] 4. What were free speech, press, and religion? [Name two.] 5. What were the French and American Revolutions?
10	6. What was Venice or Genoa? [Name one.] 7. What was London or Amsterdam? [Name one.] 8. What was the Commercial Revolution? 9. Who was a stockholder (or shareholder)? 10. What were dividends?	6. Who was Nicholas Copernicus? 7. Who was Galileo Galilei? 8. What was circulation of the blood? 9. What were bacteria (microscopic life)? 10. What were gases?	6. What were the natural laws of justice? 7. What was rationalism? 8. What was religion? 9. What was civilization? 10. What was the *Encyclopédie* (the *Encyclopedia*)?	6. What was the U.S. Constitution or the Declaration of Independence? [Name one.] 7. Who was Jean-Jacques Rousseau? 8. Who was John Locke? 9. Who was Thomas Hobbes? 10. What was how people should be governed?
15	11. What was capital? 12. What were tariffs? 13. What was the Columbian Exchange? 14. What were colonies? 15. What were precious metals and/or raw materials?	11. What was oxygen? 12. What was the microscope? 13. What was the mercury thermometer? 14. What was vaccination? 15. Who was Isaac Newton?	11. What was the land? 12. What was laissez-faire? 13. What was science, modern languages, or modern history? [Name one.] 14. Who was Alexander Pope? 15. Who were the *philosophes*?	11. What was anarchy, or a state of nature? 12. What was the English government? 13. What was the separation of powers? 14. What were checks and balances? 15. What was limited monarchy?
20	16. What were manufactured goods? 17. What were banks of deposit (or bills of exchange)? 18. Who were the Dutch? 19. What was mercantilism? 20. What was a joint stock company?	16. Who was Robert Boyle? 17. What was classification? 18. Who was Vesalius? 19. What was the heliocentric theory? 20. Who was Ambroise Paré?	16. What was a *tabula rasa* (blank slate)? 17. What were salons? 18. Who was René Descartes? 19. Who was Francis Bacon?	16. What was the people's will (or the general will)? 17. What was popular sovereignty? 18. What were enlightened despots? 19. What was the Declaration of the Rights of Man?

23 Revolution in North America

	Steps to Revolution	Revolutionary People	Revolutionary Places	Elements and Results of the Revolution
5	1. What was an assembly? 2. What was the Sugar Act? 3. What was the Boston Tea Party? 4. What was "no taxation without representation"? 5. What was Parliament?	1. Who was George Washington? 2. Who was Thomas Jefferson? 3. Who was George III? 4. Who was Paul Revere? 5. What was redcoat (or lobsterback)? 6. Who were Minutemen?	1. What was Philadelphia? 2. What was Valley Forge? 3. What was Bunker Hill (Breed's Hill)? 4. What was West Point? 5. What was Massachusetts? 6. What was the Atlantic?	1. What was the Declaration of Independence? 2. What was the United States of America? 3. What was the Constitution of the United States? 4. What was a republic? 5. What is the Bill of Rights?
10	6. What were rights of Englishmen? 7. What was the French and Indian War? 8. What was the Treaty of Paris? 9. What was the Stamp Act? 10. What was a boycott?	7. Who were Hessians? 8. Who were Tories (or Loyalists)? 9. Who were Patriots? 10. Who was John Hancock? 11. Who was the Marquis de Lafayette?	7. What was Boston Harbor? 8. What was the Mississippi? 9. What were Lexington and Concord? 10. What was the Hudson? 11. What was Saratoga? 12. What was Yorktown?	6. What were its army and navy? 7. What was a federal system? 8. What was the Second Continental Congress? 9. What was "created equal and/or with unalienable rights"? 10. What was the power to tax?
15	11. What was the Boston Massacre? 12. What was the British East India Company? 13. What were the Intolerable Acts? 14. What was the First Continental Congress? 15. What were royal, proprietary, and self-governing colonies? [Name two.]	12. Who was Baron von Steuben? 13. Who was Thomas Paine? 14. Who was Lord Cornwallis? 15. Who was Benjamin Franklin? 16. Who was Patrick Henry?	13. What was Paris? 14. What were the Great Lakes? 15. What was Florida? 16. What was Canada? 17. What were Connecticut and Rhode Island?	11. What was France? 12. What were the Articles of Confederation? 13. What was the militia? 14. What were U.S. (federal) courts? 15. What was guerilla style (or "Indian style")?
20	16. What was mercantilism? 17. What were the Navigation Acts? 18. What was the Declaratory Act? 19. What were the Townshend Acts? 20. What was the Quebec Act?	17. Who was James Madison? 18. Who was Samuel Adams? 19. Who was Casimir Pulaski or Thaddeus Kosciusko? [Name one.] 20. Who were Benjamin Franklin, John Jay, and John Adams? [Name two.] 21. Who was John Adams?	18. What were Quebec and Montreal? 19. What was Boston? 20. What was New York? 21. What was Philadelphia? 22. What was Rhode Island?	16. What were untrained, poorly organized, and inadequately equipped? [Name two.] 17. What was the Peace of Paris? 18. What was the Constitutional Act? 19. What were Great Britain, France, Spain, and Russia?

24 The French Revolution and Napoleon

	Steps to Revolution	Revolutionary Events	Napoleon's Rise and Empire	Napoleon's Decline and Fall
5	1. What were the estates? 2. What were taxes? 3. What was the middle class? 4. Who was Marie Antoinette? 5. Who were the clergy? 6. Who were the nobility?	1. What was the Bastille? 2. What was "Liberty, Equality, Fraternity"? 3. Who were the people? 4. What was the Reign of Terror? 5. What was the guillotine? 6. What was beheading?	1. What was a dictator? 2. What was the legislature? 3. What was a strong central government? 4. What was emperor? 5. Who were his relatives? 6. What was Corsica?	1. What was the French Revolution? 2. What was smuggling? 3. What was Russia? 4. What was Elba? 5. What was Waterloo?
10	7. Who was everyone except the clergy and nobility? 8. What were individual rights (or personal liberties)? 9. What was the American Revolution? 10. What was the American Revolutionary War? 11. What was the Estates-General?	7. What was the Directory? 8. Who was Jean-Paul Marat? 9. Who were Robespierre and Danton? 10. What were Austria and Prussia? 11. What were the radicals, moderates, and conservatives (or left, center, and right)?	7. What was Egypt? 8. What were the Coalitions? 9. What was the Napoleonic Code? 10. What were freedom of speech and the press? 11. What was Notre Dame Cathedral?	6. What was nationalism? 7. Who were non-Frenchmen? 8. What were Portugal and Spain? 9. What was the severe Russian winter? 10. What was the retreat from Moscow (Russia)?
15	12. Who was Louis XVI? 13. What was credit (or money)? 14. What was one? 15. What was Versailles? 16. What were the bourgeoisie, manual workers, and serfs and peasants?	12. What was a constitutional (limited) monarchy? 13. What was the Church? 14. What was Paris? 15. What was the Declaration of the Rights of Man (and of the Citizen)? 16. What was the tricolor?	12. What was conscription (the draft)? 13. What were Austria and England? 14. What was Louisiana? 15. Who was Admiral Horatio Nelson? 16. What was First Consul?	11. What was St. Helena? 12. Who was the Duke of Wellington? 13. What were Germany and Italy? 14. What was being an army of citizens, not professionals? 15. What was the Peninsular War (or Campaign)?
20	17. What was the Old Regime? 18. What was the Enlightenment? 19. What was together, not separately? 20. What was the National Assembly? 21. What was the Tennis Court Oath?	17. What was abolishing both serfdom and tax exemptions for nobles and clergy? 18. What was the Commune? 19. What was the National Convention? 20. What was the Revolutionary Tribunal? 21. What was the Committee of Public Safety?	17. What was "a nation of shopkeepers"? 18. What was the Continental System? 19. What was the Holy Roman Empire? 20. What was the Confederation of the Rhine? 21. What was Austerlitz?	16. What was guerrilla warfare? 17. What was the "Battle of the Nations" at Leipzig? 18. Who were the Bourbons? 19. Who was Louis XVIII? 20. What were the Hundred Days?

25 The Industrial Revolution

	Agriculture and Manufacturing	Transportation and Communication	Conditions and Effects	Reform
5	1. What was the textile industry? 2. What was in their own cottages (at home)? 3. What were rivers or streams? 4. What were factories? 5. What was the cotton gin? 6. What was the flying shuttle?	1. What was steam? 2. Who was Robert Fulton? 3. What were canals? 4. What were barges? 5. What were railroads? 6. What was Morse code?	1. What was the middle class? 2. What was the industrial working class (proletariat)? 3. Who were children? 4. What were cities? 5. What were going to school and playing? 6. What was population growth?	1. What was child labor? 2. What were trade unions? 3. What were strikes? 4. Who was Charles Dickens? 5. What was 10 hours? 6. What was collective bargaining?
10	7. What was the spinning jenny? 8. Who was James Watt? 9. What was steam? 10. Who was Eli Whitney? 11. What was mass production? 12. What were interchangeable parts?	7. Who was Samuel Morse? 8. What were macadam roads? 9. What are locks? 10. What was the *Clermont*? 11. What was the telegraph? 12. What were cables?	7. What were noisy, dirty, dangerous, and uncomfortable? [Name two or three.] 8. Who were women and children? 9. What was their labor? 10. Who were farm workers (or self-employed workers)? 11. Who were managers?	7. What were cheap factory (consumer) goods? 8. What was the aristocracy? 9. What was socialism? 10. Who were Utopian socialists? 11. Who was Robert Owen?
15	13. Who was Henry Bessemer? 14. What was steel? 15. What was coal? 16. Who was Cyrus McCormick? 17. What was the enclosure system?	13. What were raw materials and finished goods? 14. What was by horse or cart (over roads)? 15. What were locomotives? 16. What was the automobile? 17. What was the *Great Western*?	12. What was move their homes? 13. What was unskilled labor? 14. What was unemployment? 15. What was polluted? 16. What was the aristocracy (upper classes)?	12. Who was Karl Marx? 13. What was the *Communist Manifesto*? 14. Who were the bourgeoisie (capitalists) and proletariat (workers)? 15. What was laissez-faire? 16. Who was Thomas Malthus?
20	18. Who was John Key? 19. Who was James Hargreaves? 20. Who was Thomas Newcomen? 21. Who was Richard Arkwright? 22. What was the power loom?	18. Who was George Stephenson? 19. What was the *Rocket*? 20. Who was Alessandro Volta? 21. Who was Cyrus Field? 22. Who was Michael Faraday?	17. What were factories? 18. What was 12 to 14 (or 16) hours? 19. What was 6 to 7 days? 20. What were tenements? 21. Who were capitalists?	17. Who was David Ricardo? 18. Who was John Stuart Mill? 19. What was New Lanark? 20. Who was Friedrich Engels? 21. What was *Das Kapital*?

26 Latin America and the Struggle for Freedom

	Colonial Times	Revolution in Mexico, Central America, and the Islands	Brazil	Revolution in Spanish South America
5	1. What is Latin America? 2. What is Brazil? 3. Who were the Indians? 4. What were gold and silver? 5. What were high government offices? 6. What were finished (manufactured) products?	1. Who were the Indians and mestizos? 2. What was a republic? 3. What was Central America? 4. What was Spain? 5. What was the Monroe Doctrine?	1. What was brazilwood? 2. What was Africa? 3. What was bloodshed? 4. What is the Amazon? 5. Who were criminals? 6. What was Roman Catholicism?	1. Who was Simón Bolívar? 2. What was Spain? 3. What were the Andes? 4. What is Lima? 5. What was Bolivia? 6. What was Venezuela?
10	7. What were raw materials? 8. Who were the Aztecs and Incas? 9. What are the pampas? 10. What was Mexico City? 11. Who was a viceroy?	6. What was Haiti? 7. Who was Toussaint L'Ouverture? 8. What was France's (Napoleon's) invasion of Spain? 9. What was Mexico City? 10. What are Guatemala, El Salvador, Honduras, Nicaragua, and Costa Rica? [Name three.] 11. What was Santo Domingo?	7. What was Portugal? 8. What was sugar cane? 9. What were gold and diamonds? 10. What was the Portuguese royal family? 11. What was Portuguese? 12. What was Rio de Janeiro?	7. What was Caracas? 8. Who were the creoles? 9. What were the United Provinces of La Plata? 10. Who was José de San Martín? 11. Who was Bernardo O'Higgins? 12. Who was José de San Martín?
15	12. Who were people born in Spain (*peninsulares*)? 13. Who were creoles? 14. Who were mestizos? 15. What was the Roman Catholic Church? 16. Who were mulattos?	12. What was France? 13. Who was Santa Anna? 14. Who was Benito Juárez? 15. What were abolition of slavery and redistribution of land? 16. What was Hispaniola?	13. What were coffee and rubber? 14. What was development (of agriculture and industry)? 15. Who was Napoleon? 16. Who was King John VI (João VI)? 17. Who was Pedro I?	13. Who was Simón Bolívar? 14. What was a union of South American states? 15. Who was Tupac Amaru? 16. What was Argentina? 17. What were Paraguay and Uruguay?
20	17. What was North America? 18. What are llanos? 19. What was New Spain? 20. What were New Granada, La Plata, and Peru? 21. What were tithes?	17. What were the United Provinces of Central America? 18. Who was Father Miguel Hidalgo? 19. Who was Father José María Morelos? 20. Who was Augustín de Iturbide? 21. Who was Jean Jacques Dessalines?	18. What was a constitutional monarchy? 19. Who was Pedro II? 20. Who was the governor general? 21. What was England? 22. What were captaincies?	18. What was Buenos Aires? 19. What was Peru? 20. What was Chile? 21. What was Gran (Great) Colombia? 22. What are Colombia, Venezuela, Ecuador, and Panama? [Name three.]

27 Conflict and Democracy in the English-Speaking World

	Great Britain Becomes a Democracy	Canada, New Zealand, and Australia	Growth of the United States	Civil War and Reunion in the United States
5	1. What was voting reform? 2. What was debt? 3. Who was Queen Victoria? 4. What was the Victorian era? 5. What was the potato crop? 6. What was a salary?	1. What is the United States–Canada boundary? 2. What was a penal colony? 3. What is an island and a continent? 4. Who were the Aborigines? 5. What was gold?	1. Who were Washington, Jefferson, and Adams? [Name two.] 2. What were reservations? 3. What was the Gold Rush? 4. What were the Rockies? 5. What were Canada and Mexico? 6. What was the Alamo?	1. What was industry? 2. What was agriculture? 3. What were plantations? 4. What was slavery? 5. Who was Abraham Lincoln? 6. Who was Robert E. Lee?
10	7. What was the Whig party? 8. What was the Liberal party? 9. What was the Conservative party? 10. What was grain? 11. Who was Benjamin Disraeli? 12. Who was William Gladstone?	6. Who were the French and the British? 7. What was the Klondike Gold Rush? 8. What was the Northwest Territory? 9. What was a dominion? 10. What was the "White Australia" policy? 11. What were New South Wales, Tasmania, Western Australia, South Australia, Queensland, and Victoria? [Name four.]	7. What was power changing hands peacefully? 8. Who were adult white males? 9. What was the Louisiana Territory? 10. What was Florida? 11. What was Mexico?	7. Who was Ulysses S. Grant? 8. What was the Emancipation Proclamation? 9. What were cotton and tobacco? 10. Who were abolitionists? 11. What was to secede?
15	13. What was home rule? 14. What was the British Labour party? 15. What was social welfare legislation? 16. What were rotten boroughs? 17. What were pocket boroughs?	12. Who were the Maori? 13. What was the Netherlands? 14. Who was Captain James Cook? 15. What was ethnic tension? 16. What was the Canadian Pacific (transcontinental) Railway?	12. What was France? 13. What was California? 14. What were the Mississippi River and the Rocky Mountains? 15. What was Texas? 16. What was New Orleans?	12. What was the Republican party? 13. Who were carpetbaggers? 14. What was the Confederate States of America? 15. Who was Jefferson Davis? 16. What was the War Between the States?
20	18. What was the Reform Bill of 1832? 19. Who were the Chartists? 20. Who were male city industrial workers? 21. Who were male agricultural workers? 22. What was the Parliament Bill of 1911?	17. What was the Durham Report? 18. What was the Act of Union? 19. What was a federal union? 20. What was nine? 21. What was woman suffrage?	17. What were territory and population? 18. What was the Republic of Texas? 19. What was the Oregon Country? 20. What were Oregon, Washington, and Idaho? [Name two.] 21. What was the Gadsden Purchase?	17. What were industry and railroads? 18. What was Reconstruction? 19. What was South Carolina? 20. What was the spread of slavery to the new territories? 21. What was Great Britain?

28 Reaction and Revolution in Europe

	The Congress of Vienna	Alliances and the Age of Metternich	France: Empire, War, and Republic	Revolt and Revolution
5	1. What was the Congress of Vienna? 2. Who was Prince von Metternich? 3. Who was Prince Talleyrand? 4. What was (divine-right) monarchy? 5. What were overseas territories? 6. What was France?	1. What was peace (or stability)? 2. Who was Prince von Metternich? 3. What was revolution, (or liberal ideas)? 4. What was balance of power? 5. What was the status quo?	1. What was being emperor? 2. What was Napoleon III? 3. What was the Suez Canal? 4. What was Mexico? 5. What was the Franco-Prussian War?	1. What were constitutions? 2. Who was Lord Byron? 3. What was Paris? 4. What was Spain? 5. What was Naples?
10	7. What were Austria, Prussia, Russia, and Great Britain? 8. Who was Tsar Alexander I? 9. What was Poland? 10. What was Switzerland? 11. What was the Congress System?	6. What was the secret police? 7. What was absolute monarchy? 8. What was the Quadruple Alliance? 9. Who was the king of England, Turkish sultan, or pope? [Name one.] 10. What was the Quintuple Alliance?	6. Who were the workers and the middle class? 7. What were a constitution, a legislative body, and universal male suffrage? [Name two.] 8. What were only the emperor could propose laws; the legislature had no power over spending; no free speech; trials not required? [Name two.] 9. What was the Crimean War? 10. What was Algeria?	6. What was Portugal? 7. Who were the Greeks? 8. Who were the Ottoman Turks? 9. Who were Serbs and Romanians? 10. What was Belgium? 11. What was England?
15	12. What was Italy? 13. What was Denmark? 14. What was Norway? 15. What was legitimacy? 16. Who was Lord Castlereagh?	11. Who were the Bourbons? 12. Who were the Hapsburgs? 13. What was being a representative government? 14. What was suppression (repression)? 15. What was reaction?	11. What was Cambodia? 12. Who was Maximilian? 13. Who was Benito Juárez? 14. What was the Commune? 15. What was the Panama (Canal) Company?	12. What was the middle class? 13. What was universal manhood suffrage (right of all males to vote)? 14. What were Austria, Germany, and Hungary? [Name two.] 15. Who was Louis Napoleon? 16. What was nationalism?
20	17. Who was King Frederick William III? 18. Who was Louis XVIII? 19. What were Belgium and Holland? 20. What was Saxony? 21. What was an indemnity?	16. What was the Holy Alliance? 17. Who was Tsar Alexander I of Russia? 18. What was the Concert of Europe? 19. What was Great Britain? 20. What was foreign minister of Austria?	16. What was the large number of political parties? 17. What was Louis's uncle? 18. What was the Second Empire? 19. Who were Roman Catholics? 20. What was to become a prisoner of war?	17. Who was Charles X? 18. Who was Louis Philippe? 19. What was the Second French Republic? 20. Who were the Poles? 21. What was the Frankfurt Assembly?

29 Unification and Nationalism

	A United Germany	A United Italy	Central Europe	Russia
5	1. Who was Otto von Bismarck? 2. What was the army? 3. What was prime minister, or chancellor? 4. What was Kaiser? 5. What was Prussia? 6. What was Austria?	1. What were the Papal States? 2. What was Sicily? 3. What was Rome? 4. What was industry? 5. What was agriculture? 6. What was the Mafia (or Camorra)?	1. What was the Austrian Empire? 2. Who were the Hapsburgs? 3. What was Hungary? 4. What was Austria-Hungary? 5. What was nationalism?	1. What was autocracy? 2. What was serfdom? 3. What was emancipation? 4. What was assassination? 5. Who were terrorists?
10	7. What was Berlin? 8. What was the Franco-Prussian War? 9. What were German industries? 10. Who were socialists? 11. What was the Franco-Prussian War? 12. What was Denmark?	7. Who was the pope? 8. What was Rome? 9. Who was Giuseppe Garibaldi? 10. What was the Kingdom of the Two Sicilies? 11. Who were the Red Shirts? 12. What was Naples?	6. What was Magyar? 7. What was German? 8. What was the Ottoman Empire? 9. What was "The Sick Man of Europe"? 10. What was autocratic? 11. What was Russia?	6. What was the Mediterranean? 7. What was Russification? 8. What was Pan-Slavism? 9. What was the Crimean War? 10. What was the Black Sea? 11. What was the creation of modern field hospitals and/or professional nursing of the wounded?
15	13. What was the Iron Chancellor? 14. What was the German Confederation? 15. What was the Seven Weeks' War? 16. What was the North German Confederation? 17. Who was William I? 18. Who were Junkers?	13. Who was Victor Emmanuel II? 14. Who was Napoleon III? 15. Who was Count di Cavour? 16. What was France? 17. What was Austria? 18. Who was Giuseppe Mazzini?	12. What was the Congress of Berlin? 13. Who was the sultan? 14. What was Russia? 15. What was Great Britain? 16. Who was Franz Josef I?	12. Who was Alexander II? 13. Who were socialists? 14. What was Slavic? 15. Who were Finns and Poles? 16. Who were middle-class industrialists?
20	19. What was the Zollverein? 20. What were Schleswig and Holstein? 21. What was Realpolitik? 22. What was the Ems dispatch? 23. What were the Bundesrat and the Reichstag?	19. What was *Risorgimento*? 20. What was Lombardy? 21. What was the Carbonari? 22. What was Young Italy? 23. What was Venetia?	17. What was the Seven Weeks' War? 18. Who were Serbs, Bulgarians, Romanians, and Greeks? [Name three.] 19. What was the Treaty of San Stefano? 20. What was Cyprus? 21. What was Bulgaria?	17. What was Sevastopol (or Sebastopol)? 18. Who were Nihilists (or anarchists)? 19. Who were Populists? 20. What were pogroms? 21. Who were Orthodox Christians?

30 Latin America, the Pacific Islands, and Imperialism

	All About Imperialism	The Pacific Islands	Spain Yields to the United States	The United States Steps into Latin America
5	1. What is imperialism? 2. What are raw materials? 3. What were tropical foods (or foods from Asia and Africa)? 4. What were new markets? 5. What was nationalism?	1. What was steam? 2. What were the Hawaiian Islands? 3. What was monarchy? 4. What were sugar cane and pineapple? 5. Who were American planters?	1. What was the *Maine*? 2. What was independence? 3. Who was Theodore Roosevelt? 4. Who were the Rough Riders? 5. What was independent? 6. What were newspapers?	1. What was experience? 2. What was defense? 3. What was the Panama Canal? 4. What was the mosquito? 5. What was yellow fever?
10	6. What was to spread religion? 7. What was a colony? 8. What were tariffs? 9. What was surplus capital (profits)? 10. What was manpower?	6. What was American Samoa? 7. What was coal? 8. What were the Midway Islands? 9. What was the U.S. Navy? 10. What was a territory?	7. What was Cuba? 8. What was Havana? 9. Who was William McKinley? 10. What was the Spanish-American War? 11. What were Cuba and Puerto Rico?	6. What were the Atlantic (or Caribbean) and Pacific? 7. Who was Pancho Villa? 8. What was the Monroe Doctrine? 9. What was the Roosevelt Corollary? 10. What was the Isthmus of Panama?
15	11. What were refueling stations and/or naval bases? 12. What was to "civilize" them? 13. What was World War I? 14. What was a protectorate? 15. What were treaty ports?	11. Who was Queen Liliuokalani? 12. What were the Aleutians? 13. Who was Captain James Cook? 14. What was Pago Pago? 15. What was Wake Island?	12. What were the Philippines and Guam? 13. What is Manila? 14. What were the Philippines and Puerto Rico? 15. Who was an appointed governor? 16. What is the Caribbean?	11. What was nonpayment of debts? 12. What was Venezuela? 13. What was Colombia? 14. What was the Dominican Republic? 15. What was Haiti?
20	16. What was mercantilism? 17. What was economic imperialism? 18. What was political imperialism? 19. What was a sphere of influence? 20. What was Social Darwinism?	16. What was Western Samoa? 17. What were the Marquesas, Tahiti (Society Islands), and New Caledonia? [Name two.] 18. What were the Fijis, Gilberts, Solomons, and Cooks? [Name two.] 19. What were the Solomons, Marshalls, Carolines, and Marianas? [Name two.] 20. What were the Samoan Islands?	17. What was the Platt Amendment? 18. What was Guantánamo Bay? 19. What was Guam? 20. What was Luzon? 21. Who was Emilio Aguinaldo?	16. What were the Virgin Islands? 17. What was Nicaragua? 18. What was the Pan American Union? 19. What was an "international police power"? 20. What was Veracruz?

31 Asia and Imperialism

	India	Southeast Asia	China	Japan
5	1. Who were Indians? 2. Who were Hindus and Muslims? 3. Who was Queen Victoria? 4. What was superior? 5. What were states (or native princes)? 6. Who was the viceroy?	1. What is Indochina (or Southeast Asia)? 2. What was India or China? [Name one.] 3. What were spices? 4. What were coffee and tea? 5. What was China? 6. What was forced labor?	1. What was isolation? 2. What was opium? 3. What was Peking? 4. What was Russia? 5. What was a republic?	1. What was isolation? 2. Who were shipwrecked sailors? 3. What was to open up trade? 4. What was population? 5. What were raw materials and food?
10	7. What was Portugal? 8. What was the British East India Company? 9. What was the Black Hole of Calcutta? 10. What was Bengal? 11. What were the caste system and religious differences? 12. Who were the Muslims?	7. What was the Indian Ocean? 8. Who were the Portuguese and the Dutch? 9. What was Great Britain? 10. What was Singapore? 11. What was Siam? 12. What is Thailand?	6. What was the Manchu dynasty? 7. What was the Opium War? 8. What was Hong Kong? 9. What was Korea? 10. What was Japan? 11. What was Manchuria?	6. What was universal public education? 7. Who was Commodore Matthew Perry? 8. What was industrialization and/ or modernization? 9. What was constitutional (but absolute) monarchy? 10. What was China or Russia? [Name one.]
15	13. What was British education? 14. What was the British Crown (or government)? 15. Who was Ram Mohun Roy? 16. What was the Muslim League? 17. Who was Robert Clive?	13. What was France? 14. What was French Indochina? 15. What was the Dutch East India Company? 16. What were the Dutch (Netherlands) East Indies? 17. What was Burma?	12. What was the Open Door Policy? 13. What was the Boxer Rebellion? 14. Who was Sun Yixian (Sun Yat-sen)? 15. What were "unequal treaties"? 16. What was the Taiping Rebellion?	11. What was Lüshun (Port Arthur)? 12. What was Taiwan? 13. Who was Theodore Roosevelt? 14. What was Manchuria? 15. What was Korea?
20	18. Who were sepoys? 19. What was the Sepoy Rebellion? 20. What was the Indian National Congress? 21. What was Pondicherry? 22. What was Madras?	18. What was the Malay Peninsula? 19. What was Borneo? 20. What was New Guinea? 21. What was the South China Sea? 22. What were Sumatra, Java, Borneo, Celebes, Timor, and New Guinea? [Name three.]	17. What was Vladivostok? 18. Who was Cixi? 19. What was reform? 20. What was the Kuomintang? 21. What is the Yellow Sea?	16. What was Nagasaki? 17. What was Meiji (or the Meiji Era)? 18. Who was Mutsuhito? 19. What was the Liaotung Peninsula? 20. What was Portsmouth, New Hampshire?

32 Africa and Imperialism

	North Africa	West Africa	East Africa	Southern Africa
5	1. What was the Barbary Coast? 2. What is the Mediterranean? 3. What was France? 4. What was the Suez Canal? 5. What was the Sahara Desert? 6. What was Algeria?	1. What is sub-Saharan Africa? 2. What was French West Africa? 3. What was the Gold Coast? 4. What was the Belgian Congo? 5. What was Liberia? 6. What is the Atlantic Ocean?	1. Who was David Livingstone? 2. Who was Henry Stanley? 3. What was "Dr. Livingstone, I presume?" 4. What was German East Africa? 5. What was British East Africa? 6. What was Italian Somaliland?	1. Who were the Boers? 2. Who was Cecil Rhodes? 3. What were diamonds? 4. What was gold? 5. What was Rhodesia? 6. What was Cape Town?
10	7. What is Morocco? 8. Who were the Berbers? 9. What was the Egyptian government? 10. What are the Red and Mediterranean Seas? 11. What was Great Britain? 12. What was Libya?	7. What was French Equatorial Africa? 8. What was Nigeria? 9. Who was Henry Stanley? 10. Who was King Leopold II of Belgium? 11. What was Monrovia? 12. What was Portuguese Guinea?	7. What is the Indian Ocean? 8. What is the Red Sea? 9. What was Ethiopia? 10. What is the Sudan? 11. What was French Somaliland? 12. What was Ethiopia?	7. What was the Boer War? 8. What was Afrikaans? 9. What was the Union of South Africa? 10. What was Mozambique? 11. What was German Southwest Africa? 12. What was Angola?
15	13. What was Islam? 14. What was Spain? 15. What was Tunisia? 16. What was the Ottoman Empire? 17. What are the Atlas Mountains?	13. What was Lagos? 14. What were Senegal, French Guinea, Cote d'Ivoire, and Dahomey? [Name two.] 15. What was Timbuktu? 16. What was the Senegal? 17. What was the (French) Congo?	13. What were France and Great Britain? 14. What is the Nile? 15. What is Lake Victoria? 16. What was Anglo-Egyptian Sudan? 17. What was the Maji Maji rebellion?	13. What are Victoria Falls? 14. What was Cape Colony? 15. What were the Orange Free State and the Transvaal? 16. What was a north-south railway (through a chain of British colonies)? 17. What was Bechuanaland?
20	18. What was the Algeciras Conference? 19. Who was Ferdinand de Lesseps? 20. What was Alexandria? 21. Who was the Mahdi? 22. What was a dey (or bey)?	18. What was the Congo? 19. What was the Asante? 20. Who was Samori Touré? 21. What were Togo and the Cameroons? 22. What were Río de Oro and Río Muni?	18. What was Madagascar? 19. What was Uganda? 20. What was Eritrea? 21. What was Khartoum? 22. Who was Menelik II?	18. What were Cape Colony, Natal, the Transvaal, and the Orange Free State? 19. Who were the Hottentots and Hereros? 20. What was the Zambezi? 21. Who was Shaka? 22. What was Portuguese East Africa?

33 The Growth of Science and Technology in the Nineteenth Century

	The Physical Sciences	The Biological Sciences	The Social Sciences and Psychology	Industrial Advances
5	1. What are the physical sciences? 2. What are astronomy, geology, physics, and chemistry? [Name two.] 3. What is the atomic theory? 4. What is atomic weight? 5. What is radium or polonium? [Name one.] 6. What are subatomic particles?	1. What are the biological sciences? 2. What is the nucleus? 3. Who was Charles Darwin? 4. What is the theory of evolution? 5. What was at least millions of years?	1. What are the social sciences? 2. What is political science? 3. What is sociology? 4. What is psychology? 5. What is economics? 6. What is history?	1. What was electricity? 2. Who was Thomas Edison? 3. What were electric light bulbs? 4. What was hydroelectric power? 5. Who was Alexander Graham Bell?
10	7. What was Greece? 8. What are formulas? 9. What is the Periodic Table of Elements? 10. What is geology? 11. What is physics? 12. What is chemistry?	6. What were dinosaurs? 7. What was the general cell theory? 8. What was *On the Origin of Species by Means of Natural Selection*? 9. What is "survival of the fittest," or natural selection? 10. What is genetics?	7. What was archaeology? 8. What were dogs? 9. Who were Karl Marx and Friedrich Engels? 10. What is socialism? 11. What is anthropology?	6. What were waterfalls? 7. What was the internal combustion engine? 8. Who was Rudolf Diesel? 9. What was structural steel? 10. What was a phone network and/or long-distance lines?
15	13. What are X rays? 14. What is an electron? 15. What is radioactivity? 16. Who were Pierre and Marie Curie? 17. Who was John Dalton?	11. Who was Gregor Mendel? 12. What were pea plants? 13. What are chromosomes? 14. What is disease? 15. What is inheritance of acquired characteristics?	12. What is Social Darwinism? 13. What were utopias? 14. What were the bourgeoisie and the proletariat? 15. Who was Ivan Pavlov? 16. Who was Thomas Macaulay?	11. What was the radio? 12. What was the phonograph? 13. What were industrial research labs? 14. What was the electrical industry? 15. Who were Karl Benz and Gottlieb Daimler?
20	18. Who was Dmitri Mendeleyev? 19. Who was Wilhelm Roentgen? 20. Who was Maria Mitchell? 21. What was Neptune? 22. What was heat?	16. What were universities and colleges? 17. Who was Robert Brown? 18. What was "special creation," or creation all at one time? 19. Who was Jean Baptiste Lamarck? 20. Who was Walther Flemming?	17. Who was Auguste Comte? 18. Who was Herbert Spencer? 19. What was conditioned reflex? 20. What was laissez-faire? 21. What was the scientific method?	16. Who were Charles and Frank Duryea? 17. What was artificial dye? 18. What was Germany? 19. Who was George Eastman? 20. What was the dynamo (electric generator)?

34 Western Culture in the Nineteenth Century

	Public Health and Medicine	The Life of the People	Literature and Philosophy	The Fine Arts
5	1. What was two? 2. What were epidemics (or contagious diseases)? 3. What were bacteria (or germs)? 4. What was rabies? 5. What was population? 6. What was surgery?	1. What was Europe? 2. What was refrigeration? 3. What were residential suburbs? 4. Who was the father? 5. What was food?	1. Who was Lord Byron? 2. What was nationalism? 3. Who were the Grimm brothers (Jakob and Wilhelm)? 4. Who was Edgar Allan Poe? 5. What was *War and Peace*? 6. Who was Mark Twain?	1. What was romanticism (or the Romantic Movement)? 2. What was realism? 3. What was Impressionism? 4. What was Paris? 5. Who was Ludwig van Beethoven?
10	7. Who was Florence Nightingale? 8. Who was Edward Jenner? 9. What was smallpox? 10. Who was Louis Pasteur? 11. What was cowpox? 12. What was ether or chloroform? [Name one.]	6. What was illiteracy? 7. What was 10 million? 8. What were economic conditions and minority oppression? 9. What were refrigerator cars? 10. What were voting and holding public office?	7. Who was Samuel Taylor Coleridge? 8. Who were Shelley and Keats? 9. Who was Sir Walter Scott? 10. Who was Goethe? 11. Who was James Fenimore Cooper? 12. Who was Henrik Ibsen?	6. Who was Frédéric Chopin? 7. Who was Peter Ilyich Tchaikovsky? 8. Who was Giuseppe Verdi? 9. Who was Richard Wagner? 10. Who was Johannes Brahms? 11. Who were Claude Monet and Pierre-Auguste Renoir?
15	13. What was infection? 14. What was childbirth? 15. What was sanitation? 16. What were battle wounds? 17. What was pasteurization?	11. What were the American and French revolutions? 12. What was free public education? 13. What was local (or state) government? 14. What was the central government? 15. What were jobs?	13. Who was Alfred, Lord Tennyson? 14. Who was Thomas Hardy? 15. Who was Mary Shelley? 16. Who were the Brontë sisters (Charlotte, Emily, and Anne)? 17. Who were the Three Musketeers?	12. Who was Auguste Rodin? 13. Who was Paul Gauguin? 14. Who was Vincent Van Gogh? 15. What was France? 16. Who was Franz Schubert, Robert Schumann, or Felix Mendelssohn? [Name one.]
20	18. What was India? 19. What were anesthetics? 20. Who was Joseph Lister? 21. What were antiseptics? 22. Who was Robert Koch?	16. Who were women and children? 17. What was widespread literacy (or education)? 18. What was Wyoming? 19. What was New Zealand? 20. What was universal and compulsory?	18. Who was Charles Dickens? 19. What was regionalism? 20. Who were naturalists? 21. Who was Emile Zola? 22. Who was Victor Hugo?	17. What was the piano? 18. Who was Franz Liszt? 19. Who were John Constable and J.M.W. Turner? 20. Who was Paul Cézanne? 21. What were Germany and Austria?

35 World War I

	The Stage Is Set	Conflict Begins	The Fighting	The Peace and Its Aftermath
5	1. What was nationalism? 2. What was imperialism? 3. What was militarism? 4. Who were army officers? 5. What were higher taxes?	1. What was Sarajevo? 2. Who were Serbs? 3. What was Austria-Hungary? 4. What was declaring war? 5. What was Serbia? 6. What was Russia?	1. What was the machine gun? 2. What was the tank? 3. What was the airplane? 4. What was the submarine? 5. What was poison gas? 6. What were trenches?	1. Who was Woodrow Wilson? 2. What was the armistice? 3. What was Versailles? 4. What were its colonies? 5. What was the civilian population?
10	6. What were secret alliances? 7. What were colonies? 8. What was mobilization? 9. What was the arms race? 10. What were (defensive) alliances?	7. Who was Archduke Franz Ferdinand? 8. What was an ultimatum? 9. What was mobilizing its troops? 10. What was Belgium? 11. What was the invasion of Belgium?	7. What was a quick victory? 8. What were the Central Powers? 9. What were the Allied Powers (or Allies)? 10. What was being citizen (non-professional) armies? 11. What was the North Sea? 12. What was the *Lusitania*?	6. What were the Fourteen Points? 7. What were Britain, France, Italy, and the United States? 8. What was Italy? 9. What were reparations? 10. What was that it alone was guilty of causing the war?
15	11. What were Germany, Austria-Hungary, and Italy? 12. What were France, Russia, and Great Britain? 13. What was an entente? 14. What were the Balkans? 15. What was the Berlin to Baghdad railroad?	12. What was Japan? 13. What was Italy? 14. What was the Ottoman Empire? 15. What was Austria? 16. Who was Kaiser Wilhelm II?	13. What was unrestricted submarine warfare? 14. What was "to make the world safe for democracy"? 15. What was the Russian Revolution? 16. What were to observe troop movements and drop explosives? 17. What was the First Battle of the Marne?	11. What were Austria and Hungary? 12. What was Russia? 13. What was the League of Nations? 14. What was the United States? 15. What was heavy debt?
20	16. What were joint borders and a central position on the continent? 17. What were control of the seas and surrounding the Triple Alliance nations? 18. What were hostile nations on east and west and hostility between Austria-Hungary and Italy? 19. What were being an entente, not an alliance, and friction between Britain and Russia? 20. What were naval strength, colonial expansion, and world trade?	17. What was to knock France out of the war quickly? 18. Who was Gavrilo Princip? 19. What was Bulgaria? 20. What was the Black Sea? 21. What was Bosnia and Herzegovina?	18. What was Jutland? 19. What was Verdun (or the Somme)? 20. What was the Zimmerman telegram? 21. What was Gallipoli? 22. What was the Argonne?	16. What were France and Belgium? 17. What was the World Court (Permanent Court of International Justice)? 18. What were Ottoman, German, Austro-Hungarian, and Russian? [Name three.] 19. What were Czechoslovakia and Yugoslavia? 20. What were to promote international cooperation and to maintain peace?

36 The Russian Revolution

	Steps to Revolution	Revolution and Civil War	The Lenin Years	The Stalin Years
5	1. Who was Tsar Nicholas II? 2. What were strikes? 3. What was the army? 4. What was industrial development? 5. Who were students, workers, or peasants? [Name one.] 6. Who were peasants (former serfs)?	1. What were soviets? 2. Who were the Bolsheviks? 3. Who was Lenin? 4. What was the proletariat? 5. What was red? 6. What was the provisional government?	1. What was Moscow? 2. What was Petrograd (St. Petersburg)? 3. What was socialism? 4. What was execution? 5. What was starvation? 6. What was the government?	1. Who was Joseph Stalin? 2. What was a totalitarian (or police) state? 3. What was a command (completely state-controlled) economy? 4. What were consumer goods? 5. Who were the peasants? 6. What is "man of steel"?
10	7. What was absolute monarchy? 8. What was Bloody Sunday? 9. What were good equipment, supplies, and/or leadership? 10. What was Petrograd (St. Petersburg)? 11. What were civil liberties?	7. Who were the Mensheviks? 8. What were the soviets? 9. Who was Lenin? 10. What was Marxism? 11. What was in exile (in Switzerland)? 12. What was the Bolshevik Revolution (or the Second Russian Revolution)?	7. What was the Soviet Union? 8. What was the Union of Soviet Socialist Republics (U.S.S.R.)? 9. Who were Nicholas and Alexandra? 10. What were republics? 11. What was Marxism-Leninism? 12. What was "one step backward"?	7. Who were Trotsky and Stalin? 8. What was all over the world? 9. What was in the U.S.S.R. only? 10. What were Five-Year Plans? 11. What were collectives (or state-owned farms)? 12. What was the Russian Orthodox Church?
15	12. What were railroads and good roads? 13. What were strikes and street demonstrations? 14. Who were soldiers? 15. What was Japan? 16. What was the Revolution of 1905?	13. What was the Communist Party? 14. What was civil war? 15. What was the Red Army? 16. Who were the Romanovs? 17. What was Germany?	13. What was foreign capital? 14. What was the Red Army? 15. What were industry and industrial workers? 16. Who were a small (minority) group of Bolsheviks? 17. What was the Communist Party?	13. What was atheism? 14. What was socialist realism? 15. What was the Politburo? 16. What were purges? 17. What was Georgia? 18. Who was Leon Trotsky?
20	17. What was the Duma? 18. What were casualties? 19. What was the October Manifesto? 20. What was to dissolve the legislature? 21. What was abdicated?	18. What was "Peace, Land, and Bread"? 19. What were the Central Powers? 20. Who were the Whites? 21. Who were the Allies (France, Britain, Japan, and the United States)? 22. What was the March Revolution?	18. What was Western capitalism? 19. What was the New Economic Policy? 20. What was free enterprise? 21. What was the Red Terror? 22. What was the National Congress?	19. What was exile? 20. What was murder (in Mexico)? 21. What was the Supreme Soviet? 22. What was the Comintern? 23. What was the Presidium?

Nationalism and Communism in Asia and Africa

	China	Japan	India	Africa and the Middle East
5	1. What was the Chinese Communist party? 2. Who was Mao Zedong (Mao Tse-tung)? 3. Who were peasants? 4. What was civil war? 5. Who was Sun Yixian (Sun Yat-sen)?	1. Who was the emperor? 2. What was the navy? 3. What was the military? 4. What were raw materials, or markets for its products? [Name one.] 5. What was the population?	1. Who was Mohandas Gandhi? 2. What was Mahatma? 3. What was Great Britain? 4. What was with nonviolence? 5. What was the caste system?	1. What was Palestine? 2. What was Atatürk? 3. What was Iran? 4. What was apartheid? 5. Who were Arabs and Jews?
10	6. Who was Jiang Jieshi (Chiang Kai-shek)? 7. What was the U.S.S.R. (Soviet Union)? 8. What were the western democracies? 9. What was the Long March? 10. Who were socialists and communists (or peasants and workers)?	6. What was China? 7. What was trade? 8. Who was Hirohito? 9. What was democratic? 10. Who were ultranationalists?	6. What was World War I? 7. What was cloth? 8. What was the Salt March? 9. What was civil disobedience? 10. What was law?	6. Who was Mustafa Kemal? 7. Who were the Turks? 8. What was westernization? 9. What was Egypt? 10. What was Pan-Arabism?
15	11. Who were the middle class? 12. What was the Red Army? 13. What was Japan? 14. What was northern China? 15. What was the Nationalist party, or the Kuomintang (Guomindang)?	11. What was Manchuria? 12. What was war? 13. What was China? 14. Who were powerful business leaders?	11. What was the Muslim League? 12. What was nonviolent noncooperation? 13. What was the Indian National Congress (or Congress party)? 14. What was Punjab? 15. What were local self-government and/or limited democratic elections?	11. What was Pan-Africanism? 12. What was Saudi Arabia? 13. What were mandates? 14. What was the Ottoman Empire? 15. What was Iraq?
20	16. What was the Qing dynasty? 17. What was the May Fourth Movement? 18. What was Manchuria? 19. Who was Lenin? 20. What was Nanjing?	15. What was the Diet? 16. What were traditional values? 17. What was Manchukuo? 18. What was the League of Nations?	16. Who was Muhammad Ali Jinnah? 17. What was a separate independent state? 18. What was racial discrimination? 19. What was the dhoti (or a simple and traditional white garment)?	16. What was the Balfour Declaration? 17. Who was Reza Khan (Reza Shah Pahlavi)? 18. What was négritude? 19. Who was Marcus Garvey?

38 The Western World Before and Between the Wars

	The Americas	Economic Conditions	Europe	The Rise of Fascism
5	1. Who was Franklin D. Roosevelt? 2. Who were flappers? 3. What were the Roaring Twenties? 4. What was immigration? 5. Who was Pancho Villa?	1. What was the government? 2. What was heavily indebted? 3. What were taxes? 4. What was the Great Depression? 5. What were banks?	1. What was less than a year? 2. Who were coal miners? 3. What was the Labour Party? 4. What was the Irish Republican Army? 5. What was Northern Ireland? 6. What was the Maginot Line?	1. What were raw materials? 2. Who was Benito Mussolini? 3. Who was Adolf Hitler? 4. Who were the Jews? 5. What was *Mein Kampf* (*My Struggle*)? 6. What was the Gestapo?
10	6. What was the Republican party? 7. What was Prohibition? 8. Who was Herbert Hoover? 9. Who was Diego Rivera?	6. What was unemployed? 7. What was unemployment? 8. What was inflation? 9. What were tariffs? 10. What was the stock market?	7. What was the Ruhr Valley? 8. Who was Ramsay MacDonald? 9. What was the Easter Rising? 10. What was the Irish Free State (Eire)? 11. What was agriculture? 12. What was *Anschluss*?	7. What was the Third Reich? 8. What was *der Führer*? 9. What was *Il Duce*? 10. What was fascism? 11. What was Munich? 12. What was the Reichstag?
15	10. What were Mexico and Venezuela? 11. Who was Emiliano Zapata? 12. What was Haiti or the Dominican Republic? [Name one.] 13. What was the Red Scare? 14. What was Nicaragua?	11. What was the New Deal? 12. What was the Social Security Act? 13. What was organized labor? 14. What was a general strike? 15. What was overproduction?	13. What was a military dictatorship? 14. What was a military dictatorship? 15. Who were wealthy aristocrats? 16. What were coalition governments? 17. What was the Locarno Pact?	13. What were poor land and a large population? 14. What was totalitarianism? 15. What was extreme nationalism? 16. What was a police state? 17. What was communism?
20	15. What was the PRI (Institutional Revolutionary party)? 16. What was *soldaderas*? 17. What was the Good Neighbor policy? 18. What was "Colossus of the North"?	16. What was financial cooperation? 17. What were public works? 18. What was world trade? 19. What was economic nationalism? 20. What was buying on margin?	18. What was the Popular Front? 19. Who was Léon Blum? 20. Who was Béla Kun? 21. What was Finland, the Baltic States, or Czechoslovakia? [Name one.] 22. What was the Kellogg-Briand Pact?	18. What was the Nazi Party? 19. What was government control over everything ("dictatorship of the state")? 20. What were the middle and upper classes? 21. Who were the Black Shirts? 22. What was the Weimar Republic? 23. What were the Storm Troopers (or Brown Shirts)?

39 World War II

	The Road to War	Conflict Begins	The War in Europe and North Africa	The War in Asia
5	1. What was Ethiopia? 2. What was Manchuria? 3. Who was General Francisco Franco? 4. What was the Munich Conference? 5. What was the Rhineland? 6. What was appeasement?	1. What were Germany, Italy, and Japan? 2. Who was Winston Churchill? 3. What was France? 4. Who was General Charles de Gaulle? 5. What was the Soviet Union? 6. What was the Polish Corridor?	1. What was neutrality? 2. What was the Soviet Union? 3. Who were Roosevelt, Churchill, and Stalin? 4. What was the Holocaust? 5. What was Normandy?	1. What was Pearl Harbor? 2. What was Australia? 3. What were aircraft carriers? 4. Who was General Douglas MacArthur? 5. What was the atomic bomb? 6. What was Hiroshima?
10	7. What was (only) to condemn it? 8. What was China? 9. Who was Haile Selassie? 10. What were Italy and Japan? 11. What was nonintervention? 12. What was Austria?	7. What was Poland? 8. What was *Blitzkrieg*? 9. What were Great Britain, the U.S., the U.S.S.R., and China (plus France)? 10. What were Denmark and Norway? 11. What were the Netherlands, Belgium, and Luxembourg? 12. What was Dunkirk?	6. What was the Battle of Britain? 7. What was the Royal Air Force? 8. Who was Erwin Rommel? 9. Who was Bernard Montgomery? 10. Who was Dwight Eisenhower? 11. What was Stalingrad?	7. What were kamikaze attacks? 8. What was Nagasaki? 9. What was V-J Day (September 2, 1945)? 10. What were the Philippines? 11. What was island-hopping?
15	13. What was the Sudetenland? 14. Who was Neville Chamberlain? 15. What was Czechoslovakia? 16. What was "living space"? 17. What was the Rome-Berlin Axis?	13. What were the Free French? 14. What were Great Britain and France? 15. What was Danzig? 16. What was the Siegfried Line? 17. What was Poland?	12. What was sonar? 13. What was radar? 14. What was D-day (June 6, 1944)? 15. What was V-E Day (May 8, 1945)? 16. What was Berlin?	12. What was Guadalcanal? 13. What were the Aleutians? 14. What was the Battle of Midway? 15. What was the Battle of the Coral Sea? 16. What was Guam or Wake Island? [Name one.]
20	18. What was the Kellogg-Briand Pact? 19. What were economic sanctions? 20. What was the Versailles Treaty (ending World War I)? 21. Who were the Nationalists and Loyalists (or Republicans)? 22. What was isolationism?	18. What was the Soviet Union? 19. What was the "phony war" or *Sitzkrieg* (sitting war)? 20. What were the Baltic States? 21. What was Finland? 22. What was the Pétain (or Vichy) government?	17. What was Operation Sea Lion? 18. What was Lend-Lease? 19. What was El Alamein? 20. What was the Battle of the Bulge? 21. What was Italy?	17. What was Manchuria? 18. What was "Asia for Asians"? 19. What was the Netherlands East Indies? 20. What was French Indochina? 21. Who was Isoroku Yamamoto?

40 The Cold War and Postwar Europe

	Postwar Settlements	Cold War Politics	Economic Recovery	The Eastern Bloc
5	1. What were occupying armies? 2. What was a republic? 3. What were territories taken in the war? 4. What were war criminals? 5. Who was Charles de Gaulle?	1. What were the United States and the Soviet Union? 2. What was the Cold War? 3. What was an airlift? 4. What was the Berlin Wall? 5. What was the Iron Curtain?	1. What was the automobile industry? 2. What was the Labour Party? 3. What was a welfare state? 4. What were strikes? 5. What was the Marshall Plan?	1. Who was Marshal Josip Tito? 2. What were satellites? 3. What was Yugoslavia? 4. Who was Nikita Khrushchev? 5. What was Titoism?
10	6. What was nationalism? 7. What were the Nuremburg trials? 8. What was genocide? 9. What was France? 10. What were refugees?	6. Who was Winston Churchill? 7. What was East Germany? 8. What was containment? 9. What was Greece? 10. What was the Berlin blockade? 11. What were refugees?	6. What was the mark? 7. What was "nationalization"? 8. What was the European Economic Community? 9. What was the Common Market? 10. What were tariffs and/or import quotas?	6. What was an army of occupation? 7. What were Poland and the Soviet Union? 8. What was the Red Army? 9. What was the German Democratic Republic? 10. What was Hungary?
15	11. What were reparations? 12. What was the Potsdam Conference? 13. What was the Yalta Conference? 14. What was four? 15. What was Trieste? 16. What was Austria?	12. What was NATO (the North Atlantic Treaty Organization)? 13. What was the Warsaw Pact? 14. What was "peaceful coexistence"? 15. What were summit conferences? 16. What was South Korea?	11. What was Great Britain? 12. What were tariffs? 13. What was Africa? 14. Who was Secretary of State George C. Marshall? 15. What was agricultural policy?	11. What was Poland? 12. What were Bulgaria, Czechoslovakia, East Germany, Hungary, Poland, and Romania? [Name four.] 13. Who were workers? 14. What was Poland? 15. What was Czechoslovakia?
20	17. Who was Konrad Adenauer? 18. What was the Fifth French Republic? 19. Who was Clement Atlee? 20. What was the Federal Republic of Germany? 21. Who were foreign ministers?	17. What was détente? 18. What was the Comintern? 19. What was the Truman Doctrine? 20. What was brinkmanship? 21. What was the U-2 incident?	16. What was Comecon (Council for Mutual Economic Assistance)? 17. What was France? 18. What was the European Coal and Steel Community? 19. What was "the German miracle"? 20. What was the United Nations Relief and Rehabilitation Administration?	16. What were the Baltic States? 17. What were Latvia, Estonia, and Lithuania? [Name two.] 18. What were Albania and Yugoslavia? 19. What was Czechoslovakia? 20. What was East Germany?

41 Revolution in Asia

	China and Korea	The Indian Subcontinent	The Island Nations	Southeast Asia
5	1. Who was Mao Zedong (Mao Tse-tung)? 2. What were communes? 3. What was Seoul? 4. Who was Deng Xiaoping? 5. What was South Korea? 6. What was the pro-democracy movement?	1. What were religious preferences? 2. What was population growth? 3. What are floods? 4. Who was Indira Gandhi? 5. What were nuclear devices?	1. What was Japan? 2. What was the United States? 3. What were exports? 4. Who was Ferdinand Marcos? 5. What were military bases?	1. Who was Ho Chi Minh? 2. Who were the Viet Cong? 3. Who was Lyndon Johnson? 4. What is Hanoi? 5. What was Saigon? 6. Who were boat people?
10	7. What was Taiwan? 8. What was the People's Republic of China? 9. What was Zhou Enlai (Chou En-lai)? 10. Who was Richard Nixon? 11. What was the Cultural Revolution?	6. Who were Muslims? 7. Who were Hindus? 8. Who was Jawaharlal Nehru? 9. What were language differences? 10. What is Bangladesh? 11. Who were the Sikhs?	6. Who was Hirohito? 7. What are earthquakes? 8. What was Sri Lanka? 9. What was democratic, parliamentary, or constitutional monarchy? 10. What was Nationalist China (the republic of China) (Taiwan)? 11. What was the Philippines?	7. What were refugees? 8. What is the Pacific Rim? 9. What was Ho Chi Minh City? 10. What was Cambodia? 11. Who was Dwight Eisenhower?
15	12. Who were the Red Guards? 13. What was the United Nations? 14. What was isolation? 15. Who was Kim Il Sung? 16. What was Tiananmen Square?	12. Who was her son, Rajiv Gandhi? 13. What were India and Pakistan? 14. Who was Benazir Bhutto? 15. Who was the Dalai Lama? 16. What was the Indus River Valley? 17. What was the Ganges Delta?	12. What was martial law? 13. What was SEATO (the Southeast Asia Treaty Organization)? 14. Who were communist and/or Muslim guerrillas? 15. What was Singapore? 16. Who was Corazón Aquino? 17. What was Indonesia?	12. Who were the Khmer Rouge? 13. What was Vietnam? 14. Who was Norodom Sihanouk? 15. What was Dienbienphu? 16. What was the Pathet Lao?
20	17. What was the demilitarized zone? 18. What was Hong Kong? 19. What was private enterprise? 20. What was the 38th parallel? 21. What was the United Nations army?	18. What was Kashmir? 19. What was the Congress Party? 20. Who was General Zia (Mohammed Zia-ul-Haq)? 21. What was Bhopal? 22. Who were the Taliban?	18. What were Borneo, Sumatra, Irian Jaya (New Guinea), Sulawesi, and Java? [Name two.] 19. Who was Suharto? 20. Who are the Tamil (or Tigers)? 21. What was Malaysia? 22. Who was Sukarno?	17. What was Thailand? 18. What was Burma? 19. What was Myanmar? 20. What were Laos, Cambodia, and Vietnam? 21. Who was Aung San Suu Kyi?

42 Independent Africa

	Independence Politics	Former British Africa	Leaders	Former Non-British Africa
5	1. What were trade unions? 2. What is one? 3. Who are army (military) leaders? 4. What is socialism? 5. What are skilled workers? 6. What is underdeveloped?	1. What was Ghana? 2. What was the Commonwealth? 3. Who were the Mau Mau? 4. What was Uganda?	1. Who was Jomo Kenyatta? 2. Who was Nelson Mandela? 3. Who was Desmond Tutu? 4. Who was Charles de Gaulle? 5. Who was Idi Amin? 6. Who was Haile Selassie?	1. What was by referendum (vote)? 2. What was forced labor? 3. What was Portugal? 4. Who were the Portuguese army?
10	7. What was apartheid? 8. What is the Organization of African Unity (OAU)? 9. What was Israel? 10. What was the EEC? 11. What was the PLO?	5. What was Ghana? 6. Who were the Kikuyu? 7. What were Tanganyika and Zanzibar? 8. What is oil? 9. What was Sharpeville?	7. Who was Kwame Nkrumah? 8. Who was Léopold Senghor? 9. Who was Sékou Touré? 10. Who was Patrice Lumumba? 11. Who was Julius Nyerere?	5. What were Angola, Guinea-Bissau, and Mozambique? [Name two.] 6. What was Guinea-Bissau? 7. What was the Cote d'Ivoire? 8. What was Namibia? 9. What was French Equatorial Africa?
15	12. What was neocolonialism? 13. What are ethnic/ tribal divisions? 14. What were Nigeria and Ghana? 15. What were industry and agriculture? 16. Who were American and West Indian blacks?	10. What was Soweto? 11. What was Rhodesia? 12. What was the Gold Coast? 13. What was Entebbe? 14. What were sexual relations and marriage between races?	12. Who was Milton Obote? 13. Who was Ian Smith? 14. Who was Kenneth Kaunda? 15. Who was Félix Houphouët-Boigny? 16. Who was Joshua Nkomo or Robert Mugabe? [Name one.]	10. What was Somalia? 11. What was the United Nations? 12. What was Rwanda? 13. What was Katanga? 14. What was Liberia?
20	17. What was the Pan-African Congress? 18. What was the Lomé Convention? 19. What was the Economic Commission for Africa (ECA)? 20. What was World War II? 21. What was the Brazzaville Conference?	15. What is Nigeria? 16. What was the Central African Federation? 17. What were Bantustans? 18. What was Zimbabwe? 19. What was the African National Congress or the Pan-African Congress? [Name one.]	17. Who was Albert Luthuli? 18. Who was Hendrik Verwoerd? 19. Who was Eduardo Mondlane? 20. Who was Mobutu Sese Seko (Joseph Mobutu)? 21. Who was F.W. de Klerk?	15. What was Eritrea? 16. What is Djibouti? 17. What is Burkina Faso? 18. What was Angola? 19. What was Benin?

43 North Africa and the Middle East: Tensions and Conflict

	North Africa	Arab-Israeli Conflict	The Middle Eastern States	The Saudi Peninsula and the Politics of Oil
5	1. What is Islam? 2. Who was Muammar al-Qaddafi? 3. What is oil production? 4. What is terrorism? 5. What was Iran? 6. What is a kingdom?	1. What was Palestine? 2. What was war? 3. What is the PLO (Palestine Liberation Organization)? 4. Who was Yasir Arafat? 5. What was refugee?	1. What is a kibbutz? 2. What is water? 3. Who were Muslims and Christians? 4. Who was the Ayatollah Ruhollah Khomeini? 5. What was Beirut? 6. Who was Saddam Hussein?	1. What is OPEC (Organization of Petroleum Exporting Countries)? 2. What was to raise the price of oil (by reducing production)? 3. What is Saudi Arabia? 4. What is the Persian Gulf? 5. What was Mecca?
10	7. Who was King Hassan II? 8. Who was Gamal Abdel Nasser? 9. What was the Aswan High Dam? 10. What was the Suez Canal? 11. What was Libya? 12. Who was Anwar el-Sadat?	6. What was the Gaza Strip? 7. What was the Sinai Peninsula? 8. What was the United Nations? 9. What is the intifada? 10. What was the Suez Canal and/or the Gulf of Aqaba? 11. What was the Six-Day War?	7. What was Syria? 8. What was Iran? 9. What were Iran and Iraq? 10. What was a suicide bombing? 11. What is the socialist party (Arab Ba'ath Socialist Party)? 12. What is the Arab League?	6. What was the Persian Gulf? 7. What was the Persian Gulf War? 8. What was Kuwait? 9. What is Abu Dhabi, Iran, Iraq, or Kuwait? [Name one.] 10. Who was King Faisal?
15	13. What was assassination? 14. What were Great Britain and France? 15. Who was Nasser? 16. What was a constitutional monarchy? 17. What was Algeria?	12. What was the West Bank (or Gaza Strip)? 13. What was the Yom Kippur War? 14. Who were Sadat and Begin? 15. Who was Jimmy Carter? 16. Who was Ariel Sharon? 17. What was Jordan?	13. Who were the Palestinians? 14. Who was King Hussein? 15. Who was Golda Meir? 16. Who were the Kurds? 17. Who was Muhammad Khatami? 18. What were Jordan, Lebanon, and Syria?	11. What was the United States? 12. What is the Arabian Sea? 13. What is the Gulf of Oman? 14. What are Algeria, Iraq, Kuwait, Libya, Qatar, Saudi Arabia, and the United Arab Emirates? [Name three.] 15. Who was King Fahd?
20	18. What was the OAS (Secret Army Organization)? 19. Who was Ben Bella, Boumediène, or Bendjedid? [Name one.] 20. What was the United Arab Republic? 21. Who was Richard Nixon? 22. Who was Hosni Mubarak? 23. Who was Haile Selassie?	18. What were the Golan Heights? 19. What was Palestinian self-rule? 20. What were the Camp David Accords? 21. What was Lebanon? 22. What was Jordan? 23. Who were Arafat, Rabin, and Peres?	19. Who was Chaim Weizmann? 20. Who was David Ben-Gurion? 21. Who was Hafez al-Assad? 22. What was a kingdom (monarchy)? 23. Who was Yitzhak Rabin, Shimon Peres, Benjamin Netanyahu, or Ariel Sharon? [Name one.] 24. Who were Islamic reformers?	16. What is Bahrain? 17. What is Oman? 18. What is Qatar? 19. What is the United Arab Emirates? 20. What was (the Republic of) Yemen?

44 The Western Democracies Since 1960

	Western Europe	The United States Abroad	The United States at Home	Canada, Australia, and New Zealand
5	1. Who was Francisco Franco? 2. Who was Kurt Waldheim? 3. What is Berlin? 4. What is the Channel Tunnel (or Chunnel)? 5. Who was Margaret Thatcher?	1. What was the Peace Corps? 2. What was the Cuban Missile Crisis? 3. What was the Vietnam War? 4. What was the Persian Gulf War? 5. What was Iran?	1. What were recessions? 2. What were civil rights? 3. Who was Martin Luther King, Jr.? 4. What were riots? 5. Who were college students? 6. What was segregation in schools?	1. What is the British Commonwealth of Nations? 2. What is Quebec? 3. What was French? 4. What is voting? 5. What is the Saint Lawrence Seaway?
10	6. What was Northern Ireland? 7. Who was Charles de Gaulle? 8. What was Germany? 9. Who was Willy Brandt? 10. What was East Germany?	6. Who was the shah? 7. What were China and the Soviet Union? 8. What was Afghanistan? 9. What was the Bay of Pigs? 10. What was Panama?	7. Who were George H. W. and George W. Bush? 8. Who was Malcolm X? 9. Who was Bill Clinton? 10. What were school shootings? 11. What was terrorism? 12. Who was Ronald Reagan?	6. What are favorable trade arrangements? 7. What are the Yukon and the Northwest Territory? 8. Who was Pierre Elliott Trudeau? 9. What is the Canadian constitution? 10. What was the conservative (Progressive Conservative) party? 11. Who was Jean Chrétien?
15	11. Who was Tony Blair? 12. What was nationalization? 13. Who was King Juan Carlos? 14. Who were the Basques (or Catalonians)? 15. What was Argentina?	11. Who was Jimmy Carter? 12. What were Egypt and Israel? 13. What was Nicaragua? 14. What was El Salvador? 15. What was Panama?	13. What was the Great Society? 14. Who was Al Gore? 15. What were the World Trade Center towers? 16. Who was Bobby Kennedy? 17. What was Watergate? 18. What was the Oklahoma City bombing?	12. What was the Labor Party? 13. What were nuclear-powered or nuclear-armed vessels? 14. What was the Labor Party? 15. What is Nunavut? 16. What was the Statute of Westminster?
20	16. What was the Maastricht Treaty? 17. Who was François Mitterrand? 18. Who was Antonio Salazar? 19. Who are French- and Flemish-speaking people? 20. Who was Olof Palme? 21. What is Benelux?	16. What was the Dominican Republic? 17. What was Teheran? 18. What was the Eisenhower Doctrine? 19. What was Saudi Arabia? 20. What was Cuba?	19. What was 18? 20. Who was Gerald Ford? 21. Who were Jimmy Carter and Bill Clinton? 22. Who was Richard Nixon? 23. Who was Joseph McCarthy?	17. What is 10? 18. What is 6? 19. Who is the (British) governor-general? 20. What is ANZUS? 21. What was the Meech Lake Accord?

45 Changes in the Communist World

	The Soviet Union at Home	The Soviet Union Abroad	The Eastern "Bloc"	The Soviet Empire Collapses
5	1. What was the KGB? 2. Who was Mikhail Gorbachev? 3. What was Chernobyl? 4. What were consumer goods and/or housing? 5. What was the Communist party? 6. What were harvests?	1. What was Cuba? 2. What were human rights? 3. What was the hot line? 4. What was China? 5. What was Afghanistan?	1. What was Solidarity? 2. Who was Lech Walesa? 3. What were shipyards? 4. What was West Germany? 5. What was Berlin?	1. Who was Boris Yeltsin? 2. What was an attempted coup? 3. What was the Warsaw Pact? 4. What was the Berlin Wall? 5. What was West Germany (the Federal Republic of Germany)? 6. What was Yugoslavia?
10	7. Who was Leonid Brezhnev? 8. Who was Andrei Gromyko? 9. What was Armenia? 10. Who were dissidents? 11. What was de-Stalinization?	6. Who was Leonid Brezhnev? 7. What were North Korea and North Vietnam? 8. What were the Moscow (Summer) Olympics? 9. What was grain? 10. What was the United States?	6. Who was Alexander Dubček? 7. What was Czechoslovakia? 8. What was the Warsaw Pact? 9. What was Poland? 10. What was Gdansk?	7. What were Estonia, Latvia, and Lithuania? 8. What were the Baltic republics? 9. What was noncommunist government? 10. What was the U.S.S.R. (Soviet Union)? 11. What was inflation?
15	12. What was wheat (grain)? 13. What was local control? 14. What were mental hospitals? 15. What was glasnost? 16. What were contested elections?	11. What was Africa? 12. What was détente? 13. What was natural gas? 14. What was radiation?	11. What was opened its border? 12. What were churches and mosques? 13. Who was Nicolae Ceauşescu? 14. What was Yugoslavia? 15. What was the Prague Spring?	12. What was unemployment? 13. What were the Czech Republic and Slovakia? 14. What were free elections? 15. What were the republics? 16. What was Chechnya?
20	17. Who was Yuri Andropov? 18. Who were refusniks? 19. What was perestroika? 20. What was the Communist party? 21. What was president?	15. What were the Los Angeles (Summer) Olympics? 16. What was China? 17. What were farm products and technology? 18. What was South Korea?	16. Who was Erich Honecker? 17. What was Romania or Albania? [Name one.] 18. Who was János Kadar? 19. What was invade it? 20. What was Wenceslas Square?	17. Who was Václav Havel? 18. Who were Croats and/or Slavic Muslims? 19. What were Russia and Kazakhstan? 20. What was Albania? 21. What was Romania?

46 Postwar Latin America

	Inter-American Relations and Economies	Central America and Mexico	South America	The Caribbean Islands
5	1. What is NAFTA? 2. Who are military officers? 3. What is poverty? 4. What is population? 5. What were loans for development?	1. What was Panama? 2. What was oil? 3. What was Mexico City? 4. What was the Canal Zone? 5. Who was General Manuel Noriega? 6. What was Panama?	1. Who was Juan Perón? 2. Who was Salvador Allende? 3. What was the CIA? 4. What were the Falkland Islands? 5. What was the interior? 6. What were urban areas?	1. Who is Fidel Castro? 2. What is Cuba? 3. What were missiles? 4. What was revolution? 5. What is Miami? 6. What is New York City?
10	6. What is the rain forest? 7. What is capital? 8. What are social and economic reforms? 9. What is a junta? 10. What was a communist takeover? 11. What is coffee or sugar? [Name one.]	7. What is Mexico? 8. Who were the Sandinistas? 9. Who were the contras? 10. Who were the rebels? 11. Who was Daniel Ortega?	7. What was Brazil? 8. What was Chile? 9. What was cholera? 10. Who was Eva or Isabel Perón? [Name one.] 11. Who was Isabel Perón?	7. What are hurricanes? 8. Who was Che Guevara? 9. What was the Soviet Union? 10. What were U.S.-owned businesses? 11. What was the Bay of Pigs?
15	12. What is land (agrarian) reform? 13. What were imports (oil and agricultural chemicals)? 14. What was oil? 15. What were exports? 16. What are *maquiladoras*?	12. What was Honduras? 13. Who was Vicente Fox Quesada? 14. Who was Oscar Arias Sánchez of Costa Rica? 15. Who was José Napoleon Duarte? 16. What was Belize?	12. Who are the disappeared ones? 13. What is Colombia? 14. What is Venezuela? 15. What was Bolivia or Colombia? [Name one.] 16. What was Uruguay?	12. What are the Virgin Islands? 13. What was Puerto Rico? 14. What was the United States? 15. Who was François Duvalier (Papa Doc)? 16. Who was Jean-Claude Duvalier (Baby Doc)?
20	17. What is the Organization of American States (OAS)? 18. What was the Alliance for Progress? 19. Who were wealthy landowners? 20. What was abroad? 21. What is the Montevideo Pact?	17. What was Guatemala? 18. Who were the Somozas? 19. What is Costa Rica? 20. What is Chiapas? 21. What was Guatemala?	17. What are the Malvinas? 18. What is São Paulo? 19. Who was General Augusto Pinochet? 20. What is the Shining Path (Sendero Luminoso)? 21. Who was General Alfredo Stroessner?	17. What was Haiti? 18. What was Grenada? 19. Who was Fulgencio Batista? 20. What was Angola? 21. What was the Mariel boatlift?

 International Cooperation

	The United Nations	U.N. Peacekeeping	International Associations and Agreements	Nuclear Arms Control
5	1. What is the Security Council? 2. What is New York City? 3. What is the General Assembly? 4. What is the International Court of Justice (or the World Court)? 5. Who is the Secretary-General?	1. What was Korea? 2. What were Israel and Egypt? 3. What was the Six-Day War? 4. What was the Mideast? 5. What was the Persian Gulf War?	1. What is OPEC (Organization of Petroleum-Exporting Countries)? 2. What is the International Red Cross? 3. What is Amnesty International? 4. What is Greenpeace? 5. What is NAFTA (North American Free Trade Agreement)?	1. What was SALT (Strategic Arms Limitations Talks)? 2. What was inspection? 3. What was spying? 4. What is outer space? 5. What was Western Europe?
10	6. What is to prevent war (or to keep peace)? 7. What is the World Health Organization (WHO)? 8. What is a veto? 9. What was the Soviet Union? 10. What is UNESCO?	6. What are observers? 7. What was the Suez Canal crisis? 8. What was Yugoslavia? 9. What was bankruptcy? 10. What was only recommending (not initiating) action?	6. What is the WTO (World Trade Organization)? 7. What is the Arab League? 8. What is the OAS (Organization of American States)? 9. What is the Group of Seven (G-7) (known as G-8 when Russia joins in)? 10. What is the World Bank?	6. What is the seabed (ocean floor)? 7. What were ICBMs and submarine-launched missiles? 8. What was SALT II? 9. What were medium-range missiles? 10. What is Antarctica?
15	11. What is UNICEF? 12. What are the United States, Russia, France, China, and Great Britain (United Kingdom)? 13. What is the Secretariat? 14. Who was Kofi Annan? 15. Who was U Thant?	11. What were Israel and the Arab states? 12. What was Haiti? 13. What was Cyprus? 14. What was Lebanon? 15. What was Somalia?	11. What is the European Union? 12. What is Doctors Without Borders? 13. What is the Helsinki agreement? 14. What is the IMF (International Monetary Fund)? 15. What is CARICOM (Caribbean Community and Common Market)?	11. What are the atmosphere, under water, and outer space? 12. What was SDI (Strategic Defense Initiative)? 13. What was Star Wars? 14. What was Reykjavik? 15. Who were Gorbachev and Reagan?
20	16. Who was Trygve Lie? 17. Who was Boutros Boutros-Ghali? 18. Who was Ralph Bunche? 19. What are English, Chinese, French, Russian, Spanish, and Arabic? 20. Who are refugees?	16. What is a permanent police force? 17. Who were Greeks and Turks? 18. What are special assessments? 19. What was Indonesia? 20. What was the Congo?	16. What is GATT (General Agreement on Tariffs and Trade)? 17. What is OAU (Organization of African Unity)? 18. What is ASEAN (Association of Southeast Asian Nations)? 19. What is APEC (Asian-Pacific Cooperation group)?	16. What were long-range missiles? 17. What is the Disarmament Commission? 18. What was the Nuclear Nonproliferation Treaty? 19. What was START (Strategic Arms Reduction Treaty)?

48 The New Global Economy and Environment

	Energy: Sources and Strategies	The Environment: Air and Water	The Environment: Earth	Global Business and Economics
5	1. What are fossil fuels? 2. What is nuclear energy? 3. What is solar power? 4. What is wind power? 5. What is oil (petroleum)? 6. What is natural gas?	1. What are whales? 2. What is acid rain? 3. What is smog? 4. What is drought? 5. What are oil spills? 6. What was the Persian Gulf?	1. What is a landfill? 2. What are pesticides? 3. What are herbicides? 4. What is overpopulation? 5. What is erosion?	1. What are living standards? 2. What is a monopoly? 3. What is free trade? 4. What are low wages? 5. What are public utilities?
10	7. What is tidal energy? 8. What is hydropower? 9. What is firewood (fuelwood)? 10. What is gasohol? 11. What are renewable energy sources?	7. What was Prince William Sound, or the *Exxon Valdez*? 8. What is the ozone layer? 9. What is ultraviolet light? 10. What is the greenhouse effect? 11. What are sewage treatment plants? 12. What is sea level?	6. What is irrigation? 7. What is recycling? 8. What are nuclear (radioactive) wastes? 9. What is the "green revolution"? 10. What is fertilizer?	6. What is the euro? 7. What is a protective tariff? 8. What is devaluation? 9. What is a multinational corporation? 10. What is the revolution of rising expectations?
15	12. What are nonrenewable resources? 13. What is uranium? 14. What is nuclear fusion? 15. What is radioactive waste? 16. What is coal?	13. What are automobile emissions? 14. What is skin cancer (melanoma)? 15. What is fallout? 16. What are algae? 17. What is thermal pollution?	11. What is the Environmental Protection Agency (EPA)? 12. What are endangered species? 13. What are waste materials? 14. What is the Amazon rain forest? 15. What are paper, glass, and aluminum?	11. What is the Southern Hemisphere? 12. What are raw materials? 13. What is a debtor nation? 14. What are economic summit meetings? 15. What is a tariff wall?
20	17. What is Saudi Arabia? 18. What are Norway and the United Kingdom? 19. What are photovoltaic (solar) cells? 20. What is geothermal energy? 21. What is hydrogen?	18. What are chlorofluorocarbons (CFCs)? 19. What is Earthwatch? 20. What is carbon dioxide? 21. What are catalytic converters? 22. What is sulphur dioxide?	16. What are soil conservation programs? 17. What is family planning? 18. What is lead? 19. What was the Earth Summit? 20. What is habitat destruction?	16. What were free trade agreements? 17. What were South Korea, Taiwan, Hong Kong, and Singapore? 18. What were information industries? 19. What is dumping? 20. What is protectionism?

Science and Technology in the Twentieth Century

	Technology	The Physical Sciences	The Biological and Psychological Sciences	The Space Age
5	1. What was Kitty Hawk? 2. Who were Wilbur and Orville Wright? 3. What was the Model T Ford? 4. What was television? 5. What is the Internet? 6. What is a cell(ular) phone?	1. Who was Albert Einstein? 2. What is the theory of relativity? 3. What is the nucleus? 4. What is the big bang theory? 5. What is antimatter (antiparticles)?	1. What is chemotherapy? 2. What was penicillin? 3. What are genes? 4. What was polio? 5. Who was Sigmund Freud? 6. What is AIDS?	1. What was *Sputnik I*? 2. What is the space shuttle? 3. What is the aerospace industry? 4. What was a cosmonaut? 5. What was *Challenger*? 6. What is the National Aeronautics and Space Administration (NASA)?
10	7. What is e-mail? 8. What were natural gas and electricity? 9. What was radio? 10. What was sound? 11. What was the assembly line (or mass production)? 12. What are transistors?	6. What are cosmic rays? 7. What is superconductivity? 8. What is a proton? 9. What is $E = mc^2$? 10. What is geophysics? 11. What are subatomic particles?	7. What is bioterrorism? 8. What is genetics? 9. What are chromosomes? 10. What is cloning? 11. What is DNA? 12. What are antibiotics?	7. Who were Neil Armstrong and Edwin Aldrin? 8. What was *Apollo 11*? 9. What was *Skylab*? 10. Who was Yuri Gagarin? 11. Who was John Glenn? 12. What is interstellar space?
15	13. What is a laser? 14. What is a microprocessor? 15. What is an electric engine? 16. What is silicon? 17. What are robots?	12. What are optical fibers? 13. Who was Enrico Fermi? 14. What is the quantum theory? 15. Who was Ernest Rutherford? 16. What is a pulsar?	13. What is a CAT scanner? 14. What is microsurgery? 15. What is Alzheimer's disease? 16. What is organ transplant? 17. What is molecular medicine?	13. What is a space station? 14. What are space probes? 15. What was *Telstar*? 16. What was Venus? 17. What was *Mir*? 18. What was the *Hubble* space telescope?
20	18. What were consumer goods? 19. What was the diesel engine? 20. What is a semiconductor? 21. What were "second generation" computers (or personal computers)? 22. What is a catalytic converter?	17. What is a quasar? 18. What is a quark? 19. What is a nanosecond? 20. What is the plate tectonic theory? 21. What is a particle accelerator?	18. What is MRI (magnetic resonance imaging)? 19. What is genetic engineering? 20. What is the human genome project? 21. What is cryogenics? 22. Who are neonatologists?	19. What is the Van Allen belt? 20. What were *Apollo* and *Soyuz*? 21. What was Laika? 22. Who was Valentina Tereshkova? 23. What was *Columbia*?

50 Western Culture in the Twentieth Century

	Literature, Philosophy, and Religion	Music, Poetry, and Theater	Painting and Photography	Architecture and Sculpture
5	1. What is the occult? 2. Who was Ernest Hemingway? 3. Who was F. Scott Fitzgerald? 4. Who was William Faulkner? 5. Who was John Steinbeck? 6. What was the Harlem Renaissance?	1. Who were the Beats? 2. Who was Robert Frost? 3. Who was Tennessee Williams? 4. Who was Arthur Miller? 5. What is Broadway? 6. What was rock and roll?	1. What is microfilm? 2. What was postimpressionism? 3. What was cubism? 4. What was expressionism? 5. What was pop art? 6. What was op art?	1. What is environmental sculpture? 2. Who was Frank Lloyd Wright? 3. What is landmark status? 4. What was the World Trade Center? 5. What is the Empire State Building?
10	7. What is the New Age movement? 8. What is existentialism? 9. Who were Black Muslims? 10. Who were the Lost Generation? 11. Who was James Joyce?	7. Who was T.S. Eliot? 8. Who was Dylan Thomas? 9. Who was Eugene O'Neill? 10. What is theater of the absurd? 11. What was jazz? 12. What is Off-Off-Broadway?	7. What is folk art (or primitive art)? 8. Who was Grandma Moses? 9. What was surrealism? 10. What was the Armory Show? 11. What was abstract expressionism? 12. What is minimal art?	6. What is the Sears Tower? 7. What are organic forms? 8. Who was Henry Moore? 9. What was Chicago? 10. What was the Bauhaus? 11. What is the international style?
15	12. What is stream of consciousness? 13. What is symbolism? 14. What were magazines? 15. What are Judaism and Islam? 16. Who was Jean-Paul Sartre?	13. What was the National Theatre? 14. What is the Royal Shakespeare Company? 15. What was vaudeville? 16. What was *Tommy*? 17. What is the National Endowment for the Arts?	13. What is new realism? 14. Who was Andrew Wyeth? 15. Who was Norman Rockwell? 16. Who was Andy Warhol? 17. What was the Leica?	12. What is reinforced concrete? 13. Who was Le Corbusier? 14. Who was I. M. Pei? 15. What is postmodernism? 16. What is the mobile?
20	17. What is the ecumenical movement? 18. What was Vatican Council II? 19. Who was Toni Morrison? 20. What is magic realism? 21. What is liberation theology?	18. Who was Sylvia Plath? 19. Who was Yevgeny Yevtushenko? 20. Who was Bertolt Brecht? 21. Who was Lorraine Hansberry? 22. What is Germany?	18. Who was Walker Evans or Dorothea Lange? [Name one.] 19. Who was Alfred Stieglitz or Edward Steichen? [Name one.] 20. What was fauvism? 21. What was dadaism? 22. What was the Ashcan School?	17. Who was Constantin Brancusi? 18. Who was Louise Nevelson? 19. What was the Chicago School? 20. Who was Walter Gropius? 21. Who was Ludwig Mies van der Rohe? 22. What were prairie houses?

Share Your Bright Ideas

We want to hear from you!

Your name_______________________________________ Date_______________

School name____

School address____

City ______________________ State ____ Zip________ Phone number (_____)__________

Grade level(s) taught________ Subject area(s) taught______________________

Where did you purchase this publication?___________________________

In what month do you purchase a majority of your supplements?__________________

What moneys were used to purchase this product?

___School supplemental budget ___Federal/state funding ___Personal

Please "grade" this Walch publication in the following areas:

Quality of service you received when purchasing .... A B C D
Ease of use........ A B C D
Quality of content........ A B C D
Page layout .... A B C D
Organization of material........ A B C D
Suitability for grade level........ A B C D
Instructional value........ A B C D

COMMENTS:____

____

What specific supplemental materials would help you meet your current—or future—instructional needs?

____

Have you used other Walch publications? If so, which ones?_____________________

May we use your comments in upcoming communications? ___Yes ___No

Please **FAX** this completed form to **888-991-5755**, or mail it to

Customer Service, Walch Publishing, P. O. Box 658, Portland, ME 04104-0658

We will send you a **FREE GIFT** in appreciation of your feedback. **THANK YOU!**